THE FINAL FRONTIERSMAN

THE FINAL FRONTIERSMAN

HEIMO KORTH AND HIS FAMILY, ALONE IN
ALASKA'S ARCTIC WILDERNESS

JAMES CAMPBELL

ATRIA BOOKS

NEW YORK LONDON TORONTO SYDNEY

ATRIA BOOKS
1230 Avenue of the Americas
New York, NY 10020

ISBN: 0-7434-5313-1

First Atria Books hardcover edition May 2004

10 9 8 7 6 5 4 3 2 1

ATRIA BOOKS is a trademark of Simon & Schuster, Inc.

Interior design by Davina Mock
Map by Paul J. Pugliese

Credits for photo insert: page 1 courtesy of Gale Sunderland; pages 2, 3 (top), and 4 courtesy
of Heimo Korth; page 3 (bottom) courtesy of Shannon and Richard Hayden; pages 5–8
courtesy of the author.

Manufactured in the United States of America

For information regarding special discounts for bulk purchases,
please contact Simon & Schuster Special Sales at 1-800-456-6798
or business@simonandschuster.com

To My Mother and Father, Who Have Always Believed
and to the Memory of Coleen Ann Korth

Acknowledgments

First on my list of people to thank are the Korths, for taking me in, feeding me, courageously revealing their lives to me. I have tried to honor their lives with this book.

Next is Elizabeth, my wife, love of my life, fellow adventurer, the woman who faithfully sticks by me, and first reader of all my work, who challenged me, always, to make this book better. And to my daughters, Aidan and Rachel, who each day make me grateful.

Thanks to David McCormick, my agent, who believed in this book's potential from the very beginning and then helped to make it a reality. Thanks also to Leslie Falk, who endured the ignorance of a first-time book writer, and to David Sobel, my occasional publishing advisor.

Writers write, and editors edit, or so a writer-friend once told me. The truth is he was wrong. The humbling fact is that writing is ultimately a collaborative act. At the top of the list of people who helped me to shape this story is Luke Dempsey, my editor, who aside from being a master craftsman is also a helluva guy—friendly, patient, always supportive, unflappable.

Thanks to my old Boulder, Colorado, buddies: Burns Ellison, astute reader, lover of Alaska, traveling companion, a second brother to me; and to dear friend, fellow writer, and now fellow father, too, David Gessner, who took time away from his own book to read early drafts of this book. I am indebted to writer-friends Dean King and Carolyn

Kremers, whose close reads and incisive comments made this book so much better; to trail bum Tim Malzhan; to wilderness man Stu Pechek; to the big-hearted Lucia Berlin for encouraging me when I was young, raw, and dreamy-eyed; and to the incomparable Reg Saner, poet and essayist, who took a group of us writers in, reminding us always that we must offer the reader the sweat from our brows.

Many thanks to a host of Alaskans who shared their stories and helped to make this book possible: Steve Ulvi and Lynette Roberts for their generosity of spirit, the camaraderie, the drink, and the discourse; to Dave Musgrave for his friendship and hospitality; to Dan O'Neill and Sarah Campbell for the thoughtful conversation, the moose stew, and the occasional dram of whiskey; Alex and Nancy Tarnai, too, for the Sunday breakfasts and their generosity; pilot-philosopher Kirk Sweetsir; Roger Kaye with his poet's heart; Bill Schneider for his willingness, always, to help, and to Sid and Willa Schneider, too; Paul and Dawn Jagow, Randy and Karen Kallen-Brown, Dean Wilson, Harry Bader, Alonzo Kelly, Don Ross, Fran Mauer, Joe Dart, Ron Long, John Peterson, Ron Bennett, David Schlesinger, Lou Swenson, Scott Fischer, Randy Zarnke, Pete Buist, Rick Schikora, Gene Hume, Dick Bishop, Percy Dyke, Simon Francis, Paul Herbert, Sarah James, Katherine Peter, Fred Thomas, Bill Pfisterer, Joe Matesi, and the Alaska Native Language Center.

Thanks, also, to Bert and Janie Gildart for showing me Alaska and to the always-informed, indefatigable Allen Smith.

Thanks to Heimo's sister Lisa for making my reunion with Heimo possible, and for her assistance and candor, to Heimo's sister Angie for her willingness to talk with me, and to Heimo's childhood friends, Jim Kryzmarcik, Roland Pruno, and Steve Laabs.

I am grateful to my brother and sidekick, Jeffrey, who missed this adventure, but was there for so many of the others; to my sisters, Jill and Jennifer, whose unfailing support means the world to me; and to my parents-in-law and faithful supporters, Daggett and Ellie Harvey.

Thanks to the librarians at the Woman's Club Public Library in town and to Marsha Monaco-Bletsch, my travel agent.

And finally, a world of thanks to those writers who came before me whose thoughts inform this book.

Contents

"It is not on any map. True places never are."
> —Herman Melville, *Moby Dick*

"I wanted movement and not a calm course of existence. I wanted excitement and danger and the chance to sacrifice myself for my love."
> —Leo Tolstoy, *Family Happiness*

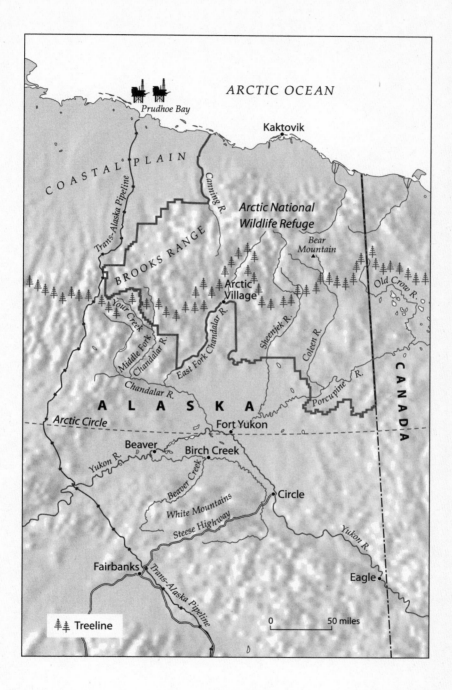

ARCTIC OCEAN

Prudhoe Bay

Kaktovik

COASTAL PLAIN

Trans-Alaska Pipeline

Canning R.

Arctic National
Wildlife Refuge

Bear
Mountain

BROOKS RANGE

Old Crow R.

Arctic
Village

Your Creek

Sheenjek R.

Coleen R.

Middle Fork
Chandalar R.

East Fork Chandalar R.

Chandalar R.

Porcupine R.

ALASKA

CANADA

Arctic Circle

Fort Yukon

Beaver

Birch Creek

Yukon R.

Beaver Creek

Circle

White Mountains

Steese Highway

Yukon R.

Fairbanks

Trans-Alaska Pipeline

Eagle

‡‡ Treeline

0   50 miles

Prologue

He had a backpack, a sleeping bag, a space blanket, a sheet of plastic, his shotgun, a can of tuna, and six pieces of bread. Not much food to sustain him on an eighty-mile hike, but he was counting on hunting along the way.

"You're going to be okay?" the bush pilot asked.

"Sure," he answered. "I'll be okay."

"See ya then," the bush pilot said.

He'd only been walking for a mile when he came upon a grizzly. The grizzly had rolled in a caribou kill, and even at forty yards, he could smell the bear. The raw stench almost made him retch. The grizzly hadn't caught his scent though, and instead of pressing his luck, he stayed downwind. The bear never even knew he was there.

The first night he came upon a no-name creek roiling with spring runoff. He knew he had to wait. If the water went down overnight, he would try to cross in the morning. If not, he would hike up to the headwaters. It meant ten extra miles, but that was better than drowning. Besides, he was in new territory, and he liked the look of it—the 6,000-foot mountains, the occasional Dall sheep sure-footing its way over the scree, the tall white spruce lining the river, and lots of wolf sign.

He built a lean-to, covered it with the sheet of plastic, and grabbed his gun. Walking for eighteen hours across a waterlogged landscape of forest, tundra, and tussock had taken its toll. He had planned to shoot some ducks, but he was past being picky now. He would settle for anything, even a ground squirrel or two.

When he spotted a small flock of ducks swimming lazily in a mountain lake, he hoped his luck was about to change. It would have to. He had to cover another sixty miles and he was already out of food. He put in five shells of No. 4 birdshot and ground-swatted them, splattering BBs across the water. He squeezed off three shots before the ducks flushed and fled, and he shot one last time as they flew away. Then he waded out into the lake to retrieve his dinner—two drake bluebills. He had meat.

Introduction

Alaska. The United States practically stole it from the Russians in 1867 for $7.2 million, the equivalent of about two cents an acre. For years it was widely regarded as a laughably errant land buy. "Seward's Folly," the purchase was called, after President Abraham Lincoln's Secretary of State, William Henry Seward, who negotiated the deal for the frozen wasteland. However, by the time I attended grade school, students were taught to think of the acquisition of Alaska as the visionary achievement of a man who understood before anyone else did that Alaska was our nation's destiny.

Ala-aska, the Aleut Indians called it—"the great land." It is a word that carries mythic overtones, that totes on its back all of our hopeful notions about Americans being a frontier people. Despite our soft suburban ways, Alaska and its 375 million acres, covering an area one-fifth as large as the total area of the lower forty-eight states, is there, way up there, a shining symbol that we are the capable offspring of courageous explorers and pioneers.

Heimo Korth has lived in the Alaskan bush for nearly three decades. His story is the exception in Alaska, one that is vastly outnumbered by the stories of those who left in a hurry after their first encounter with winter, by those who never intended to stay. People have always come to Alaska: for gold; for fast cash on the pipeline; to get rich quick and get out; to live out a romantic dream; to patch incomplete and unfulfilling lives; to outrun the law; for the sheer adventure of it; because they don't fit in anywhere else. Most of them resettled in Alaska's coastal or Interior towns and cities, or in the bush villages. Some became "sourdoughs," people, as the Alaskan joke goes, who have "soured on the country and ain't got the dough to get out." But only a few made it farther into the woods than the state's negligible road system allows. The handful who made it deep into the country, and stayed, learned the truth of the old maxim: "If you live in Alaska two years, your feet will be frozen in."

Heimo Korth never intended to do anything else but stay. When he came from Wisconsin to Alaska, he knew it would be forever, and he adapted to its harsh conditions out of a mixture of heartfelt ideology and brute necessity.

The Alaska that he inhabits, however, is not Anchorage or Fairbanks, Juneau, the North Slope boomtown of Barrow, or even the bush villages. He calls the far northeastern Interior of Alaska home, 150 miles above the Arctic Circle, in the southern foothills of the Brooks Range.

Northeast Alaska is one of the world's last great, intact ecosystems. The narrow and embattled coastal plain of the far north is the ancient calving grounds for the 126,000 porcupine caribou herd. Moving south, the coastal plain gives way to foothills, which, in turn, abut the Brooks Range, a dramatic, wind-beaten, 700-mile-long mountain chain lying entirely above the Arctic Circle, where treeless slopes rise abruptly to 9,000 feet. Immediately to the south of the mountains, glaciers and talus wander into Alaska's Interior, an expansive area of high, rounded hills, tundra, and tussock as large as New York, Pennsylvania, Ohio, and Indiana combined, bounded by the Brooks Range to the north and the Alaska Range to the south. The vast Interior is strung together by snow-frosted forests of spruce, birch, willow, alder, tamarack, trembling aspen, and balsam poplar, and wild, limpid rivers, some so cold that only the super-adapted grayling can survive them.

The Interior is the hottest and coldest place in all of Alaska. Winter temperatures can lock in at 50 below and not budge for weeks at a time, and windchill can cause them to plunge to minus 90. In summer, on the other hand, when the sun refuses to set, temperatures can soar into the high 80s. The Interior is one of America's last repositories of wildness, so large and its winter weather so brutal that it is *terra incognita*, unknowable, except to a select few wilderness people who have chosen to make their lives here.

Heimo Korth lives more remotely than any other person in Alaska, more than one hundred miles from anything resembling civilization. In 1882, a United States Census Bureau geographer classified the frontier as a place containing fewer than two people per square mile, but the definition is absurd here. Heimo and his family are the only settlers for more than 500 square miles. The nearest road is the Steese Highway, 250 miles away, on the southside of the White Mountains. The nearest hospital is in Fairbanks, 300 miles away.

Heimo Korth is one of only seven hunter-trappers with a cabin permit in the Arctic National Wildlife Refuge, which at 19.5 million acres is almost as large as the state of South Carolina. For Heimo the refuge is a permanent home. The others reside elsewhere, visiting their cabins for months, or only weeks, at a time. Fittingly, Heimo has become something of a legend in Alaska. Alaskans have always been proud of their latter-day mountain men—modern incarnations of past American heroes such as John Colter, Jim Bridger, Hugh Glass, Jedediah Smith, men who wandered the untamed wilds of the Shining Mountains (the Rockies) in search of fur and adventure—and they accord them a special kind of respect.

Heimo Korth is part of what Judith Kleinfeld, director of the University of Alaska Fairbanks Northern Studies Program, calls a "unique generational moment"—a movement of daring and idealistic young men who set out in the sixties and seventies for the Alaskan bush in search of raw reality, to recreate the kind of life that hadn't been lived since the early days of the fur trade in the American West. In a book by the same name, John McPhee called this occurrence "Coming into the Country." Up and down the mighty Yukon River, this wilderness generation took to the woods; they hunted, trapped, fished, and lived by their wits in one of the world's harshest climates. Most of these men are gone now, disillusioned, burntout, threatened with trespass and chased off by the U.S. government, married and living in cities across the United States. The ones who remember the bush experience with some fondness left simply because it was time to go, like Henry David Thoreau, because they had "several more lives to live." Heimo Korth is married now, too, with a wife and family of his own, yet he remains. He is one of the last of Alaska's hunter-trappers, making a living almost entirely off the land, the keeper of an American tradition of self-sufficiency.

I first approached Heimo Korth to write about him in 1994. In the letter I sent him, I called him a noble adventurer, a free spirit, a visionary rebel, a fugitive from civilization, and finally a frontiersman, and tried to convince him that I was the writer to tell his life story. He sent back a letter saying he wasn't interested. It was more of a note, terse and impersonal, which given the fact that I am his cousin might surprise some. But we were never close.

Heimo grew up wild. His "old man," as he always called his father, wanted him to follow in his footsteps, to take up a trade, to get a steady union job with good benefits. But Heimo had seen what that life had done for his father, and early on he vowed that he'd take a different path. His father resented his rebellion and was more inclined to use the belt than gentle persuasion. And the more Heimo resisted, the more his volatile father beat him. The story I heard was that one day Heimo had enough of his father's anger and the threats, his disapproval, the stifling boredom of a life he regarded as a dead end. The story was short on details, but I got the gist of it—Heimo took off for Alaska to be a wilderness man, a woodsman and a trapper. Though I was only twelve, I was inspired by his example. I, too, I told myself, would one day go to Canada's Yukon Territory or Alaska to homestead. I never made it, which may account for why I was unwilling to let Heimo go.

CHAPTER 1

Winter

I arrive at Heimo Korth's cabin on the Old Crow drainage in the far northeastern corner of Alaska in early January 2002 after a three-hour, 300-mile flight from Fairbanks. Although I expected stomach-churning air currents, the flight was a smooth one, and the two-seater 1954 Cessna 170B skids to an easy stop in a tundra field two feet deep in snow. In the Alaskan bush, the plane functions as a time machine, and only thirty minutes outside of Fairbanks, Rick, the bush pilot, and I had left behind civilization. Even the seismic lines, slashed across the countryside during decades of oil exploration, disappeared. For the next two and a half hours, there was not even a building to mar the harsh beauty of the Alaskan winter, and I had the feeling that I was being transported straight back into the nineteenth century.

"Heimo and his family are the only subsistence family I know," Rick said as we crossed Stranglewoman Creek. " 'Subsistence' gets a lot of lip service in Alaska, but the Korths live almost strictly off the land. You got to respect them for that. Hell, their closest neighbor is a hundred miles downriver on the Porcupine."

Looking out the window at the endless sweep of land, at the trees bent double under the weight of snow, and the cow moose bedded down in the frozen creek bed, I tried to imagine it: New York City to Philadelphia; Chicago to Milwaukee; Los Angeles to San Diego—not a soul in between.

Heimo heard the plane approaching—in the Arctic winter, when stillness is nearly absolute, sounds are magnified—and he is at the runway waiting for us.

I have not seen Heimo in twenty-seven years, and I've been imagining this day since the previous summer when Heimo was in Fort Yukon and he and I worked out the details of my visit by phone. I zip up my coat, pull my fleece hat over my ears, and pop open the door. Squeezing out of the seat, I nearly fall from the plane. But my reunion with Heimo will have to wait. First we unload the plane, and then we outfit the wings and engine with insulated covers to keep them warm and ice-free for the hour that Rick will be on the ground.

Once the work is finished, it is time for greetings. Rick and Heimo shake hands and discuss the weather—in winter Alaskans are at the mercy of Mother Nature, and the talk is often of temperature, snow, wind, ice. I listen and look on. Heimo wears canvas pants with gleaming, blue vinyl kneepads, moose-and-caribou-hide mukluks with wolf trim and sealskin liners, thick beaver mitts, and a canvas parka with a wolverine ruff and seams held together by bright white dental floss. Dental floss is stronger than sewing thread. Though it may look foolish, over one hundred miles from the nearest neighbor, appearances are apparently something Heimo cares little about. Ice has crystallized in his beard, which he wears like an Amish farmer, long and unruly, with only a faint trace of a mustache. He also wears a wool hat, which sits on his head in a cock-eyed fashion like Randall P. McMurphy, Jack Nicholson's character in *One Flew Over the Cuckoo's Nest*.

Heimo comes over to say hi. Even in the cold, he moves like an athlete. "Nice weather we got, eh?" He smiles. "Early January and it's only fifteen below." Then he gestures in the distance at the white peaks of the Brooks Range, which are silhouetted against a faint gray-blue sky that stretches to the horizon. "What do ya think?" he asks.

"Best backyard in America," I answer. He seems to like my response and shakes my hand heartily.

Heimo ferries my bags and me back to the cabin in a sled behind his Ski-Doo snowmachine, while Rick waits at the plane until Heimo returns. The trail winds through the tundra, and I bounce around and struggle to hold on until half a mile or so later we come to a stop at a large hollow in the snow colored a faint red by blood. "Shot a moose here in fall time. Called him from a mile away." Heimo simulates the call of a cow moose in estrus looking for a mate, a low bawl of longing, a groaning, "awhhhh, awhhhh" like a fishing boat's foghorn. "I hid behind that tree," Heimo says, stuttering slightly, the same stutter he had as a teen who spent more time in the woods hunting, trapping, and identifying birds than he did in the classroom. He points to a weary-looking black spruce no thicker than a child's ankle surrounded by snow-topped tussocks. "Moose can't see very good. They can smell, but their eyes ain't very good. The big bull came in swinging his horns, lookin' for a cow. Dropped him with one shot. Best thing about it was I didn't have to pack him out. I was only a quarter of a mile from the cabin."

We cut through a maze of willows and then dip down into a creek bed. After a quarter of a mile we climb the creek bank and Heimo stops the snowmachine. "See that," he says, pointing out an area where it looks as if a team of sled dogs has been urinating for days. Deep yellow holes pockmark the snow. But I know that Heimo doesn't run dogs. "That's where you dump your honeybucket," he says, clearing up my confusion. The honeybucket is an essential fixture of the Alaskan bush, usually a five-gallon plastic pail, though just about anything will do in a pinch, in which people relieve themselves at night when it's too cold to make a trip outside. In winter, at 30 and 40 below, the honeybucket is a savior. Extending his arm in the direction of an orange tent nestled among a stand of black spruce, he says, "And there's your place—the Arctic oven." The ten-foot by ten-foot double-walled tent outfitted with a small woodstove is to be my home away from home for the next three and a half weeks.

Heimo helps me get my gear into the tent, and then he shows me how to operate the woodstove. He lights a fire and then adjusts the stove's vents. After the fire is crackling, he leaves. I sit on my cot as close to the stove as I can, trying to absorb the heat. After I warm up, I arrange my gear quickly, walk outside the tent, zip the double fly, and follow a trail that leads away from the creek. Forty yards down, I discover the cabin, sitting at the base of a hill, concealed on three sides by a cluster of top-heavy spruce trees. Roger Kaye, a twenty-six-year veteran of the U.S Fish and Wildlife Service, informed me of Heimo's tendency to hide his cabins. "Trappers are a paranoid bunch in general," Roger said, "but there's nobody who tucks his cabins away like Heimo." I can see what Roger meant. I could have walked the creek not more than a stone's throw away and never noticed the cabin at all had it not been for the sweet, comforting smell of woodsmoke.

Compared to the cabins I've seen farther south in Alaska, where builders have larger trees to work with, Heimo's looks unassuming, even frail, as if a polar wind or the Big Bad Wolf could do considerable damage. The wall logs are thin and chinked with moss. Moss covers the roof, too. The cabin's obvious asset is its location. To the north thick black spruce and to the south a 1,000-foot hill protect it from the frigid winds that pummel this landscape. Twenty feet from the cabin, a winter's supply of cordwood is stacked neatly, and snowshoes and an exterior-frame backpack lean against the woodpile. A moose leg lies suspended between two roughly fashioned sawhorses. Bags of furs and leghold traps hang from racks and caribou antlers, and the foreleg of a caribou rests against the cabin's front wall near a metal washtub. Another caribou flank hangs from a tree branch. Boreal chickadees peck at it, leaving a dusting of reddish brown flesh on the snow. Two willow ptarmigan swing from a string that has been tied around a roof pole, and propped against the cabin wall are an ice pick, a scoop shovel, and two iron rakes. A second snowmachine sits idle behind the cabin near the meat cache.

Heimo is standing outside the cabin's front door. "Come on, warm up," he says, inviting me in. "You can look around later." He ducks in through the shoulder-high doorway, which is cut small to conserve the cabin's heat, and removes a wool blanket draped across the opening. I follow, bending deeply at the waist.

Heimo introduces me to Edna, his wife, who is kneeling by the woodstove, frying bread in a cast-iron skillet. Edna rises quietly and shakes my hand. She has broad, high cheekbones, a strong, muscular jaw, braided raven-black hair, and dark Mongolian eyes. She is Eskimo, a Siberian Yupik Eskimo from St. Lawrence Island, an island of rock and lava stranded in the middle of the Bering Sea, 120 miles off the west coast of Alaska, forty miles from Siberia's Chukchi Peninsula.

Heimo then introduces me to his youngest daughter, Krin, who sits in the corner of the cabin, watching me intently. When I approach she looks down at a notebook and begins scribbling. "What kind of greeting is that?" Heimo asks her. Krin stands and shakes my hand and smiles shyly. She has almond-shaped eyes, Heimo's angular nose, and Edna's lovely cheekbones and complexion. Nearly as tall as Heimo, she is a willowy twelve-year-old with long legs and arms. Edna invites me to sit down, and Krin returns her attention to her notebook. Since there are no chairs in the cabin, I sit on a bucket near the simple sheet-metal woodstove, and Edna hands me two sandwiches of fry bread and cheese. Heimo grabs a piece of bread and explains that his eldest daughter, Rhonda, is still out on the trapline. Then, suddenly, he jumps, as if he's been shocked by an electric fence. "Oh shit!" he exclaims, lunging for the door. "I forgot about Rick. He's gonna be pissed. He's gonna think I'm screwin' with him."

The cabin is no larger than a conventional suburban kitchen, ten by sixteen, four steps across, six and a half steps long, necessarily small in a climate where heat is precious. Sitting on the bucket, I remember what bush pilot Kirk Sweetsir, who was raised in the Yukon River village of Ruby, 450 miles downriver from Fort Yukon, said about the Korths. "You visit Heimo and Edna's place and there stuff amounts to nothing. Theirs is not a sedentary life. Their lifestyle reflects an awareness that life in the Arctic exists on the margin. Every season they move, and they understand that the key to surviving in the Arctic is living light."

Edna apologizes for the plywood floor, which has a hole in it the size of a frying pan and has begun to sag. The floor was damaged in a spring flood, and Heimo, she explains, has been too busy hunting and trapping to fix it. Otherwise the cabin is comfortable, cluttered but clean and homey with one large window that faces south and captures the reluctant winter light and another small one, looking west. Space is at a premium, and nearly every square foot has a purpose. Three sleeping platforms, each two and a half feet off the cabin floor, with curtains that can be let down for privacy, form a horseshoe around the perimeter of the cabin. Above the platforms is a storage loft, where books and most of the clothes are kept. Underneath the platforms, clothes, headlamps, pencils, pens, boots, books, and notepads lie scattered about the floor. Edna has decorated the walls of the cabin with the girls' artwork, and next to their sleeping platforms the girls have tacked up photos from teen magazines and splashy promotional shots of their favorite music stars—Eminem, Britney Spears, Snoop Dogg. Above a rough-hewn wood counter, which holds two plastic tubs filled with water, is a shelf with two small mirrors, cups, dishes, bowls, plates, and toothbrushes. A chain basket containing soaps, lotions, toothpaste, vitamins, shampoo, and other bathroom items hangs from the wall in the corner. Cast-iron pots and pans decorate another wall, and a radio hangs from a nail at the head of the largest sleeping platform. The radio is attached to an aerial wire that runs through a small hole Heimo has bored into one of the logs of the cabin. Once outside, the wire attaches to a nylon cord and climbs a spruce pole. Then it cuts across a small clearing and attaches to a second nylon cord hanging from another tall spruce pole. Lots of wire improves radio reception, and the nylon cords prevent the wire from grounding out on the wooden poles.

Krin's giggling jars me from my observations. I look at her and she turns her head downward toward her notebook and puts her hand over her mouth. I look at Edna and she is trying to stifle a laugh, too. Finally Edna says, guffawing, "Krinny saw you leaning back on the bucket, almost touching your coat to the woodstove." I turn and realize that I was only inches from the blazing hot stove. I am a stranger, and as far as Krin is concerned a silly city boy, and she wasn't going to tell me that I was about to catch fire.

Books, candles, the girls' CDs, cassettes, writing supplies, sketchpads, a deck of cards, batteries, and ammunition are arranged on top of another shelf. Long poles of debarked spruce dangle horizontally from wires attached to the seven-foot-high ceiling. Two wet washrags, a towel, and a T-shirt are draped across one of the poles to dry. They are steaming from the heat of the woodstove. From another pole hangs the cabin's only kerosene lamp. Above the door, guns are pegged to the wall, shotguns and large- and small-caliber rifles. To the door's left, parkas are slung over long nails. To the right, a lynx pelt and three marten pelts dry from hooks. A chain saw lies on the floor. The snowmachine and chain saw, it seems, are the Korths' only concessions to the notion of hard work made easier. Edna dips out a cup of drinking water for me from a large plastic garbage can next to the woodstove and tells me that Krin hauled in the fresh ice for my arrival. The ice, she explains, has to be brought from the creek, a half-mile away.

Heimo and Rick return and they, too, grab buckets. "Lucky it isn't cold today," Rick laughs. "This son of a bitch forgot all about me," he says, elbowing Heimo, who is sitting next to him. But Heimo isn't listening. Rick has brought in three months' worth of mail and two large boxes of Christmas presents and cards. Heimo is tearing into a small box of candy, picking out chocolates. He grabs two or three and then holds out the box, urging everyone to take a few.

"Save some for Rhonda," Edna says, reminding him that Rhonda is still out on her trapline. Looking like a kid who's just been caught with his hand in the cookie jar, Heimo puts the cover on the chocolates and sets them aside. Rick finishes his sandwiches and a cup of water and announces that it is time to go; he wants to get back to Fairbanks while he still has light.

It is just after 1:00 P.M. when I follow Rick out of the cabin, say goodbye, and retire to my tent. Heimo has told me that until the sun returns, five hours per day of something resembling light is all we can hope for. In early January, that light, he said, rarely lingers past 2:30 P.M., so before darkness falls, I unpack my gear and acquaint myself with the small woodstove. Since it is my first day, Heimo allows me to take a night's worth of wood from their winter supply. But that's it—only one night. Their wood supply is limited, enough to get them to March, figuring in cold spells, meaning at least a week or two with temperatures lower than minus 40. Finding, cutting, hauling, and splitting wood to last me until late January is to be my responsibility.

I test out my army cot and do an inventory check—polar gear, hand and foot warmers, PowerBars, one for each day on the trapline, matches, knife—and then I close down the vents of the Yukon stove, now churning out heat, and go back to the cabin. I knock at the front door, and from inside I hear Heimo say, "Oh, who could it be? A neighbor stopping by to visit?" Then I hear laughter.

I remain outside until Heimo shouts, "Just shuffle your feet like an Eskimo, so we know you're there, and come on in." I enter, unclipping the blanket, and then I clip it again before the heat can escape. Edna explains that no one in her village of Savoonga on St. Lawrence Island ever bothers to knock. "They just shuffle their feet or kick them like they're trying to get snow off their boots," she says, "so everyone knows there's someone coming. Then they just walk right in."

Rhonda is back and is sitting on her sleeping platform. Still windblown and cold from the day, she's wrapped in a sleeping bag and is telling the story of losing a marten to a prowling lynx. She stops long enough to get up and say hello. She tosses the bag onto her bed and thrusts out her hand and smiles as if she is genuinely happy to have a visitor. Then she sits back down and resumes her story, wrapping herself in the sleeping bag again. She found fur in the jaws of the trap, but the marten was gone. Leading to and from the poleset, she discovered the cat's tracks, and guesses that the trap was robbed the day before. "Maybe I'll have that lynx in one of my snares next week," she says, looking at Heimo and grinning.

Rhonda is darker complected than Krin and has a wide, friendly face. She is also several inches shorter and powerfully built like an Olympic bobsledder. She looks like she could walk for days. At fifteen, she will be my escort across the tundra when I don't join Heimo on the trapline. Heimo has no way of knowing whether or not I've come to Alaska with any wilderness skills, and he won't risk allowing me to roam the countryside on my own. But he trusts Rhonda. She has been running her own trapline for two years.

Looking at Rhonda, I remember the story Roger Kaye told me about her. "When the Korths are at their Old Crow cabin," he said, "they are, without a doubt, the most isolated bush family in America, and maybe North America, too. Once, when Rhonda was only three, I was doing aerial reconnaissance and decided to drop in before going back to Fairbanks. I was inside the cabin, and Rhonda couldn't take her eyes off of me. She just kept staring. Edna, Heimo's wife, noticed and apologized.

'She hasn't seen anybody else in six months,' she said to me. And I remember being so struck by that—a child who hadn't seen another human being outside her immediate family in six months. She sat right next to me in the cabin, practically touching me, and then when I left she followed me outside. Of course, six months for a child seems like a lifetime. A child forgets that there is anybody else in the world."

On my first night in the Arctic we eat a supper of rice and lynx, which has a familiar taste, like the dark meat of a Thanksgiving turkey. After the meal, Heimo insists I stay while they open their Christmas gifts. Had Rick the pilot not delivered the presents when he dropped me off, the Korths would have had to wait until March, when the next pilot flies out, to receive them. Christmas in January is an unexpected treat, and they tear into the gifts. Friends and relatives have sent candles, batteries, boxes of chocolate, ceramic figurines, and typical Christmas cards of themselves posed in front of mountain scenes or dressed in their holiday finery kneeling next to the tree. I ask Heimo how it is that America's most isolated family has so many well-wishers across the country. He just shrugs and bites into a cream-filled chocolate candy.

Before returning to my tent to stoke the fire, I stop next to the woodpile to watch the sky. The entire sky is exuberant, full of blinking and beaming stars. Then I crane my head and there it is, the North Star, near its zenith, an unreliable bearing in the Arctic, more uncertain even than a compass, which at this latitude wobbles indefinitely to a magnetic north, a full 34 degrees east of true north.

Later, after succumbing to the warmth of my tent and dozing off, I return to the cabin. Shortly after 9:00 P.M., Krin turns the radio dial to KJNP, a religious station out of North Pole, Alaska, just east of Fairbanks, and everyone grows silent for *Trapline Chatter*. Seven nights a week, "King Jesus North Pole" kicks in its 50,000-watt signal and broadcasts personal messages throughout Alaska's vast bush. For some families like the Korths, KJNP's *Trapline Chatter* is the only regular connection to the outside world. People send messages from home, holiday and birthday greetings, gossip, everyday news, and weather updates, which Bev Olson at KJNP dutifully reads over the air once or twice a day. Listening to KJNP is like sneaking into someone's mailbox and reading a letter from a much-loved aunt or listening to the trivial messages on someone's answering machine. Usually there is not much in the way of voyeurism; KJNP is, after all, "God's Tower of Power; The Gospel Station at the Top of the Nation." Occasionally, there'll be a message from a girlfriend who has been left behind in the city, telling her man, who's gone back to the trapline or a mining claim, how much he is missed. The language is platonic, containing little of the juicy longing or abandonment she perhaps feels. Still, people are often as interested in others' news as they are their own, and even as satellite phones become more common in the bush and the messages have reduced from fifty a night to no more than a dozen, *Trapline Chatter* is still a comforting nightly ritual for many Alaskan families.

After *Trapline Chatter*, Heimo tells stories about his early days on the trapline, talking well past his usual 9:30 P.M. bedtime. When he gets up to get a cup of water, Rhonda jumps in. "I should tell you about the first time I snared a wolverine. Wanna hear?" she asks.

"Sure," I answer.

"I couldn't believe it," she says, not bothering with the details. "When I saw it in my snare, I kept yelling, 'I can't believe it, I can't believe it.' Of course, there wasn't a soul around to hear me." She giggles at this, as if realizing how comical she must have looked, jumping up and down, celebrating in the middle of nowhere. "But that didn't stop me. When I finally calmed down, it hit me, 'Shoot, now I have to carry this thing all the way home.' It was frozen, so I couldn't skin it, so I stuck as much of it as I could in my backpack and started walking. When I got near the cabin, Daddy saw me coming and ran out onto the tundra to meet me. I thought he'd take the backpack, but he was so excited, he ran all the way back to drag Mom and Krin out to see me."

"Yeah," Heimo says when Rhonda finishes her story, "she's my little woodsman." Encouraged by her father's compliment, Rhonda reaches under her sleeping platform. She grabs a stack of photographs and shuffles them onto her sleeping bag as if she's dealing cards. Then she finds the one she's been looking for—a photo that Heimo took of her on her trapline. Surrounded by black spruce trees, she is carrying a 30.30 rifle and a backpack. It is cold, nearly 30 below. Though she is wearing a hat and a hood, her bangs are covered in frost. I tell her that she looks like a real trapper, and she is clearly pleased. Then she turns and grabs her portable CD player and shows me her new Lauryn Hill CD. Adjusting her headphones, she slips the disc into the machine, flicks on the music, and whispers the rhyming words.

I say good night and walk from the warm cabin. Earlier, Heimo, who checks the temperature once a day for the National Oceanographic and Aeronautics Administration (NOAA) and sends his reports out every three months by bush plane, announced that the temperature had dropped to minus 22. Despite the slap of the cold, I linger outside my tent, amazed by the spectral colors of the aurora borealis (literally "dawn of the north"), charged by cosmic particles unable to escape the earth's magnetic field. Radiant pinks, pulsating whites, and luminous greens light up the Alaskan night like the swirling phosphorescence of a Cape Cod bay after the sun has set. The northern lights dance, whirl, and shimmer, then they fade. The Inland Eskimos of Anaktuvuk Pass call the aurora "spirit light," and I feel a sense of grace on this, my first night in the Interior.

At 9:00 A.M. the blue shadows of twilight are disappearing, yielding to the dim light of day. Dawn is an occurrence that is happening somewhere else, farther south, that we will not see for nearly another week, when the sun breaks from its winter hibernation. At 68 degrees latitude north, the sun slips unceremoniously below the horizon near the end of November and isn't seen again until the middle of January, and even then its appearance is brief, nothing more than a flash of light in a day dominated by gray.

Off to the east, in the direction of what Rhonda and Krin have christened Thunder Mountain, a broad, treeless, snow-covered peak that rises coldly out of the tundra, the sun flirts with the horizon and the sky has a distinct painted-desert glow. Heimo stops to wrestle his snowmachine out of a snow drift. Annoyed, he pulls the machine's skis back onto the trail and blows a string of snot from his nose. "Sometimes I hate it," he growls. "Just when I think I have my trails cleared, it snows, and then I spend the rest of the week pulling my machine out of the drifts, understand?" Heimo punctuates many of his sentences with "Understand what I'm saying?" or the shorter version, "Understand?" as if he's unsure whether someone from the Outside—which Alaskans amorphously call anything beyond the state's borders—can even begin to comprehend his life. He tells me about the time in the late 1980s when the snow didn't melt until June and came again in great, wet gobs in early September and stayed again until late the following May. "I heard about the seven feet of snow in Buffalo. Hell, you couldn't pay me enough money to live in Buffalo," he says, and smirks, fully aware of the irony of his statement. "I don't mind the cold, but snow makes life miserable. You never heard of a guy dying of a heart attack from shoveling too much cold, have you?"

Eager to change the subject, Heimo says, "We should see it on January thirteenth, if we're lucky, if a low doesn't settle in." I know he is talking about the sun now. Each day, for the past five days, the sea of light has crawled resolutely across the land, coming closer and closer to the tundra valley, tinting the sky with color, and this has been the topic of our dinner conversations since my arrival. For a man who hasn't laid his eyes on the sun for six weeks, however, Heimo seems to be taking its absence in stride. "Some years it gets to you more than others," he admits.

Alaska's Interior is definitely no place for fair-weather fans. There are two seasons up here, people joke, "Fourth of July and winter." Summer, it has been said, is "nothing more than a sweet dream," an evanescent eight weeks between breakup and freeze-up, when mosquitoes rise like thick smoke out of the muskeg's cotton-grass sedges, and flowers bloom at a frantic pace and go to seed by early August. Despite the unnerving hordes of mosquitoes in summer, winter is the season when even the strongest psyches are challenged. In August, when the willows and balsam poplars are already turning yellow, bearberry blazes a bright crimson, alders turn a muddy brown, and the first killing frost comes, everyone knows that summer has, once again, ended too quickly. As the earth's northern axis turns away from the sun, a reckoning occurs. Winter is the all-consuming fact of life in Alaska's Interior, a vital, physical, force. Those who suffer from seasonal affective disorder (SAD), which is believed to be caused by too little exposure to sunlight, would find their own private hell here.

Though the temperature is mild today by the Interior's standards, only 28 below, I can feel the cold's uncaring stab even with my layers of expensive, high-tech inner gear, a full-body polar suit, a badger fur bomber hat with earflaps, big, clunky Trans Alaska boots, a balaclava, expedition-rated mittens. But there is no room for bellyachers out here. Once the cabin is out of sight, there is nowhere to warm up. If the wind is shrieking across the tundra, as it often does, Heimo may occasionally seek refuge among the trees, but he won't linger long. There are traps to check and very little light in which to do so.

I'm aware that I should be thankful for this brief January warm spell. I've heard the stories. In the savage winter of 1989–1990 it was 56 below or colder for a month and a half. In February it "warmed up" to 46 below, and Heimo seized the opportunity to check his traps. Though there was a wind—the new windchill chart postulates that a mild 15 mile-per-hour wind transforms a temperature of minus 45 to an almost unbearable 77 below, where exposed skin suffers frostbite in less than two minutes—Heimo hadn't checked his traps in nearly three weeks, and he'd been feeling stir-crazy. When a spring broke on the snow-machine, Heimo was forced to stop and fix it with his bare hands. He froze his heel, his nose, the tips of his fingers, and his cheeks that day.

In the Arctic, the weather can assert its primacy at any time, as if to make it completely clear that this is not a land that man was intended to inhabit. Exploring the realm of subzero cold, for those who have never experienced it, is like learning a new language or like being plopped down in another country in which you lack even a vague understanding of the local tongue.

Though I was raised in Wisconsin, where the cold is something we're proud of—"Keeps out the whiners" an old friend says—I discovered that Interior Alaska required a complete readjustment of my cold quotient. In Wisconsin it can reach 10 below, but at that temperature we all huddle under blankets in our warm, gas-heated houses, leaving the couch only long enough to go to the window and watch for signs of life

outside. But for residents of Alaska's Interior, 10 below is considered re-
freshing; they split wood in flannel shirts or sweatshirts at 10 below. Between minus 10 and 20, there's very little difference. Perhaps a person
would throw on a jacket for another layer and smile about how easily
the wood splits. But as the temperature nears 30 below, blood retreats
from appendages. Take off your gloves for more than five minutes or so
and your fingers will probably be frostbitten. This is the temperature at
which a person achieves a vivid understanding of just how ill-prepared
the human body is to handle the cold. Even trees suffer at 30 below.
Moisture beneath tree bark can freeze and swell, causing bark to snap
like the sound of a flat hand slapping the water's surface. At minus 40
the air has the quality of fire. Snow is as dry as flour. But there is almost
nothing harsher than a high pressure, when the winds barrel out of the
high Canadian Arctic, bringing with it the northern latitudes' bitter
chill, or a "Siberian Express," charging full-steam out of Russia's icy
hinterlands. Worse perhaps is when the winds south of the Brooks
Range simply stop circulating. Temperatures in the Interior can then
plunge to 50 and 60 below, a desolate cold for which we have no vocab-
ulary, one that saps the spirit. The still air has a bite that can literally
burn the lungs. Breath crackles with each exhalation and muscles react
slowly, sluggishly, to orders from the brain. Worst of all, 50 below
makes no allowances for mistakes.

Even in my tent at night, I became well acquainted with the Interior's
cold—my woodstove was small enough that the fire required my attention about every two hours. At first, invariably, I slept through the embers, waking only after a deep chill invaded my bones. I crawled out of
my sleeping bag and worked bare-handed, tearing thin strips of paper
and then arranging the paper and kindling inside the belly of the stove.
Lighting the match and touching it to the paper became an act of fer-
vent hope. Even before the kindling caught, I scrambled back to my bag
and watched the fire, blowing at it from a distance, trying to coax it to
life. On more than one occasion, when the kindling failed to light, I
scrambled out of my bag, shivering and cursing, reluctant to start the
process again. When the kindling caught, I put on mittens, a hat, a neck
gaiter, an extra pair of socks, and sometimes a coat, and buried myself in

my bag and fed small logs into the fire. The whole procedure, if performed unerringly, took a few minutes. However, an hour later, after the
tent was hot, I would wake up to shed my extra clothes, aware that the
whole process would have to be repeated again in another hour.

After those first few days, though, my internal clock adjusted to the
demands of the fire. I woke every two hours or so, as if on cue, to catch
the embers while they were still glowing. When I caught them in time,
I threw in two or three small logs, opened the stove vents long enough
for the fire to blaze, then closed down the vents to the point where only
a whisper of air could sneak into the stove. If I did it right, the tent
stayed relatively warm—though I could still see my breath—and I'd be
snuggled deep in my bag with sleep overtaking me in a minute or so,
hardly time enough to catch a chill.

Today, ten days after my arrival on the Old Crow, Heimo pulls me in a
sled behind his snow machine. I'm wedged among longspring leghold
traps; wire snares for wolf, fox, wolverine, and lynx; skinned marten carcasses, which Heimo will put near the base of a tree as bait—a week ago,
he noticed wolverine tracks near the tree—a small-caliber .22 rifle; an
ax; an extra drive belt; a spare backpack with emergency rations,
matches, and extra clothes; and our snowshoes. We use the sled instead
of the second snowmachine because we are headed east across the tundra to the Old Crow Flats along the Canadian border and because
Heimo's winter gasoline supply is getting dangerously low. He uses
about ten gallons a week, and he's figured out that he's got just enough
to get him to March. Years ago, when Heimo ran shorter lines, fifty to
seventy miles long, he checked all his traps by snowshoe, but now with
200 to 250 traps and 120 to 170 miles of line, he makes the rounds by
snow machine, stopping often to check the short side lines on foot. For
that reason, Heimo is emphatic about calling his snowmobile a snowmachine, though I persist in calling it by its Lower Forty-eight name.
"It's strictly a work vehicle," he says. "I'd never own one if I didn't need
it. How many guys down in the Lower Forty-eight use theirs for work?
There, it's a recreational vehicle, neon to neon, you know," he laughs,
"tavern to tavern. And there ain't a tavern up here for over 300 miles."

As we near the Old Crow Flats, the Richardson Mountains take shape far to the east. They are large and ominously white, rising out of the Flats' snow-covered marshland. We stop for a moment, and Heimo sets a blindset, a coilspring trap that he lays just under the snow, hoping to surprise an unsuspecting lynx or wolverine that has taken to our trail because of the ease of travel. Though I should be paying close attention, I am in love with the rarefied light and the silence, which is as wide as the country, oceanic, and I am remembering what John Muir said. In Alaska, Muir marveled, "it is the morning of creation."

Heimo tugs at my snowsuit, breaking my reverie, and points to a small clearing where some caribou had bedded down the night before. We walk over and he shows me the white tufts of their bleached winter hair, which lie matted in the snow. Minutes later, we're off again. We cross a lake, and Heimo takes the opportunity to open up the throttle, a bit of a joy ride. Snow flies straight back, and I pull the ruff of my fur hat over my eyes and adjust my face mask. Before the mask froze, it strained the biting cold, but now it is nothing more than a shield of ice. My eyelashes are freezing shut, and pinpricks, like the burn of stinging nettles, warn me that my cheeks are near freezing. Once over the lake, I look up just in time to swat away the supple alders and willows that line the trail and slap at me. By the end of my stay, I will develop an intense dislike of alders, the black sheep of the birch family, which resist human intrusion with whiplike lashes. When Zeus killed Phaëthon with a thunderbolt, he later punished Phaëthon's sisters for mourning their brother's death by turning them into alders. Offspring of the sisters flank nearly every trail and seem to be doing their best to punish me, displacing their anger, exacting some sort of belated revenge.

I'm relieved when a few minutes later Heimo slows and shuts off the snowmachine. Heimo has stopped here because he's eager to show me the international boundary line, an improbable thirty-foot swath cut through the trees. We forgo the snowshoes and slip up the riverbank to a clearing. Heimo makes it up first, and when I arrive I see his vapor trail and him posed next to a three-foot cylindrical cement marker, marker #32, designating the boundary between the United States and Canada, the 141st parallel. "Go ahead," he says, pointing to a clearing that extends to the south as far as I can see. "It'll be the only time you can cross over into Canada and get back to American soil without having to clear customs. I do it whenever I'm here. In fact, I always piss on the Canadian side. Not because I don't like Canada, but because I can't stand parks, and this is the Vuntut National Park. They set up parks, and they take out the people," Heimo says, echoing a sentiment I have heard regularly in Alaska.

The Arctic is a wilderness, but it has been inhabited for perhaps as long as 10,000 years by descendents of those who crossed the Bering Land Bridge. Modern definitions of wilderness won't allow for the presence of people, however; in fact, they demand their absence. By that standard only Antarctica is a true, undefiled wilderness, though with research stations appearing on the Antarctic ice pack and a steady supply of tourists, this, too, is up for debate.

It has been two days since our trip to the Canadian border, and Heimo is all business. He sets a wolverine snare, adjusting the guide sticks carefully, so that if the wolverine chooses the trail, there's only one direction for it to go. "I'll get 'em with this," he says, and pushes one last stick into place.

Though many of Alaska's trappers use leghold traps for wolverine, Heimo usually prefers the snare. It is effective and easy to use. Heimo explains how the stiff end of the wire snare is fastened to a tree, while the malleable loop dangles from a stick placed near the middle of the trail eight inches from the ground. When a wolverine enters the loop and continues walking, the loop slips closed around its neck, which activates a small locking device and prevents the snare from reopening. When the snare works as it's supposed to, the loop pulls tighter as the wolverine struggles, and the animal dies swiftly of suffocation.

Having set the last guide stick, Heimo walks back to the snowmachine. Before he can start the machine, I venture a question that I've been meaning to ask, and now seems as good a time as any.

"What about groups like PETA [People for the Ethical Treatment of Animals]," I say, "which claim that you're putting the animal through a lot of unnecessary pain?"

"PETA"—Heimo winces at the word. "If the PETA people had their way, I'd be working in Fairbanks at Jiffy Lube instead of trapping," he laughs. "Sure, an animal in a trap experiences pain, but I try to keep it to a minimum. Anyway, pain ain't new to animals; they live with it. I trap half a dozen wolves a year. My impact is nothing. Many others die of starvation or are eaten by other wolves. And don't forget, I subject myself to cold, hardship, pain, and the threat of death, too. I'm not above the natural process. The wolf kills the caribou, and I kill the wolf. But a bear could maul me, or I could drown. Some might say that I'm a killer, but most people just leave that to others. How many people butcher their own chickens? Do they ever think about all the animals killed in a combine?"

Heimo whips around in his seat—end of discussion. "Just one more set," he says, "and then we'll head for home." The news lifts my spirits. I am cold and eager to return to the Arctic oven, and fire up the wood-stove and crawl into my sleeping bag. Heimo starts the snowmachine, gives it some gas, and nearly jerks me out of the sled.

Although Heimo and I usually spend a portion of our time on the trapline telling stories, joking, and exchanging insults, today he has been a predator, checking and setting traps, and examining every track he sees with the taut alertness of a wild animal. Just by looking at a track, he can determine so much: the animal's size, its age, direction of travel, how fast it's moving, if it's breeding. And his ability to remember where all his traps are situated is nothing short of extraordinary. He wrestles his machine through a featureless forest and suddenly he stops, and I'm left wondering why. Then I see him clear the trail of a snare. Even when we're checking a side line on snowshoes, I fail to notice these snares. I walk right into them, realizing my mistake only when I hear the guide sticks snap or get tripped up in the wire. Heimo finds my ineptitude amusing. To me the forest has a bewildering uniformity, and one spruce tree looks no different from the next. For him, it is an intimate world that reveals itself in nuance.

Because he feels that maps impose an artificial order on the world, Heimo is not in the habit of using them. When he first came to Alaska he did so, but that was in the 1970s and early 1980s, when he was still developing an eye, and a feel, for the country. His map now is a mental one, as reliable as a topographic map, covering 500 square miles from the Yukon Flats, north over the elevations of the Brooks Range, to the foothills and the coastal plain, from the Chandalar River east to the Old Crow drainage and the Canadian border, an area larger than all of Grand Teton National Park.

One hundred feet before we reach his last set, Heimo whoops. He stops the snowmachine. "Wolverine!" he shouts, and celebrates with a short victory dance. He points in the direction of his trap and even I can tell he's caught a wolverine. The area has been denuded as if a Biblical cloud of locusts swooped in and devoured everything. In its struggle, the wolverine has cleared the six-foot-high tree of every one of its branches and torn up all the brush within a twenty-foot circumference. As we approach the site, called a "catch circle" by trappers, I feel my pulse quicken. Twenty feet away I can smell the pungent musk from the wolverine's anal glands, which it has sprayed all around the trap site. I dare to walk closer, and I see the wolverine's eyes staring at me, watching my every move. I imagine that its eyes burn with something like hatred. As I approach, it snarls and lunges at me. I step back and study it. It has short legs, a long snout for rooting, a small, flat head, a bushy tail, paws the size of salad plates, and it is built powerfully, low to the ground. It seems entirely unafraid, hunkered down in the dirt and snow as if it is preparing to spring on me. I have the unnerving suspicion that if the chain that attaches the leghold trap to the tree were longer, it would shred me with its rapier claws and its one-and-a-half-inch canines, and then crush my bones in its massive jaw.

Heimo tells me to step back, positions himself, and dispatches the animal with a .22 shot to the heart. The wolverine collapses and heaves twice before it dies. Heimo kneels beside it and shows me the small bullet hole, which hasn't damaged the fur. He separates the jaws of the trap, removes the animal's foot, and then skins the beast where it lies, making quick work of it, deftly cutting the thick, pungent, yogurt-colored fat and then peeling back the fur and fat from the purple-blue flesh and sinew. Wolverine fur, Heimo tells me, is the finest there is. It doesn't mat or freeze to the skin, so Alaskans use it to make hood ruffs or for anything else that may touch the face.

The wolverine fur is a lush, beautiful brown with a band of gold running from its front shoulders to the base of its tail. I run my hands along the gold strip. "That's called the 'diamond,' " Heimo says. "Fur buyers love that."

Wolverine fur brings remarkably good money. A fur buyer will pay $350 for a large male, according to Heimo. When I express surprise at the sum, he explains that in addition to the time he puts in on the line, it will take him at least eight hours to prepare the fur. "My philosophy is that you take the animal's life, so you should treat the fur with respect," he says. "And that takes time."

Heimo is fond of the wolverine, there's no doubt about that. The wolverine is a solitary, seldom-seen animal—a bit like Heimo in his early years—with a range as large as the wolf's. Early French trappers called it the "devil bear," and some Eskimos call it *gulu gulu*, the glutton. The Indians of north-central Alaska's Koyukuk River call it *doyon*, which derives from the Russian word *toyon*, meaning chief, and they regard the wolverine with reverence. Wolves and even grizzlies are common sights in Alaska compared to the loner wolverine. The naturalist Ernest Thompson Seton only saw two wolverines in his entire time in the field in the Canadian Arctic in the late 1800s. Wolverines are stinky and surly and decidedly not cute, but Heimo admires them for their versatility. Though they are not even half the size of an adult wolf, they are pound for pound the strongest mammals in the Arctic, and they have been known to scare off bears and bring down caribou and Dall sheep. One day they are top predators; the next, lowly and insatiable scavengers.

To think that Heimo would pass up trapping a wolverine because he admires it, though, is to be ignorant of what motivates him. He is not shy about expressing his love for the land apart from its ability to yield fur, but he also cherishes his way of life. He can simultaneously extol the intelligence of an animal and talk of ending its life.

Heimo puts the wolverine carcass into a large flour bag and sets it in the sled. He says he'll sell the head to a skull buyer for $35 or to a university, where it will be used in a biology lab. He'll use the carcass as bait for attracting other furbearers, but the wolverine is nothing that will ever grace his dinner table. Though the Korths eat lynx, beaver, muskrat, porcupine, and sometimes grizzly bear, they observe the old Athabaskan Indian taboo against eating wolves or wolverines or any other member of the weasel family because they sometimes carry trichinosis.

"You can watch me work on the wolverine tonight after supper," Heimo says, straddling the snowmachine. "You might like that. Now let's get the hell outta here. I'm hungry."

It is January 20 and we are above treeline, beyond Rundown Mountain, another peak that Rhonda and Krin named as little girls. January 13 came and went, and the sun didn't arrive, but today, for the first time since late November when the sun disappeared below the horizon, the clouds have lifted and the sun fills the land with light. Heimo shuts off the snowmachine and bounds out into the snow. He's been waiting for this day since November 27 and is as excited as a child by the sight of his shadow. He chases it briefly and then stops as if he's suddenly aware that I've been watching. High above, a transarctic jet etches a white line across the electric-blue sky. At 35 below, its roar, even at 30,000 feet, is almost deafening. Heimo waits for it to pass. "I listened to Enya last night," he says, closing his eyes and raising his face to the sun. Since his musical tastes usually gravitate toward Jimi Hendrix and Led Zeppelin, I express my surprise. "Yeah, that's right," he says. "Enya. It suits the landscape." To the north the peaks of the Brooks Range look like gleaming white gods, and in the valley frosted spruce trees are glistening in the sun's brittle light.

We are finished checking the traps for the day and must now only reset the trail snares on the way back to the cabin. This is our third day in a row without so much as a marten, the Alaskan trapper's bread and butter, but Heimo looks far from unhappy. He has driven the snowmachine and sled into the sun and hasn't said a word for the last five minutes, which is unusual for him. Heimo is garrulous and good-natured—a real talker—hardly what I expected from a reclusive hunter-trapper. But to live deep in the Alaskan bush requires, if anything, a healthy sense of absurdity and a lissome capacity for happiness. Sweat the little things and you won't enjoy a moment of peace. Fail to appreciate the warmth of the returning sun, the brief moments of joy, and you disavow your reason for being here.

I am on the trapline with Edna, who once a week leaves the cooking, all of which she does on a woodstove, to the girls. Given the option of cooking a meal on a woodstove and checking a trapline by snowshoe, I'd choose the less taxing of the two—the trapline. One of the myths about Alaska is that it's a man's world, but Edna is as capable and tough as most men.

This wasn't always the case. When Edna first arrived in the bush in 1981, she was a woman on the mend. She had a girl and a boy from previous relationships. Melinda, or Millie, who was six, was the daughter of Edna and a Swedish biologist, to whom Edna was engaged shortly before he was killed in a plane crash. Merlin, her son, was born in late November 1977. He was the child of Edna and a ne'er-do-well Eskimo from Nome. Millie accompanied Edna when she first joined Heimo in the bush. Later she lived with them for only part of the year and spent the rest of the year with Edna's parents in Savoonga, where she felt most at home. Merlin, on the other hand, stayed with Edna's parents full-time. In Savoonga it was not uncommon to pass on children to one's parents or relatives. Still, it went against Edna's instincts to leave either child behind, even if it was for only a few months at a time, and it saddened her, but reason eventually won out. She'd be making a new life in an unfamiliar and dangerous place, and she had no idea what to expect. The children, her parents told her—and she knew it, too—would be better off in Savoonga with them. So Edna let go.

After checking most of her traps, Edna and I return to the mountain that overlooks the cabin. The afternoon sun shines on us at an oblique angle, filling the forest with orange shadows and a beneficent glow. For the past week, the days have been nothing more than rose-tinted promises, but now the sun has returned, and the snow reflects hundreds of smaller suns. Ahead of me, Edna moves agilely, economically, like a dancer, her long ponytail swishing against the synthetic material of her parka as she walks. "It's nice to see the sun," Edna says so quietly that I can barely hear her over the scraping of my snowshoes. Like many Eskimos, Edna's English is slow and soft with a musical, singsong quality. The words originate deep in her throat, a melodic gargling sound, and her lips and jaw hardly move at all. A raven cries somewhere in the distance and suddenly Edna stops. "The raven?" I ask. "Sshhh," Edna whispers, and points in the direction of a clump of small black spruce trees. "Siberian tit, I think," she says, speaking of a bird that many birders spend decades trying to add to their life lists. Like Heimo and the girls, Edna is fond of birds, and she is clearly excited by the prospect of seeing the rare Siberian tit. Then she makes a gentle whistling sound, like wind leaking in through a little crack in a car window, a long expulsion of air like the shriek of a hawk, but soft. Standing perfectly still, we watch the trees for nearly a minute. Then Edna takes her snow stick, which she uses to rid overhanging spruce boughs of sabotaging snow buildup, and hits the trunk of a tree with it, hoping to scare the bird from its hiding place. Still no bird. She does it again and then shrugs her shoulders. "I don't know. Maybe a Siberian tit. Maybe not." Just before Edna's last snare we run into fresh lynx tracks, and when I suggest that perhaps she's caught it, Edna smiles broadly. "Lynk," she says, using the Alaskan trapper's name for the cat. "That would be good." When we reach the last snare, there is nothing. We check three more polesets and discover marten fur in the final one. A marten has sprung the trap and stolen the bait. "Marten never get too trap smart," she explains. "Maybe I'll get him next week."

Before we get back to the cabin, I hear the sound of sawing. When we get close enough, I discover its source. Krin has the large hind leg of a caribou propped up on the sawhorses and is using a bow saw to cut steaks for supper. At 35 below, Krin is dressed only in jeans, a sweater, and mukluks, which the Korths call *kamiks*, pronounced "gummocks," preferring the Yupik name for the sealskin-lined boots. Krin has already cut three steaks and is on her fourth one when I ask her if I can try.

"Sure," she says, handing me the saw. "And don't forget to bring in the steaks." Then she grabs Edna's hand and the two of them skip away like little girls.

Very quickly I realize that Krin stuck me with a tough job. Sawing frozen, rock-solid steaks is harder than it looks, and I am sweating by the time I finish the fourth steak, though I know I shouldn't be surprised. There is nothing easy about this life; everything in the bush is labor intensive.

I saw through the fifth steak, trying not to bend the blade, and by the time I return to the Arctic oven, the sun has moved briskly beyond the hills. Though it is only 3:30 the light resembles the last embers of a dying fire. Thirty minutes later the orange light of dusk has been replaced by the blue shadows of night.

For supper I eat a large, delicious caribou steak, fry bread, and a plate of white rice to replenish the calories I lost on the trail. And after a day on Edna's trapline, I am dehydrated, so I drink nearly a half-gallon of ice water, which earlier in the day I helped the girls to haul.

Hauling ice is no easy task either. At a special gathering spot on the creek, the girls use a six-foot pick to break away the ice in large chunks. Along a line that divides the cloudy overflow from the new ice, whose interior is pure and blue, the girls chip with the precision of diamond cutters. The ice must be chipped and then lugged to the sled barehanded, regardless of the temperature—a sensation that feels like holding your hands to a candle flame—so that their gloves, which the girls use for everything from fetching wood to setting traps, will not taint it. Back at the cabin the ice is added to a plastic tub and boiling water is added to melt it. Hauling ice is hard work, and it's a job that the girls do every day.

After supper I walk back to my tent to stoke the fire, and then I return to the cabin. Approaching the front door, I hear a drumbeat, strong and resonant, and the sound of laughter. I shuffle my feet loudly, then knock just in case, and everything inside comes to a stop. "Come in," I hear Heimo say, and when I do, they all burst out laughing. Edna is quick to tell me that they are not laughing at me. The radio is tuned to a station out of Barrow, a coastal town on Alaska's North Slope, which is playing Eskimo music. Rhonda says that Edna and Heimo have been dancing. When I encourage them to continue, they look at each other sheepishly. Then the girls weigh in, "Please, pretty please!" Heimo and Edna agree, and Krin turns up the music. "Ready, Mom?" Heimo says. Edna moves her arms in slow, beautiful arcs, as if she were a longtime follower of the Grateful Dead. Rhonda tells me that in Eskimo dances women imitate the movement of waves. Heimo's motions, on the other hand, are abrupt and powerful. Men, Rhonda explains again, enact the story of the hunt, the violent spearing and harpooning of walrus and seal. When the music stops, Heimo, who spent every spring from 1976 to 1981 with the Eskimo hunters of Savoonga on St. Lawrence Island, adds that fifty years ago, when a young man from Savoonga killed his first seal, the elders removed his left nipple to commemorate the occasion; when he killed his first walrus, they removed his right one. When drums introduce the next song, everyone encourages me to dance. Edna, again, moves like the ocean, and Heimo teaches me my steps. I follow as closely as I can, but manage only the savage lunges, the simulated harpooning. The girls laugh at my efforts, hooting and nearly falling off their sleeping platforms.

We listen to a few more songs, and then Heimo puts on a long, plastic butcher's apron and rubber surgical gloves. He has been working on the wolverine fur for the last three nights and tonight he is determined to finish it. His sinewy forearms strain and bulge with each sweeping knife stroke, as he "fleshes" the fur. The fat and flesh curl like wood shavings. When he's done with the body, he fleshes the wolverine's foot pads. Then with his knife, he splits the lips. Only the ears remain. He makes a fine cut on each ear and turns them inside out. Then he tacks the fur, skin side up, using pushpins, onto a five-foot stretching board shaped like the blade of a canoe paddle. Lifting the stretching board toward the ceiling, he hooks it onto a nail.

Heimo sweeps up the shavings of fat and flesh into a dustpan, throws the mess outside, and returns to the cabin. "Done," he announces, wiping the sweat from his forehead with his wrist. "Finally."

Nobody pays attention though. Edna is sewing, Rhonda reads a teen magazine, and Krin is sounding out words from the dictionary. Trying to grasp the nuances of a new word, Krin announces, lisping slightly, "You all are so con-spir-a-tor-ial." Rhonda looks up from her book, getting the gist of the word, smiling mischievously, and suggests that since this is one of my last nights with them until April we should all go sledding. Heimo is scrubbing his hands in the plastic washbasin. "Not at 44 below," he says. Krin agrees to go, setting the dictionary aside, then

Edna, then I. "We're feeling conspiratorial," I say to Heimo. "Are you in or out?" Krin challenges him. "Out," Heimo shouts, "definitely out," at which Krin and Rhonda jump up and tug at his shirt and pat his bald head. "Okay, okay," he says, relenting. "I give up. Sledding it is."

Ten minutes later, bundled against the bitter cold, we gather on the slope of what the girls call House Hill. The full moon, which won't set until morning, hangs just above the spruce trees, casting the Brooks Range in a hauntingly blue light. Heimo looks on while Edna and Rhonda get settled on a large piece of plastic, hoping to be the first ones down. But Krin is too quick. "Look out for the Suicide Sled," she shouts, grabbing another piece of plastic. Then she lets out a triumphant scream and hurls herself headfirst down the hill.

CHAPTER 2

Growing Up Wild

It is late January 2002, two days after our sledding adventure, and Heimo and I are traveling by snowmachine along one of his trails, which winds its way north along Krin Creek to a bald mountaintop. Heimo named the creek after his daughter, at her birth. Krin Creek is prime marten and wolverine country. However, when we go to check Heimo's last snare, it, as the others, is empty. So we drive to the mountain, not in the hopes of finding fur, but to feel the sun on our backs and see its dim, salmon-pink reflection off the Brooks Range to the north. The valley below is still cloaked in a somber gray and will be for another month until the sun climbs high enough to shower it in light.

We abandon the snowmachine when we near the top of the mountain and posthole through three feet of snow, racing to see who can get to the top first. It isn't much as races go. With each step we sink in up to our hips. We should be wearing snowshoes, but Heimo didn't want to spend the time putting them on. Though there isn't a cloud in the sky, he is worried about the weather. The weather in the Interior can turn quickly; it is moody, like a man who hasn't seen the sun in almost two months. After the sun's long absence, Heimo is determined not to miss a moment of it.

I am ten feet behind Heimo when suddenly he stops. Fresh caribou tracks. The caribou, it appears, came down from the ridge and wandered into the valley. Without a word, Heimo bounds back to the snowmachine, quicker this time, following our fresh trail. The sun will have to wait. With the winter meat supply running low, Heimo has been hoping to run across caribou.

I follow the tracks and see where they've crossed the trail twenty feet in front of where we've left the snowmachine. Heimo joins me, clutching his snowshoes and the .22 rifle. Surely, I think, he isn't going to try and shoot a caribou with the .22. Heimo notices me looking at it skeptically. "A neck shot," he says. "We'll creep up, and I'll take one with a shot where the neck connects to the skull. I don't want to shoot it in the heart and ruin the ribs and the brisket or the heart. That's the best part. Caribou can't see good, so we can get close if we can come at them from downwind."

The wind is out of the south, so we are in luck. We follow the tracks for thirty yards and then Heimo turns and holds out his arm, instructing me to stop. "Your snowsuit's too loud," he says. "You'll scare them. Stay here." I am glad for the reprieve. Without snowshoes, I am having a hard time keeping up.

Heimo disappears into the thick forest of head-high black spruce. Then I hear them—two shots, not in rapid succession, the second one nearly a ten count after the first. I wait for a shout of joy or another shot, and then I see the caribou wander out of the trees, their tawny coats outlined against the glistening snow. They are coming right for me, but there is nothing for me to do but watch. Heimo took both guns, the .44 magnum, which he always wears in a holster, and the .22 rifle. He emerges from the woods, following them. The caribou are moving slowly, stopping to paw away the snow with their hooves and graze on moss and lichens, as if their lives are not in imminent danger. Heimo raises his gun and takes aim. But before I hear a shot ring out, one of the caribou drops not more than fifty yards from where I stand. It falls to its knees and then rolls over on its side.

I struggle through the snow to where it lies dead. It shed its horns in December and would not get them back until April, but I can tell that it is a bull by its size. Heimo, panting and sweating from the exertion of the hunt, joins me. He rolls the caribou onto its other side, and shows me the two bullet holes, both of them neck shots, dead on target, separated by no more than an inch.

Heimo pulls out his freshly sharpened jackknife and kneels next to the caribou, as if he might pray over it, and then draws his knife swiftly across its neck. Dark blood pours from the cut, transforming the snow into red-colored crystals. Next, he severs the head, and then he begins to skin the animal. He cuts the hide on one side of the caribou and peels it back like a winter blanket and then he cuts off the front and back legs on that side. Next, he skins the other side and cuts off the legs. Though he usually uses the skin, this time of year it is almost worthless. The hair falls out like strands of straw, and the larvae of warble flies, which in summer burrowed down through the hair to lay their eggs, have transformed the hide's smoothness into a series of irregular ridges.

Once he's skinned it, he makes a long, vertical cut up the caribou's midsection, stopping at its breastbone. He spreads open its belly, and steam rises from the cavity. "Hands cold?" he asks. "Put them right here and they'll warm up fast." I do, and am glad. The tips of my numbed fingers tingle with life again. Pulling out the guts halfway, Heimo cuts off the ribs where they attach to the backbone and the breastbone. Once he has one side of ribs completely off, he cuts the windpipe and the esophagus. Since the guts are no longer attached, he pulls them down and severs them from the pelvis. Then he digs out the heart, liver, and kidneys. "These are my favorites," he says, wrapping the organs in the caribou hide. "We'll bring them home with us, and Edna will fry them up tonight. You ain't sqeamish about eating organs, are you?" Had he shot the animal in summer, near water, he would have taken one of the caribou's four stomachs and eaten it raw. "That's the real treat," he tells me. "The 'Bible.'"

The "Bible" is shaped like a football, but only half the size. Inside it is layered and looks, as the name would suggest, like the pages of the Good Book. Heimo explains how he would cut the stomach, making a long incision. Then he would wash out the moss and the lichens, carve out tender chunks, and pop them into his mouth as if they were pieces of watermelon.

When he finishes with the butchering, we stand over the steaming gut pile and watch a rare winter raven appear out of nowhere. Heimo scrubs his hands all the way up to the elbow with snow and then wipes them on a bandana. While he cleans off his knife with the same bandana he explains his plan for the meat. "I'll find a place to cache it, and then if you want you can pick it up with the snowmachine tomorrow. Think you can find your way?" "Sure," I answer, but he is already looking for a place to hide the meat and isn't listening.

Nearby, the raven hovers. Though ravens are said to have thirty distinct calls, this raven is cannily silent, cruising over the site, hoping not to be noticed. We know, though, when it is overhead by the whoosh of its wings. It is keeping a safe distance, but it is clearly interested in the kill. Heimo glances at the raven again and tells me how most ravens, though supremely adapted to the cold, choose to spend their winters in Fairbanks, Fort Yukon, and the villages, scavenging food from dumpsters.

Heimo is scanning the terrain, looking for an inconspicuous spot to stash the meat, when the raven drops down for a closer look, making a faint gurgling sound. Heimo catches it out of the corner of his eye and whirls. "Yee-haahhh," he yells, throwing his hands up as if trying to clear a dusty road of milling cattle or a campsite of a marauding raccoon. The raven spooks and croaks its displeasure. "Damn raven, " Heimo says, "he's going to try to get at the meat." Turning away from me, Heimo draws his knife across his pants and slips it into his pocket. Without saying a word, he walks back to the snowmachine, starts it, and carves a new trail to where the caribou lies. We load it onto the sled, and I clear out a spot where I can kneel between one of the hindquarters and the head. The sun has swung down below the mountains, and the land is now wrapped in a lambent light. I grip the side of the sled for balance and prepare for the jerk as Heimo pulls back on the throttle. But the jerk does not come. Heimo cuts the engine and swings around on his seat, facing me. "You know," he says, looking at the sky, "never once, not even once, did the old man ever tell me that he loved me."

I look away, not sure what to make of this sudden confession. "The old man was mean, you know." Heimo takes his knife from his pocket, opens the blade, wipes it on his pants again, puts it back into his pocket, and then pulls a small, thin piece of drymeat from his coat. Sticking it into his mouth, he clamps down with his back teeth and tears off a bite.

"Mom tried to make excuses for him." His voice is soft now, a near whisper, as if he is concerned that someone might be listening. "She said it was the war that made him that way—but she knew it, too, and she protected us from him. He was mean and had a terrible temper to go with it. Not a good combination, huh?"

Like most Alaskans, Heimo Korth is from somewhere else. He came from the "Outside," first as an emigrant to the United States and then to Alaska. Heimo was born in Frankfurt, Germany, on April 17, 1955, the oldest child of Erich and Irene Korth. Erich Korth wanted his son's name to be Erich, Jr., but Irene insisted on Heimo (pronounced *HI-mo*, with a long *i* and a long *o*), a Finnish name she'd always been fond of. When Heimo was three, the family—by then including a brother, Erich, Jr., and sister Angie—emigrated to the United States, to Appleton, Wisconsin, where Irene's oldest sister, Erika, had settled after marrying an American GI. Erich Korth resisted the move. He could hardly read or speak English. He and a partner were starting a plumbing business outside of Frankfurt, and he had high hopes for it, but Irene Korth prevailed upon him, and ultimately he agreed.

Appleton, like many of the towns and cities of the Fox River Valley, was a quiet, hardworking place, a city of 45,000 dominated by one of the Midwest's leading liberal arts colleges and a paper mill industry that tamed the picturesque Fox River with a series of locks and tainted its waters with PCBs. Appleton had a flourishing downtown with two movie theaters and attractive storefronts and had not yet felt the sting of neglect that would come as the city expanded and businesses located nearer U.S. Highway 41, draining the downtown of its customer base. In fact, in the fifties, the city's downtown was busy, particularly on Friday nights, when stores stayed open until 9:00 P.M. and area farmers came to town to do their once-a-week shopping. Appleton had a "good side" of the tracks and a "bad side." However, the dividing line was not the railroad but the Fox River, which coursed through the city, creating a wide chasm with striking bluffs on either side. The Southside, by larger cities' standards, was hardly bad, but it never quite measured up to its counterpart across the river. The Korths moved to Weimar Street on the Southside, only blocks from the pretty woods and expansive fields at the town's edge.

Heimo grew up in a cream-colored old farmhouse with a large front porch that was trellised with grapevines. Five big horse chestnut trees shaded the yard, four in front and one in back. Two ancient apple trees, a crab and a Macintosh, which hung heavy with juicy apples in September, leaned over the sandbox in the backyard.

Behind the backyard was "Old Rosie's field," a large meadow of native grasses and wildflowers, strawberries, rabbits, bees, and butterflies during the summer. Old Rosie was a loud, surly woman, and she and Erich Korth traded insults and fought about whether or not the children had a right to play in her field. The kids ignored her threats. Heimo and his friends used it for playing army, tag, hide-and-seek, flying their kites, and shooting their BB guns.

Appleton was a good place for a young boy to grow up, particularly one like Heimo, who had a yearning to be outdoors, even if the hot summer winds sometimes brought in the sulfurous stench of the Fox Valley's many paper mills. Tree-filled ravines fed the Fox River, and Heimo explored every one of them. He discovered which ravines had the most frogs and which creeks the painted turtles liked best, which wild trees had apples with the fewest wormholes, and where to gather hickory nuts in fall.

When he turned twelve, Heimo bought a spear at a local sporting goods store and made solo trips to the Fox River, where he prowled the tangled brush of the river's banks like a young Huck Finn and speared spawning carp wallowing in the river's shallow backwaters. He loved that river. Sometimes his friends joined him, but Heimo usually kept to himself, and he preferred it that way. He laughs about it now. While his friends flirted with girls in the park, he explored the river, testing his balance on logs and wading in knee-deep muck.

Despite his mother's frequent warnings, he was playing on the train trestles that spanned the river, too. Every boy who played on the train trestles knew the dangers—one misstep meant a twenty-foot fall into the river's powerful current—and he knew the stories. Once in a while one of the men who operated the locks would find the body of some unlucky kid who'd drowned bumping up against one of the lock walls like a bloated fish.

At age twelve, Heimo mustered up the courage to jump his first train. Although Heimo remembers the Fox River being full of floating logs, increasingly trains instead of the river were being used to supply the paper companies with timber. The train was ten cars long and slowly rumbled past the Riverside Paper Company and then over Lawe Street—an easy one, Heimo's friends said. Many of them were older, and some of the boys had been jumping trains for two or three years. It was a hot July day, and Heimo could feel the sweat building in his hands. What if he jumped and his hands slipped? With all of his friends looking on, Heimo had no choice but to try. He picked the last boxcar, so that if he fell there wouldn't be another car to roll over him. When he was certain that the brakeman wasn't looking, Heimo made his dash from behind the building. He ran alongside the train at a good pace, but he didn't have to sprint to keep up. Then he saw the ladder attached to the back end of the car. Grabbing on to one of the iron rungs with his inside hand, he jumped. Next thing he knew, he was traveling with the car. He rode it for one hundred yards, jumping off before the car reached the river, but when he hit the gravel he lost his footing. He had the presence of mind to tuck into a roll to protect himself. When he got up and dusted himself off, his friends in the distance cheered. He had jumped his first train, and he had scraped and bleeding arms and elbows to show for it.

After that, Heimo and his friends jumped so many trains that they started a competition, a test of bravery and skill—the one who jumped the most trains in a day was the winner. Heimo entertained kids at the local pool with his acrobatic dives, and soon it became apparent that he could use these skills—agility and balance combined with fearlessness—to win the train-jumping competitions. But train jumping was perilous, and it was only a matter of time until someone got hurt. Three years later, after jumping hundreds of trains, Heimo saw what happened to a friend. Chasing a boxcar, his friend mistimed his hop and fell. He was thrown under by the speed of the train, and Heimo was sure that his friend would die. Somehow, he scrambled out just in time. But the image stayed with Heimo. He swore he was finished. He never jumped again.

Heimo remembers aspects of his childhood with fondness—even the dangerous game of jumping trains—but there are some memories he'd rather forget. Erich Korth was a drinker. He was not a hard boozer, but he liked his beer, as the saying goes, and when he was drunk he could be mean.

Though Erich Korth had five children to feed on a plumber's income, he refused to sacrifice his beer. Just about every half year, Erich Korth got into the family's white 1965 Ford station wagon and drove to the Adler Brau Brewery in downtown Appleton. Putting the backseat down for more storage space, he loaded the car with cases of discounted beer. When he was down to his last two cases, he repeated the trip. Though he did most of his drinking at home, he made an exception for the annual plumber's union picnic.

All year Erich Korth looked forward to this big summer blowout under the canopy of magnificent elm trees at Telulah Park. All the plumbers were there with their families. The barbecues coughed smoke; the air smelled of hamburgers, hotdogs, and cigars; the pop and beer flowed generously; and kids played games while their mothers looked on and played bingo and their fathers drank and talked shop. By late afternoon, the men were drunk, and then, as if on cue, the fights started. Erich Korth got as drunk as the next guy, and even as a young boy Heimo learned to recognize the signs.

Most summers, Heimo, too, looked forward to the plumber's picnic. But in 1967, he was especially excited. In the past, he had to watch while the older boys played baseball, hoping for an invitation that never came. But in July 1967, he knew that things would be different. Twelve years old now, Heimo was the starting catcher for his Little League team, and when it came to choosing sides, he was determined not to be passed over. He had a good arm, a reliable bat, and the speed to beat out an infield grounder.

Heimo was the last boy picked, but at least he'd made the cut. His team took the field first, and he was stuck out in right field, where there was very little action. Still Heimo prepared himself for every hitter. But not a ball came his way. In the bottom of the third inning, however, he finally got his chance at bat. The opposing team's pitcher, a sixteen-year-old Babe Ruth Leaguer, thought himself a hotshot. Although this was only sandlot baseball, he was throwing curveballs, sliders, and knucklers, and when the smaller boys took the plate, full-arm fastballs. Heimo hoped that he could just get his bat on one of the pitches, that he wouldn't embarrass himself.

When the first pitch came, Heimo swung hard and missed the ball badly. Then the catcalls started. "This guy can't hit! He's a whiffer!" Heimo got his bat on the second pitch, but fouled it off into the backstop. He took the plate for the third pitch and was imagining a pop fly that fell into the hole between second base and center field when he heard a scream. "Heimo, Heimo!" He whirled around and saw his mother running toward the field. All the boys were watching, and he felt like hiding. "Heimo," she called again, stopping to catch her breath. Heimo dropped his bat and ran over to her as fast as he could. The heckling of the other players followed him. "Better run to Mommy," some of them yelled out. Heimo reached his mother and by that time she was breathing so heavily, she was unable to talk and could only pull Heimo by the arm.

They ran to the beer tent, and before Heimo got there, he saw what was happening. Erich Korth and another man were squared off, screaming at each other. A small crowd had gathered around them, but no one made an effort to intervene. In fact, some of the men were drunk and were encouraging the two to fight. Irene Korth shouted at Heimo to stop his father, but when Heimo saw how mad his father was, he refused. Erich Korth was threatening the other man. They were pushing each other, and Heimo thought his dad was going to throw a punch. Finally a group of men decided they'd seen enough and dragged the two men apart.

Irene was nearly in tears. "Erich," she screamed. "Are you crazy!" *"Bist du verrückt! Sinnlos!* We're going home. *Jetzt! Sofort!"*

By early evening Erich Korth had sobered up, though he was still looking for a fight. When Heimo walked into the living room where his father was sitting, Erich Korth reminded him that it was time for a haircut. Heimo was still furious with his father about the day's events. "We'll see," he replied. That was all the provocation Erich Korth needed. He jumped out of his chair and grabbed Heimo by the back of the neck. Heimo cried out, and Irene came running out of the kitchen. "You'll do as I say," Korth yelled at his son. "You'll do as I say, won't you!" he yelled again. Irene was trying to insert herself between Heimo and his father when Erich Korth threw a punch. The blow caught Irene across the eye and her head snapped back. When Erich Korth saw what he had done, he stopped and stood there in stunned silence. Erich Korth had always reserved his anger for his children; he was never violent toward his wife. Heimo screamed at his father now, though Irene Korth insisted that she was okay. Her eye was never the same though. It always drooped a little after that.

In addition to being a drinker, Erich Korth was also an autocrat with a temper, and growing up, Heimo got the brunt of his father's rage. His father had a special belt that hung from a hook on his bedroom door that he used when he felt that Heimo was out of line. The beatings were sometimes savage and persisted for many years.

The last beating Heimo ever got was a particularly fierce one. Heimo was sixteen, a sophomore in high school, and starting to fill out, his muscles toned now by daily swim team workouts. His father scoffed at his efforts, but Heimo enjoyed swimming, especially the butterfly, where he had the strength to propel his body out of the water with a swift dolphin kick and a vigorous, near violent thrust of his arms. Heimo also loved diving. He came alive on the diving board, an actor twisting his body into sleek, beautiful forms. He loved the feeling of lifting off the board, that last step, and then the drive of his knee. Next thing he knew, he'd hit the board with both feet, feel its spring, and then he was floating. Time seemed to stop.

Heimo arrived home after swim team practice later than usual. His mother had kept his supper warm in the oven, and his father was sitting in the living room reading the paper. He had a Harvester cigar in one hand and a can of beer on the table beside him. As Heimo walked into the living room, he threw his gym bag on the floor and returned to the kitchen. Taking a seat at the table, he poured himself a glass of milk and drank it. "Two or three porkchops?" his mother asked. "Three," Heimo answered, and dug into a pile of sauerkraut. His mother set three pork-chops on his plate. From the living room, Erich Korth was listening. No one living under his roof would act like that. Erich Korth lay down his paper and came stomping into the kitchen.

"Your mother kept your goddamn food warm for you, and you don't even say please or thank you?" Heimo continued eating as if he hadn't heard his father. "You son of a bitch," his father yelled, but still Heimo wouldn't acknowledge him. Erich Korth grabbed his son's plate and jerked it from the table. Heimo got up from his chair and walked away, calmly, as if he'd finished his meal and was simply leaving the room. His father caught up with him in the living room. "You son of a bitch!" he yelled again, grabbing Heimo by the shirt collar and whirling him around. Heimo was as tall as his father now and they stood nose to nose. Heimo didn't move. He could smell his father's breath, the nauseating scent of beer and cigar. "If you want to stay in this house, get some man-ners!" Erich Korth yelled. Heimo was determined not to budge. For once he would defy his father. His father began to push him. Then came the fist across the forehead, a hit that sent Heimo to the floor. Heimo remembers seeing Angie, his sister, and her friends run from the hall into the living room. Moments later, they rushed out into the backyard. All the while, Irene Korth was screaming at her husband to stop.

Heimo curled up and protected his head with his arms, and his father kicked at him viciously. Still Heimo didn't say a word. He didn't plead or fight back or scramble away, and this angered his father even more. Erich Korth had worked himself into a pitch and Heimo felt another blow across the side of his head, just above his ear. He curled up into a tighter ball and waited. Then everything was quiet.

Heimo sat up slowly and realized that his father was gone. He could hear his mother outside yelling. He touched his head with his hand and he saw the blood. There was blood on the carpet, too. A chair lay on the floor. Heimo figured out what just happened. The hardest blow had come when his father hit him with the chair. Heimo took off his T-shirt and held it to his head. When his mother returned she took a tray of ice from the freezer. She broke the ice into a fresh towel, put it on the bleeding cut, and stroked his head with her other hand.

Heimo claims now that he's come to terms with his father's anger. "I love him, he's my dad," Heimo says. "But me and the old man, we just ground gears. He wanted me to join him in the plumbing business, but I hated the routine, eight to five. To me, that's prison. He couldn't understand that. For him it was the only way. The old man was rigid like that—his way or the highway."

Heimo says now that perhaps his father was only defending his choices, that his anger might have been nothing more than fear. Perhaps he was looking for his son's approval, for some confirmation that his life had been worthwhile, that his oldest son respected him. An aunt speculates that Erich Korth never recovered from the disappointment of having to leave Germany. "It was Irene who wanted to leave," she says. "Erich's plumbing partner in Germany became a rich man, and Erich had to start all over, learning a new language and everything. I don't think he ever got over that."

Mitigating circumstances or not, Heimo says, "If he was to come back to life, I'd give him a good chewing-out. 'What was all that shit about?' I'd ask him. For a long time, it really pissed me off. But later on he mellowed, and he tried to say he was sorry in his own way."

"Sure, Dad was sorry," says Angie Korth, Heimo's sister. "Dad ruled with a heavy hand. Later on, I think he regretted that. He just didn't know how to express his love. He never understood Heimo, but slowly he came to terms with Heimo's lifestyle. Ultimately, I think he was very proud of Heimo, and he loved him, but he just didn't know how to show it."

Lisa Korth, Heimo's youngest sister, adds, "It was Heimo's dream to go to Alaska, but there were sacrifices. He missed part of our lives. And he didn't ever really know who Mom and Dad were, especially Dad. Mom was always the loving caregiver, but there was more to her. And there was much more to Dad than Heimo ever knew. He's a lot like Dad in some ways. He hates to hear it, but it's true."

In 1977 Erich Korth called up Heimo while Heimo was in Fort

Yukon. "I have a proposition for you," he said. "I want you to come home. I'll buy you a farm in northeastern Wisconsin if you'll come home." Heimo couldn't believe what he was hearing. The old man was offering to buy him a farm? Then the thought flashed into his head— the old man's drunk. "Why?" Heimo asked. "I want you to come home," his father repeated. But he wasn't drunk; Heimo could hear that now. "You know I can't come home," Heimo answered. "Alaska, Dad, Alaska's where I live." His father struggled to find the words. "I just thought you might consider it." Then there was a dial tone, not even a good-bye. Two weeks later a large package arrived in Fort Yukon. His father had sent up a brand-new set of tools.

In 1986, Erich Korth visited Heimo and his family at their cabin, and he stayed for a month. Heimo remembers the time fondly. "The old man changed so much, I couldn't believe it. We shot a caribou, went berry picking, and fished for grayling. I never saw the old man so happy. He even helped me dig a new hole for the outhouse. When that was done he helped me put a new pole roof on the cabin. He was really willing to help, and we got along. I think he was trying to say he was sorry for all those years. We never talked about it. The old man wasn't the type to say anything." Erich Korth never visited Alaska again. He died eight years later.

Although Heimo cannot be sure what it was that caused his father's hair-trigger temper—his nature, bitterness at having to leave Germany and start all over in a new country, never having achieved financial success, the horrors of World War II and the memory of a favorite brother lost at Stalingrad, a rough childhood at the hands of his own violent father, or some angry combination of events and emotions—he does remember seeking refuge in the woods. It was the outdoors, not his father, that would have the most enduring effect on him. In the outdoors, Heimo found both deliverance and self-discovery. Thoreau called it "the tonic of wildness." For Heimo, it was the antidote to a bad situation at home— an escape to a simpler, more beautiful world—and early on Heimo cultivated his capacity for being alone.

When he was ten, Heimo and two neighborhood friends borrowed some longspring foothold traps that his friend's grandfather hadn't used in years. They set one of the traps in a field and baited it with corn, though none of them expected to catch anything. When they returned a few days later there was a half-eaten pheasant in the trap, tracks in the moist snow, and a hawk soaring overhead. "I was hooked after that," Heimo says. "I don't know why I was so interested in it. Something about being outdoors and the anticipation of it. My friends lost interest fast, and somehow I inherited the traps. I kept at it—and I enjoyed being alone. I started trapping pheasants and rabbits periodically. I'd bring them home and I'd be so proud, and the old man would just scoff, though he liked eating pheasants."

Despite his father's objections, Heimo was trapping during his free time and hunting with his uncles, which he remembers fondly. "I loved the hunting, but for the old man, if you weren't out earning money, you were wasting your time. Later on I got really serious about it. I was hunting on my own and trapping muskrats in the marshes outside of town, especially after I learned that there was a fur buyer in Appleton that paid $2.50 per muskrat skin."

The more Heimo retreated to the woods, the more resentful his father became, and Erich Korth expressed his displeasure, in part, by heaping praise on Heimo's brother Erich, Jr., setting up a sibling rivalry that continues to this day. "Erich was his pride and joy," Heimo says more than thirty years later, with a real hint of acrimony. "And Erich and I fought like hell. We never really got along." Today Erich, Jr., owns his own semitruck trailer repair company. "He's been very successful," Heimo continues. "He's worked hard. But that lifestyle, where you're married to your job, it's never been for me. I don't care if it would have made me rich."

The Korth family had been in America for only six months when, on January 3, 1959, President Dwight D. Eisenhower signed an edict admitting Alaska as the nation's forty-ninth state, ending a decade-long battle about whether or not to allow Alaska's entry into the union. Many were critical of the decision. Opponents of Alaska's statehood wondered how the state's economy could develop quickly enough to pay the bills a state government would inevitably accumulate, even though the War Department spent more than $1 billion in Alaska between 1941 and 1945 and was channeling more money into the state as a result of the Cold War. To combat this objection regarding the state's ability to raise money, a provision was included in the Alaska Statehood Act, altering the Mineral Leasing Acts of 1914 and 1920. The Bureau of Land Management would thereafter be required to compensate the state with 90 percent of the revenues acquired from the extraction of coal on federal land in Alaska and with 52.5 percent of the revenues from oil and gas extraction.

Alaska's detractors were ultimately proved correct. In February 1971, two and a half years after the Atlantic Richfield Company (ARCO) announced that it had discovered oil on Alaska's Arctic Coast, and only one and a half years after the Alaska Department of Natural Resources conducted its fourth Prudhoe Bay oil lease, Governor William Eagen testified at a hearing at the Department of the Interior. A trans-Alaska oil pipeline was urgently needed, he said. If it were not built in five years, he predicted, the state would "face bankruptcy."

On December 18, 1971, a century after the United States purchased Alaska from Russia, nearly twelve years after statehood, and only ten months after Governor Eagen's appeal, President Richard Nixon, an unlikely ally of Alaskan Natives, signed an epic bill. The Alaska Native Claims Settlement Act—ANCSA, as it came to be called—attempted to resolve aboriginal land claims and legally paved the way for the Trans-Alaska Pipeline.

With ANCSA, the Natives of Alaska—Alaskans, according to ANCSA, with one quarter or more of Indian, Eskimo, or Aleut blood—became capitalists overnight. Each Native person was represented by a village corporation and a regional corporation that had profit and investment motives. Thirteen regional corporations and more than 200 village corporations were established. Most Natives enrolled in both and were given 100 shares of stock in each. For the corporations, which quickly turned a blind eye to the longstanding traditions of communal land use and subsistence living—hunting, fishing, and gathering—it was a trial-by-fire experience. Now they would be required to post profits and to view the land as a commodity, since the land would be taxable after 1991. While ANCSA did not satisfy all Natives, and some communities opted out of the settlement entirely, the settlement was viewed by many as a model for the resolution of aboriginal land claims. The Alaska Federation of Natives (AFN) approved the bill by a vote of 511 to 45. Alaska's Natives—represented by the AFN—agreed to the extinguishing of their "aboriginal title . . . based on use and occupancy . . . including any aboriginal hunting and fishing rights." In return, ANCSA awarded them nearly $1 billion—$462 million in federal funds over eleven years, and $500 million from a 2 percent royalty on oil leases—and 44 million acres, over one-tenth of Alaska's total acreage. ANCSA gave Alaskan Natives an unprecedented opportunity for self-determination and a unique avenue into the national economy, effectively ending a 200-year-old policy isolating Natives from the business interests that drove America. By linking (cynics said "shrewdly" linking) the Native monetary settlement to the oil leases, many Natives were turned into enthusiastic proponents of the pipeline.

With Native land claims apparently settled, Alaska's boosters hoped that they could finally begin selection of, and gain title to, the 105 million acres guaranteed to the state by the Statehood Act. Prior to ANCSA, this right was denied them by section 4 of the Statehood Act, which instructed the state to "disclaim all right and title to any lands . . . the right or title to which . . . may be held by any Indians, Eskimos, or Aleuts."

Sixteen months after ANCSA became law, Heimo turned eighteen. Richard Nixon had already curtailed the draft, so instead of fighting in Vietnam, Heimo took a summer job with Wisconsin's Department of Natural Resources at Camp Mecan, a summer work camp on the Mecan River. At Camp Mecan, Heimo learned forestry and game and fish habitat maintenance skills, all of which further confirmed his love for the outdoors.

Jim Kryzmarcik, who was raised on a farm near a small town in northern Wisconsin, also attended the work camp, and he and Heimo grew to be close friends there. Kryzmarcik recalls, "Compared to me, Heimo was a city kid. But he was into nature. He wanted to know about the plants and the birds. He was real interested in learning about it and how nature worked. Camp Mecan was the turning point in his life, I think."

After Camp Mecan, the outdoors was indeed irresistible for Heimo, and he spent much of his time plotting his escape north after high school graduation. But graduation never came. Heimo explains, "Prior to my senior year, I was skipping a lot of classes, but by the middle of my senior year, I was skipping a lot of days. It wasn't that I didn't like school—I liked science and I really enjoyed geography—but I just hated the routine of it. You had to be there from 8:00 A.M. to 3:00 P.M., or whatever it was, and I couldn't stand that. So I dropped out in April of my senior year. A shrewd move, right? I had two months to go, and I left."

After dropping out, Heimo was hired on as welder at Miller Electric, a huge welding plant headquartered in Appleton. Heimo had learned the basics of welding in high school shop classes, and he attended daily advanced welding classes while working at Miller, too. As far as Erich Korth was concerned, his son had finally taken up a worthwhile trade, and he was proud of Heimo. Heimo, however, was frustrated and angry, fearful that he had become, after all, what he hated—a regular working Joe, an eight-to-fiver, living for the weekends and dreaming of that far-off day when he might be able to retire. Heimo started drinking to relieve the boredom and the disappointment, and he became a five-to six-day-a-week fixture at a tough, dimly lit, bank-turned-biker bar in Appleton called Sarge's.

Heimo had been drinking since he was fifteen, when his father got him drunk for the first time at home, but at Sarge's he was doing a different kind of drinking, serious and self-destructive. "I drank because I was bored and pissed off and because I hated what I'd become," Heimo admits.

Steve Laabs, Heimo's childhood friend, says, "Heimo was there with us every night. But he was always a little different than the rest of us. He'd been different all his life. He was always dreaming of going north."

One day in the spring of 1974, after nine months at Miller, intent on realizing his dream and following the needle pull of the compass north, Heimo quit his job and took off for the Northwest Territories. "Miller's paid well and offered good benefits and would have been a good job if I was a different kind of guy, but it was driving me crazy," Heimo says.

Roland Pruno, another childhood friend of Heimo's, says, "Heimo was making respectable money at Miller, but he was bound and determined to leave. Heimo and I had the same printing class in the eighth grade. We made some stationery, and Heimo's read, 'Heimo Korth— Guide and Trapper of the North.' He wanted to go to Canada and be a trapper and a guide, and Heimo was the only person that I ever knew that always did exactly what he said he was going to do."

Sister Angie was hardly surprised by Heimo's abrupt departure. "Heimo was always an individual," she says. "Ever since he was a boy, his room was always filled with *Field & Stream*, *Outdoor Life*, and animal and bird books. He used to take me into the woods and teach me to identify birds and animal tracks. I knew the factory job was only temporary."

While Erich Korth had always bullied and degraded Heimo, Irene Korth had instilled in him a deep belief in the possibilities of life and the conviction that he could do something unique and different with his. Angie Korth says of her mother, "Mom was born too early. She would have made a great hippie. She was worried about Heimo, but she admired free spirits, and that's what Heimo was; she knew that."

Despite Irene Korth's support of her oldest son, Lisa Korth remembers how hard it was on her mother when Heimo left. "She was very excited for him," she says. "But she worried, too. I remember Mom crying a lot."

In May 1974, Heimo packed up his Ford F150 pickup truck, which he'd outfitted with a topper, stuck $700 in his wallet, and took off for the Northwest Territories. Riding an adrenaline high, he reached International Falls, Minnesota, in less than eight hours—the 500 miles between Appleton and International Falls had been a blur. At the bridge to Canada, a customs agent pulled him over. Where was he going, the agent asked. When Heimo answered, "the Northwest Territories," the agent asked him to leave his truck and escorted Heimo to an office

where he interrogated Heimo. Where are you from? Why are you going to the Northwest Territories? What are you going to do for money?
Then it dawned on Heimo. "Jesus Christ," he thought, "I never should
have answered honestly." Canada had had problems with draft dodgers,
and now that U.S. involvement in Vietnam had ended, Canada was being flooded with disillusioned veterans. Heimo had anticipated having a
problem, so before leaving he'd made sure to shave and cut his shoul-
der-length hair. Finally the customs agent asked Heimo to open his wal-
let. Heimo dumped its contents onto the table, and the agent counted
the money slowly—$400, $500, $660. Heimo had paid for gas and food,
but his $700 was largely intact. Confident that he had no intentions of
relying on the charity of the Canadian government, the agent told
Heimo to be on his way.

After the incident at the border, Heimo gassed up and ate, then he
drove through the deep Ontario night. He stopped to sleep along a pot-
holed country road outside of Kenora, Ontario. He was too tired to
pitch his tent, so he just lay his sleeping bag under a tree. The following
day he covered all of Manitoba, crossing at night into Saskatchewan,
where he camped at Crooked Lake Provincial Park. Before dawn, he
was on the road again. He pushed himself, arriving in Calgary, Alberta,
just after sunset. Looking west in the direction of Banff National Park
and the Livingstone Range—the first mountains he'd ever seen—he felt
his heart leap. He pulled off to the side of the road and stared at the
mountains, outlined by the gray-red sky, and knew he'd never again be
happy back home in Wisconsin's flatlands.

The next morning, he headed north, past Edmonton to Peace River.
After nearly 500 miles of driving, he turned onto a gravel road, lay down
on the front seat of his truck with a sweatshirt as a pillow, and woke at
sunrise. Just west of Peace River, he went for a swim in Lac Cardinal in
Queen Elizabeth Provincial Park. Then he headed north up the
Mackenzie Highway, paralleling the Hay River just north outside the
town of Meander River. By late afternoon, he was in the Northwest
Territories. He camped that night near Hay River on Great Slave Lake.
The next morning, he arrived at the Mackenzie River, but so much ice
was rushing down from Great Slave Lake that the ferry couldn't make

the crossing. He slept in his truck that night, crossed the Mackenzie on day seven, and arrived in Yellowknife the following afternoon, 2,500 miles from Appleton.

Yellowknife itself was a disappointment to Heimo, nothing more than a jumble of buildings, jerry-rigged in the 1930s after prospectors discovered veins of gold in the local quartz. Intent on getting out of Yellowknife as soon as possible, Heimo started asking questions about trapping in the interior, in that great, wild stretch of boreal forest west of Yellowknife. The answers he received discouraged him. He was told that only Canadian citizens were allowed to trap. In a bar, Heimo met an old miner, who confided in him that there were men out there trespassing and laying low when necessary. Heimo hung around Yellowknife, debating whether or not to say the hell with the law, but a month later he returned to Wisconsin. Heimo knew that his father would gloat, and he was determined not to give him the pleasure until he had a few drinks under his belt, so instead of heading home to the inevitable "I told you so," he stopped in at Sarge's. Heimo started drinking in the afternoon, one Budweiser after another. By the time the mill crew arrived, Heimo was already drunk. He was sitting on a barstool when his friend Roland Pruno walked by. Heimo pulled Pruno toward him and wrapped a heavy arm over Pruno's shoulders. "I'm going again," Heimo said, nearly whispering. Later that night, Pruno remembers, Heimo told him and anyone else willing to listen, in a loud voice, that he wouldn't be in Wisconsin for long, that he had the guts to leave once and he'd have the guts to try again.

I am two weeks into my January visit. It is 6:30 in the morning when I hear Heimo walk by, the snow cracking under his feet. By now I know his routine. He rises at 6:15 to stoke the fire and warm the cabin and then he takes the honeybucket to the banks of the creek bed, where he dumps it. Afterward he checks the weather, reading the two thermometers that NOAA has provided him.

Despite the fact that Heimo is no longer punching a factory clock, he leads a ritualized life. Structure, he says, is essential in the bush, where at times it is so cold that getting out of bed, much less going outside and subjecting oneself to winter's cruelties, requires an act of will. It is easy to be listless in winter, particularly in January, when a person is craving the return of the sun.

Heimo is standing outside my tent now. "Ya, der, you awake or ya still snoozin'?" he asks, improvising a heavy Wisconsin accent. I try to be enthusiastic, to sound as if I've had a good night of sleep on my army cot, as if I am looking forward to bundling up against the cold. The last thing I want Heimo to think is that I am a soft city boy. "Ready and rarin'," I say, trying out my own Wisconsin accent. "Let's give 'er."

"Ooooh, Christ," Heimo continues, drawing out the long *O*. "I spent too much time at da tavern last night wit da boys. She was a late one, and I got a hangover. Aw Jeezus, da wife, she's pissed."

"Ya, der, I'm feelin' er, too. My frickin' head is poundin'," I answer. "Oooh, ders gonna be hell to pay wit da missus dis mornin'."

Heimo laughs. It has been a long time since he's been in a Wisconsin tavern, or any tavern (he hasn't touched a drop of alcohol since the fall of 1981), but he loves this routine. For two weeks now we have subjected Edna and the girls to our Wisconsin schtick. For them the humor has worn off, but Heimo loves it.

We eat a breakfast of oatmeal—"oatmeal or no meal" is Heimo's refrain—and then I return to the tent to dress, layering against the inevitable cold. By 8:30 Heimo is outside with the snowmachine and the sled. "Taxi's waiting and the meter's running," he shouts.

I get myself situated in back of the sled, using my day pack as a backrest. Today we're carrying only Heimo's pack, a few leghold traps, the ax, the .22, and two marten carcasses, so I'm able to stretch out and extend my legs. When I'm settled Heimo kisses Edna and the girls goodbye. Each morning they come out to see us off regardless of the temperature. Edna is a worrier; from experience she knows how fast things can go wrong out here. "Don't forget the plan," she says. "If you're not back by suppertime, I'll come looking for you." "Oh, Mom," Heimo replies, trying to soothe her, "we'll be okay."

Today we plan to check Heimo's longest line, a trip that will take us eight hours or more. Fortunately it is only 26 below. The temperature will be bearable, at least five degrees or so warmer once we get into the hills where Heimo has his marten sets.

Heimo has noticed significant weather changes in Alaska since he arrived in 1975. Though he expresses skepticism about the urgent warnings of a worldwide warming, his observations would probably coincide with global-climate-change models. "The winters are not nearly as cold as they once were," he tells me, wiping the snow from the #1 longspring leghold trap on his first poleset. "Years ago, forty, fifty below was common, but it's rare today. No question about it, though, the winters are longer now. They come earlier and stay later. But I can handle that. It's the snow that ticks me off. There's a lot more of it than before, and it makes my life hard. These traps get too much snow and they won't fire properly. And it's hell on my trails."

The U.N. Intergovernmental Panel on Climate Change confirms and expands upon Heimo's observations: more cloud cover, more frequent snowstorms, more moisture in the air in general, and stronger winds, which pick up moisture from the thawing ice fields of the Arctic Ocean and transport it south. A 2001 report from the panel indicates that global warming is far worse than earlier estimates, with Alaska, Greenland, and Arctic Canada witnessing warm-ups significantly higher than the rest of the world. Over the past thirty years, winter temperatures in regions of the north have risen by ten degrees compared to a worldwide average of one degree, and Arctic ice is 40 percent thinner than it was in 1960. Despite the naysayers who adhere blindly to Le Chatelier's principle—that the earth is capable of recovering on its own from devastating changes—many climatologists anticipate increases by the year 2100 "without precedent during the last 10,000 years." In other words, the earth will encounter the kinds of dramatic global climate changes that it has not seen since the last Ice Age.

By the time Heimo and I reach the fifth poleset, he is shaking his head, more puzzled than discouraged. The polesets have been empty, and he's seen very little marten sign. "There should be marten all over this hill," he says. For most trappers in Alaska's Interior, the marten is their bread and butter. It's what allows them to pay for the bush flights and their food and fuel bills. The other animals—the wolf, wolverine, lynx (or "lynk,"), fox, beaver—they're "gravy," as one old Fort Yukon trapper told me.

Heimo shuts off the snowmachine. "I'll probably catch seventy or so marten this year," he says. "At $40 or so a pelt, that's only $2800. Not much of a year unless I do well on wolves this spring. Did I ever tell you about Fred's best year?" Fred Thomas is Heimo's good friend and one of Alaska's legendary trappers, the subject of Edward Hoagland's memorable essay "Up the Black to the Chalkyitsik." Fred Thomas calls Fort Yukon home. At eighty-three, he still takes his boat up the Black River, 300-plus river miles from Fort Yukon, where he picks berries and hunts moose at his camp. He still successfully traps seventy-five miles of line around Fort Yukon, using a snowmachine, and still cuts all his own wood. "The winter of 1979-1980," Heimo continues, "Fred and his brother and son trapped 315 lynx," Heimo says the number as if it is inconceivable, the same way he might react to news of Bill Gates's net worth. "Do you wanna know what they got for each pelt? $350," he says. "$350!" Trappers in Alaska talk about the price of fur like Midwestern farmers discuss milk, corn, and soybean prices, and I knew it was the kind of payday Heimo had never seen and, considering the dismal state of the fur market, maybe never would. "With that kind of money, I'd put a chunk in the girls' college fund and then I'd buy a new snowmachine and some Alaska #9 wolf traps," he muses.

Heimo doesn't linger long over the thought. He tells me to sit down in the sled, pulls the starter on the snowmachine, lets it warm up for half a minute, and then gives the machine some gas. Every trapper has to have a bit of the gambler in him, a sense of anticipation that keeps him going in the cold, that impels him to check the next trap even when the prospects look gloomy. It isn't the same kind of mindless hopefulness of someone playing the slots, but rather the sense of expectation that a diligent blackjack player might feel. He studies the cards and knows that it's only a matter of time before he wins.

Heimo has the heart of a blackjack player. All of his marten traps are polesets. Before the season begins, he spends weeks surveying hundreds of miles of country, searching for marten tracks and the kind of terrain marten love. He's a good student, careful and observant, and even in low marten years he does well. Once he's finished scouting, Heimo lays out his lines, constructing his polesets before the season begins. The polesets are spaced fairly close together because trapping is about probabilities—the more traps you're willing to set and check, the more success you'll have. To build a poleset, Heimo locates a dead spruce tree and cuts it down at the point where the trunk begins to taper off, usually three feet above the ground. Then he notches the trunk and rests the other part of the tree, the pole, in the notch, making certain to wipe off the pitch, which can spoil a fur. Using his ax, he cuts a small, flat indentation in the pole, which will eventually contain the trap. Just before the season begins, Heimo will boil the traps in spruce boughs to take away their scent and then he'll haul them out with the snowmachine and the sled. He uses one trap per poleset, fastening the trap's chain to the pole, so that once the marten is caught it can't run off with the trap. At the end of the pole, he attaches a piece of string to which he ties bait, usually moose skin, the skin of a spruce grouse or a ptarmigan, or the fur of a snowshoe hare with the entrails wrapped inside. The bait dangles high enough from the ground that the marten can't reach it. In an effort to get at the bait, the marten will use the pole as a ramp.

We have left the polesets behind and now we're bound for a side trail to check some of Heimo's leghold traps. A quarter of a mile down the trail, Heimo stops the snowmachine and points to fresh tracks in the snow. "Wolf," he says. "Looks like a loner, traveling east. An adolescent male, I'd say," he explains, showing me the seven-inch paw prints. "He's probably after the caribou that were bedded down on the lake." Heimo steps from the snowmachine carefully. I get out of the sled. "Try to stay on the snowmachine trail," he warns me. "I don't want any fresh tracks in the snow." We walk along the trail on top of the packed snow for about one hundred yards. The wolf's tracks parallel the trail, but never once does he get closer than two feet. "Wolves are so damn smart," Heimo says. "See how he won't even step on the trail. He wants nothing to do with it."

Though wolves have ranges over 600 square miles and rarely use the same trail, Heimo thinks that this one might be coming back and decides to set two Bridger #5 longspring wolf traps in a clearing. Wolves, he tells me, are more likely to let down their guard in a clearing. First, he breaks off a rotten spruce tree at its base and pushes it into the snow so less than two feet is sticking up and sprays it with coyote urine that he orders from Fur Country Lures out of Jordan, Montana. This is the scent stick, or the "peepost," as Heimo calls it. Before setting the traps, Heimo puts on his special cloth wolf gloves, which he only uses for setting wolf traps so they won't carry any other scent, animal or human. As he prepares the wolf traps, he explains how they work. The traps have offset, rounded jaws, rather than square ones, that act like handcuffs. Rather than breaking bones or tearing into flesh, they leave a small gap, which is less painful for the wolf. Heimo sets the traps and arranges the guide sticks, then collects a film of snow on the head of his ax and gently sprinkles it over the trap lids.

"If there was wind here," he says, "I couldn't do this. I'd use a block of hard snow to hold the trap down. But you got to taper it with your ax, so there's not much snow over the pan. Otherwise the trap won't fire right."

Before leaving, he wipes snow over the chains to conceal them and then uses a small spruce bough to dust the snow clean of our footprints.

He's happy with the set and is eager to check another one a mile down the trail, where we saw fox tracks a week ago. I am hardly in the sled when he takes off. He is driving faster than usual, and I'm holding on with one hand and fending off spruce boughs with the other. When we arrive at the trap, Heimo throws his arms up as if signaling touchdown. "Got 'im," he celebrates. "A red fox." It's the same one, he says, that was prowling the hillside only eight days ago. We walk up to the fox, and unlike the wolverine, it doesn't hiss or lunge at us; it slinks low to the ground and trembles, and I feel a pang of guilt. Heimo lifts his leg and steps on it heavily, collapsing its lungs. The fox looks at me, and I turn my head and look away. "Are you okay?" Heimo asks. "Sure," I say. As he puts his weight into it and pushes the air from the fox's lungs, it emits a long, high-pitched sound like an asthmatic's wheeze.

Heimo pulls apart the jaws of the #4 double longspring trap and gives me the fox to take back to the sled. Sitting down, I hold it in my lap. I take off my mitten and glove and rub my hand along the soft, cherry-red fur along the fox's back. Though I am a hunter and have shot deer, rabbits, and countless grouse, pheasants, and waterfowl, I feel vaguely uncomfortable about the fox's death, as Aldo Leopold did when he shot a wolf and reached it in time to see a "fierce green fire" dying in its eyes. I stroke the fox and watch Heimo reset the trap. He returns to the snowmachine, straddles the seat, then turns around, facing me.

"I know," he says simply. "Sometimes it's hard."

Had Heimo been allowed to go out into the country west of Yellowknife, he would have become a fox trapper. The Northwest Territories had an abundant supply of red fox, cross fox, and Arctic fox, and their habitat was not going to be affected by oil development. While Heimo was in Yellowknife, he had learned, for the first time, of the Trans-Alaska Pipeline, a joint venture of the oil companies holding Prudhoe Bay leases. The pipeline's fate had been sealed the previous year when Vice President Spiro Agnew broke a tie vote in the Senate authorizing its construction. Though the Canadian government petitioned hard for a route through Canada via the Mackenzie River valley and into the Great Lakes, the pipeline became an all-Alaska endeavor.

The Trans-Alaska Pipeline was to be an engineering marvel. Traveling 800 miles over public domain, from Prudhoe Bay on Alaska's North Slope, across the 150-mile-wide Brooks Range, south to Valdez, a small fishing village on the Prince William Sound with a fjord deep enough to accommodate large oceangoing tankers, Rogers C.B. Morton, who was Nixon's second Secretary of the Interior, equated it with the Egyptian pyramids. For conservationists, the prospect of a pipeline was like staring into the face of the apocalypse, a scenario of industrial expansion into the far North that Bob Marshall, mountaineer, author, founder of the The Wilderness Society, and impassioned defender of the Arctic frontier, had prophesied nearly forty years earlier. Henry Pratt, Governor Keith Miller's advisor, was unmoved by their objections. Summing up what many Alaskans felt, including those in Governor Miller's administration, he said, with frontier bravado, "Hell, this country's so goddamn big that even if industry ran wild, we could never wreck it. . . ." For prodevelopment Alaskans, wary of the state's budget problems, the pipeline represented a figurative shot in the arm for the Alaskan economy. The first oil flowed south on June 20, 1977, pumping 700,000 barrels of oil a day (its capacity is two million) and millions of dollars into the foundering Alaskan economy.

For decades prior to the discovery of oil, geologists were convinced that there were significant deposits on Alaska's north coast. Early European explorers of Alaska's north coast wrote of oil seeping from the ground. After World War II, the U.S. Geological Survey was issued a directive to locate formations favorable to oil, and it produced a grid cut across the Alaskan landscape to aid in aerial surveys. Following the surveys, the federal government issued oil companies cheap leases to encourage exploration. The Israeli–Egyptian war in 1956, which shut down the Suez Canal to shipping, including all oil tanker traffic, convinced British Petroleum's executives that the company would have to search for more reliable oil supplies elsewhere. Noticing the topographic similarities between the North Slope and Iran, BP's exploration chief was confident that there was oil to be found. How much was the question.

When oil was discovered in Prudhoe Bay, talk turned swiftly to a pipeline. Robert Anderson, the chairman of the Atlantic Richfield Company (ARCO), declared that "pipeline and transportation studies would begin immediately," and the land claims issues of Alaskan Natives suddenly catapulted to national prominence. With the discovery of oil, Native claims had become much more than an Alaskan issue; they became a national one. When Arab countries cut off oil supplies to the U.S. in 1973, proponents of the pipeline used this opportunity to claim that fuel shortages and accompanying economic and national security issues made North American resource development imperative. What they failed to say is that the oil would do nothing to ameliorate the country's short-term crisis.

Shortly after oil was discovered in Prudhoe Bay, Robert Anderson, ARCO's chairman, and other oil company executives who had contributed handsomely to the Nixon campaign were pushing Nixon to appoint a Secretary of the Interior who would support their interests. Nixon came through, naming Walter J. Hickel, Alaska's prodevelopment Republican governor, to the Interior Department's top position. However, Stewart Udall, President Lyndon Johnson's outgoing Secretary of the Interior, had a trick up his sleeve. Three days before leaving office, Udall, who was determined to delay the pipeline and the land-selection process until Native land claims were settled, signed Public Land Order 4582, referred to as the "super land freeze." This order removed a whopping 262 million acres from "selection, settlement, location, sale and entry" until December 31, 1970. Udall's action pleased conservationists, who, when they realized that the subdivison of the Alaskan landscape was inevitable, set their sights on sizeable sections of the Alaskan land pie, as did Native leaders.

Prior to the discovery of oil and the ensuing land grab, the Alaska wilderness was open to anyone who wanted to line a boat up a river, peel logs, build a cabin, set up a fish camp, hunt for food. Though the land was public, few restrictions had been placed on what people could and could not do. The prospect of a pipeline set in motion an irreversible force that would end that historical freedom.

ANCSA itself was a business transaction, motivated by profit. It was an attempt by the U.S. government to satisfy the land claims of Natives, which, if left unattended, had the potential to block the building of the Trans-Alaska Pipeline. Conservationists were so outraged by plans for the pipeline and by the prospect of Native lands being administered not by the federal government but by Native corporations forced to post profits that they demanded significant conservation provisions be written into ANCSA. One conservationist summed it up this way: "You can't run a pipeline up the middle of a wilderness and still think of that place as wilderness." Congress responded, because the environmental movement, which had steadily been gaining strength since the early 1900s, was now too powerful to be ignored. Included in ANCSA was a pivotal paragraph, 17(d)(2), instructing the Secretary of the Interior to set aside 80 million acres of national interest lands, henceforth called "d-2" lands, for possible federal protection.

Disappointed but undeterred by his experience in the Northwest Territories, Heimo was back in Appleton by the end of June 1974, welding

combines, hayrakes, and other farm machinery at Fox Tractor. He had
tried to get on at Miller again, but they weren't interested in hiring him.
Two and a half months later, Fox laid him off.

Erich Korth, Sr., had been laid off, too, and the prospect of his getting back to work soon was slim. Heimo was doing nothing but hunting,
drinking, and coming home late, which only made Erich Korth more irritable. Heimo and his father hardly spoke. Mostly, they just tried to ignore each other.

Heimo was watching television one day when his father walked into
the room. "He reeked of beer," Heimo remembers. "I said, 'Jesus
Christ, Dad, you're drunk again?' " Erich Korth couldn't contain himself. The hypocrisy of it—his drunk of a son scolding him, telling him to
lay off the booze. He balled up his fist and drove his knuckles into
Heimo's head. Heimo had a choice—he could either lash out at his father or he could restrain himself and walk away. Heimo walked away,
leaving Erich Korth standing in the middle of the room. " 'Come on,
hit me,' " Heimo remembers his father screaming. " 'Just try to hit
me.' "

Heimo was tired of it. By mid-January 1975, things were about as bad
as they could get between Heimo and his father, and Heimo knew he
had to get out of the house. One evening he and some friends had plans
to drink at Sarge's. While Heimo waited at the kitchen table for a friend
to pick him up, he paged through the classifieds in the January issue of
Outdoor Life. He came upon a section for Alaskan hunting guides. The
first ad he read was from a guide by the name of Keith Koontz, who was
advertising hunting trips in Alaska's Brooks Range. Heimo decided he
would write to him. He asked Koontz if he needed a helper, someone to
do the camp stuff—prepare meals, wash dishes—and pack out the animals the hunters shot.

It was a biography of Daniel Boone that had planted the seed. After
reading that book in his early teens, Heimo was filled with the idea of
losing himself in North America's last remaining wildernesses. Early on,
he had settled on Canada's Northwest Territories. But his experience
there changed all that. While in Canada, he had heard about another
mountain range in Alaska's inhospitable Interior—the Brooks Range,

ultima Thule. From the moment he left Yellowknife, getting to the Brooks Range was his primary ambition.

Three weeks passed, and Heimo had given up all hope that Koontz would reply when a letter came. The guide expressed interest in hiring him as a packer, but he needed references. Within a few days, Heimo sent him what he wanted.

Heimo says now, "I wish Mom was around to tell the story. She was so excited for me. But she was always my ally. I watched for the mail like a kid waiting for Santa Claus. When the letter finally came, and I got the job, I was elated. I was jumping up and down. Finally, I was leaving for Alaska."

Jim Kryzmarcik, Heimo's friend from Camp Mecan, says, "God, Heimo was excited. He called me up and said he was leaving for Alaska. I thought he was crazy, but there was no stopping him. It sounded like a great adventure, but I didn't think he'd last. I thought I'd see him back in six months, to be honest with you. But he had the desire big-time. He used to walk around with a heavy backpack to train for being a packer in the Brooks Range."

Steve Laabs confirms the story. "We were shooting a lot of skeet and trap at the time—Heimo was determined to be a great shot before he left for Alaska—and Heimo would walk out to the gun club. It was eight miles from his house. He'd load his backpack with rocks. He'd walk there, shoot, and then walk home. We always offered him a ride, but he never took it."

Roland Pruno says, "I always knew he'd do it. But I was worried about him, too. He was still afraid to go into the woods at night. I knew he'd have to get over that quick."

Eight months after sending his intial letter to Keith Koontz, on a 95-degree day in early August 1975, with the air hanging heavy with humidity, Heimo left for Alaska to seek what he'd come to believe was his destiny. He and his father had had a ferocious argument that morning. Though Heimo can't recall what the argument was about, he does remember how mad his father was. "The old man was pissed. God, was he pissed. But that wasn't unusual. He was always ticked off about something. I was so happy to be getting away. I knew I wasn't coming back."

Irene Korth kissed and hugged her son, wished him luck, told him that she loved him and was proud of him, and dabbed at her tears with a tissue. She'd bought Heimo a round-trip ticket just in case something went wrong. Secretly she hoped that he'd have a change of heart. Heimo hugged his little brother, Tom, who at ten understood only that his big brother was leaving for Alaska and was excited by that. Angie, Lisa, and Erich, Jr., had said their good-byes the night before. But Erich Korth wouldn't budge. He sat on the couch reading the paper, stewing in his anger, and didn't so much as say good-bye. When Heimo left, his father didn't even look at him. To hell with him, Heimo thought. I'm outta here.

CHAPTER 3

The Final Frontier

Along the Old Crow drainage lies a tremendous chunk of wild country, dominated by hogback ridges that top out at 2,800 feet, boggy lowlands, impenetrable tundra, countless creeks, tundra lakes, and ephemeral ponds, which for nearly eight months of every year becomes a vast, navigable plain of windswept snow. At 68 degrees latitude, this is the *taiga*, a Russian word meaning, "land of little sticks," the upper limit of the world's northern forests. Four-hundred-year-old black spruces with trunks no thicker than broom handles and hip-high black spruces, almost a century old, resemble weary, white-robed mendicants. They are bent low by snow and the force of fierce southerly winds. Yet they are survivors, holding on for dear life in only centimeters of soil in the open tundra flats where no other tree can flourish. Along the river and creek beds grow balsam poplar, referred to as cottownwood, head-high willows and alders, and stands of white spruce, reaching up the waterways like God's fingers.

This is the Frigid Zone, and only ten miles north of here, the names of trees are preceded by the word *dwarf*, as in "dwarf willow" and "dwarf birch." Only thirty feet from the rivers and the tumbling creeks, the trees hug the ground, growing no higher than a few feet. Much of the land is tundra, a maze of spongy, waterlogged clumps of sphagnum moss called tussock, muskeg, hummock, or in the vernacular of old-time Alaskans "niggerheads." Walking on tussocks is like walking on a trampoline while someone is bouncing; it requires extraordinary balance.

Though people have traveled this land for perhaps as long as 10,000 years, few have done more than pass through. Prior to Heimo, there were maybe two or three other trappers who called this country home, and they lived lightly on the land. Before the trappers, small, roving bands of Athabaskan Indian subsistence hunters, members of the Gwich'in Nation, the "people of the caribou," and coastal Inupiat Eskimos followed the movement of game through this inhospitable land. They lived in caribou tents and pulled snow sleds loaded with their few possessions. Forced by weather and erratic game patterns to be perpetually on the move, they came and went, never lingering for long. For the ancient Arctic hunters, life was both a joy and a struggle, plagued by the twin dangers of hunger and death.

The Gwich'in domain extended from the Yukon River north over the Brooks Range to the Arctic Ocean and east to the Peel River in Canada. The Gwich'in culture is Alaska's oldest. Its people, anthropologists claim, are close relatives of the Navahos and Apaches of the desert Southwest. When the Gwich'in weren't fighting off famine and chasing game or warring with coastal Eskimos or far-ranging Inuit Eskimos from the Mackenzie River Delta in Canada, they lived nearer the Yukon River in caribou-skin huts.

Today the Old Crow drainage is still raw wilderness, the ne plus ultra. It is also a region without names. The Old Crow drainage, as much of Interior Alaska, was once infused with Native history and strung together with names recalling significant events or noting prominent features—to the Gwich'in, the Porcupine River was *Ch'oonjik* (pronounced *Chō* with the accent on the second syllable), or "porcupine quill along the river," and the Brooks Range was *Gwazhal*—which guided Native travelers from river bend to river bend and mountain to hill. But today those names have largely been forgotten, omitted from modern maps and unknown to a generation of Natives who no longer have a need to travel deep into the country on extended subsistence hunting journeys.

Because they use the land, Heimo and his family have names for the

Old Crow's prominent features—Rundown Mountain, Thunder Mountain, Krin Creek—but these have not made it onto modern maps either.

In early January 2002 I purchased two 1:63, 360-series topographic maps at the University of Alaska in Fairbanks. When I unrolled them on the long counter at the map office, the dizzying relief lines, the resplendent green, and the sheer number of names confused me until I realized that I'd been given the wrong quadrangles. I was looking at two maps of the Talkeetna area, a fertile, mountainous country just north of Anchorage. When the woman behind the counter returned with the correct ones of the Old Crow and Coleen River drainages, I was relieved to find vast areas awash with white and blotches of green nearly devoid of names. Even the U.S. Geological Surveyors, who superimposed a mathematical grid of six-mile squares over the landscape, refrained from the temptation to name. Perhaps they were humbled enough by what they saw from the air—the area was only cursorily field checked—and understood the meagerness of their efforts to assign names to a land they didn't know. Only the large rivers and a few of the nearby peaks are spoken for: Yankee Ridge, Horse Hill, Ammerman Mountain. Hundreds of creeks remain anonymous, as do all of the tundra ponds and lakes and the cold, detached spires of the Brooks Range, only fifteen miles away from the Korth's cabin. Pure, white, and adamantine, these peaks are the apotheosis of this epic landscape, as awesome in their physical presence as their mythic evocations.

Apart from the international boundary swath and an aborted attempt to establish a winter tractor trail during the winter of 1955-1956 to connect the Yukon River with Distant Early Warning (DEW) line sites in the Canadian Arctic, man's presence here has been inconsequential. All this unspoiled space, however, is something of an illusion. Only 115 miles north lies one of the world's largest industrial complexes, over 1,000 square miles of North Slope oil development, including Prudhoe Bay. But the 5,000- and 6,000-thousand-foot peaks of the Brooks Range protect one's view north and shield the Old Crow from the coast's brown nitrogen oxide cloud and also help to shelter the imagination from the ugly truth. The DEW line sites are the result of a military establishment that regarded Alaska as a strategic piece of property in a paranoid superpower game and erected the sites during the Cold War years to warn of a Soviet invasion from the north. But the winter tractor trail and the attempt to connect those sites with Alaska's Interior failed. Afterward the Air Force, or its civilian contractors, jettisoned much of its equipment along the Canada border. Two trailers, tanks from gas tankers, piles of chains, and tires were left along the Old Crow River. Yet, other than the junk along the border and the tractor trail, whose thirty-foot-incision through the trees and the tundra is still visible today, man has left few signs of his occupation.

The nearest villages are more than one hundred miles away—a two-to-four-day journey by snowmachine if the rivers are frozen solid and the snow isn't too deep; about the same traveling downriver by boat, much longer going upriver; almost two weeks in summer on foot, three weeks minimum in winter on snowshoes without a trail. Yet for the Korths these villages represent outposts of civilization, reference points in their physical, political, and psychic landscape.

Kaktovik, an Inupiat Eskimo village with a population of 250, lies 115 miles to the north. The Korths are separated from Kaktovik and the small island on which it is found, Barter Island, by the serrated peaks of the Brooks Range and a small swath of coastal plain, a floorboard-flat area of tundra, ponds, and rivers.

Until 1945, when Barter Island became a radar site for the Distant Early Warning system, the residents of Barter Island lived much as their ancestors did. They were whale hunters who lived in sod huts along the coast. Shortly after the DEW site was constructed, however, a school was built in Kaktovik, and people began to settle in town. Today, Kaktovik is part of the wealthy Arctic Slope Regional Corporation, the richest, by far, of Alaska's thirteen Native corporations, and one of eight villages (Wainwright, Point Lay, Point Hope, Nuiqsut, Atqasak, Anaktuvuk Pass, and the city of Barrow) encompassed by the affluent North Slope Borough, which collects taxes on oil leases. Though the people of Kaktovik still trap Arctic fox, wolves, and wolverines in the foothills of the Arctic National Wildlife Refuge and still fish and hunt along the coast for waterfowl, polar bear, caribou, bearded and hair seals, and bowhead whales, most support oil development in the refuge. Oil money has brought them a new high school and gymnasium, a swimming pool, a power plant, streetlights, running water, new homes, trucks, ATVs, boats, and countless other personal possessions. Their support for drilling, however, is qualified. Because whaling is still an important tradition, most strenuously object to offshore development in their whaling grounds.

Arctic Village, a Gwich'in Indian village of 170, lies 115 miles directly west of the Korth's cabin. It is snuggled along the East Fork of the Chandalar River and is surrounded by postcard mountains and little lakes loaded with northern pike. Despite the solitude of its setting, Arctic Village has become a battleground in the fight to determine the fate of the Arctic National Wildlife Refuge. Residents are courted by environmentalists and oil executives alike. Publicly the residents of Arctic Village struggle valiantly against the threat of oil development on the refuge's coastal plain, a place they refer to as *Vadzaih Googii Vi Dehk'it Gwanlii*, approximately "the Sacred Place Where Life Begins," and the potential disruption of the Porcupine caribou herd's calving and migration pattern. Privately a few of the villagers confess that the impoverished community, which opted out of ANCSA and the cash settlement for the right to retain their ancestral lands, could benefit from oil development.

One hundred fifty miles to the southwest is Fort Yukon, which sits just above the Arctic Circle at the confluence of the Yukon and Porcupine rivers. The Korths have a summer cabin in Fort Yukon, where they live for one and a half months of every year. Like the generations of trapping families who came before them, they spend June and a portion of July there, stocking up on supplies, reconnecting with old friends, and getting a brief dose of civilization.

Canadian traders from the Hudson Bay Company, who regarded the Yukon Flats as the richest fur territory in all of North America, established Fort Yukon in 1847. Two decades later, the United States purchased Alaska. The British fled, though Fort Yukon continued as a fur-buying center under American auspices. Later it became a stopover for hopeful shoe salesmen-turned-miners caught up in the madness of the Klondike gold rush. Today Fort Yukon is a town of 750, with a large

Gwich'in Athabaskan Indian population. It is plagued by the kinds of disquieting problems that haunt Native villages all across Alaska: alcoholism and the attendant fetal alcohol syndrome; rampant drug use; health problems ranging from tuberculosis to diabetes to heart disease; a high suicide rate; and child abuse. Despite a host of alcohol-related problems, Fort Yukon has made a deal with the devil. It is a "wet" village, the most liberal designation in a three-tiered system—dry, damp, wet—meaning alcohol can be purchased in town. Of Alaska's nearly 250 bush communities, it is one of only seventeen where booze can be bought legally. The town-owned liquor store, windowless and made of corrugated aluminum, with a thick metal door resembling that of a jail cell, is a source of considerable consternation. But even those who oppose the store don't deny that it brings in a lot of money. The store was closed in 1985, but community revenues dropped so precipitously and bootleg liquor ran so freely that it was quickly reopened.

Fairbanks (population 40,000) lies 300 miles to the southwest, and is the closest city. Downtown Fairbanks is a hodgepodge of bars, dime stores, jewelry stores, greasy spoons, seedy motels, cafés, government buildings, and now a Marriott Hotel with an upscale restaurant offering fine food and wines at Chicago prices. But despite its funky downtown and its natural beauty, Fairbanks is sprawling helter-skelter across the Tanana Valley, fueled by the Sam's Club, Home Depot, fast-food scourge that has marred cities across the country.

Fairbanks has an accidental quality about it, befitting its history. In 1901, after the Klondike had played out, eager, hell-for-leather miners floated down the Yukon, bound for Nome, on Alaska's western coast, where gold had been discovered in the sand along the beach. A small group departed from the Yukon and made its way by riverboat up a large tributary, the Tanana River, with the intention of establishing a fur-trading post. When the boat's pilot mistakenly turned up the Chena Slough, the boat got stuck on a sandbar and the captain was forced to unload cargo and passengers, too. Those left behind on the river's banks bided their time by prospecting. Some struck gold, and soon after, word got out that another rich strike had been made in a place that was later christened Fairbanks. Modern-day Fairbanks still has that feel of a city dependent on booms, bonanzas, big strikes, and huge sums of federal money capable of kick-starting an ailing economy.

The city, like much of Alaska, compromises outdoorsy, warm, generous, but tough-minded, independent people for whom the frontier is more than a distant memory. In Fairbanks, people build their own cabins and homes. They trap, hunt moose to put up winter meat, tend summer fishnets, mush dogs, heat with wood, live without indoor plumbing. Despite the fact that they live in the populous North Star Borough (population 85,000), many seek to honor values of self-reliance and simplicity. Yet, like Alaskans in general, many have struck an uneasy alliance between their ethic of individualism and their annual Permanent Fund Dividend check, a yearly gift from the state based on interest payments from oil royalty investments. In 2002, each of Alaska's 591,537 residents (those who could prove they had been there for two full calendar years) received a check for $1,540.76, only the second time in the Fund's twenty-five-year history that the dividend check was less than that of the previous year.

Fairbanks is something of an end-of-the-road town—a college town, too, with just enough university types, left-leaning liberals, and libertarian zealots to make it interesting, the kind of place where bumper stickers abound: Alaskans for Peace; Free Tibet; No Nukes North; Secede; Vote Freedom First—Vote Murkowski; Charleton Heston Is My President; Alaskan Girls Kick Ass. While sprawling Anchorage—or "Los Anchorage," as many Alaskans call it—325 miles south of Fairbanks, looks to cities like Seattle and Portland for its cues, Fairbanks dispenses with the pretense. It has earned the sobriquet "Gateway to the Interior." Anchorage is protected by the Alaska Range, the Talkeetna Mountains, and the Wrangells, while Fairbanks gets the Arctic's cold full blast, and winter lows of 20 and 30 below sometimes rival those of Fort Yukon.

If it is true that we are shaped by the landscape we inhabit, perhaps this explains why Heimo, from the very beginning, exhibited little of the bravado I'd expected. The Frigid Zone, which lies above a latitude of 66° 33' North, a theoretical line called the Arctic Circle, is an unforgiving region that doesn't tolerate recklessness or excess of any sort; it must be approached modestly.

There are few cowboys in the Arctic. An old saw about Alaska's bush pilots goes like this: "There are old pilots and bold pilots, but no old, bold pilots." The same could be said about residents of the Arctic Interior. Humility is the first virtue one learns in the high latitudes, a sense of one's inherent vulnerability, a realization that at any time nature can deliver a bad deck of cards or a fatal blow. In the Arctic one never achieves freedom from fear, because so much can go wrong—Jack London wrote that there are 1,000 ways this place can kill a man—especially in winter. For outsiders, frostbite immediately comes to mind, but few who live in the Arctic worry much about minor frostbite. Most are resigned to it, an ear or a nose or a finger, a little nip each winter.

The prospect of literally freezing to death is more real and is heightened by the combination of extreme cold and distances. But the rules to avoid this fate are axiomatic: Dress in layers; drink lots of water; don't push too hard or you may overexert and freeze to death in your own sweat; keep your core warm with calories; and beware of overflow, that insidious layer of water seeping over the ice, which is the bane of every trapper's life. Get caught in overflow, especially if it's deep, more than a few miles from the cabin, and your only choice is to build a fire, fast.

Another concern is a chimney fire, a creosote buildup in the woodstove's metal stovepipe that sets the whole cabin ablaze. Consequently, many trappers clean their chimneys compulsively, once every week, and keep a backup tent in which they can ride out the winter in case of emergency.

Snow blindness is a worry in March and April, particularly on open lakes or tundra, when the sun is strong and is reflecting off snow. Snow blindness is hard to treat—the Gwich'in once used boiled Labrador tea to soothe burned retinas. Whiteouts are a worry, too. They can obliterate every landmark in sight. In a whiteout a person only has two choices: Dig a hole in the snow and hunker down and wait or use the wind as a guide and hope that it doesn't suddenly switch.

Starvation is always a possibility, though less of one now than when the Gwich'in and Inupiat families wandered the land. Trappers haul in staples—flour, cornmeal, noodles, canned vegetables, powdered milk—which should carry them through in a pinch. Yet every bush family worries: Will the caribou come; will we get our moose; will the fish come up the rivers to spawn; will it be a good berry year; will we trap enough fur in winter to make our life possible, to pay the bills?

Cabin fever isn't talked about much, if only because it's far more common than people like to think. But cabin fever has been known to undo even the most stable trapper. One trapper told me that it can grip like superglue and suffocate the mind. Though most think of winter as the season when psyches collapse, spring also claims its share of victims. In winter, Alaskans enjoy an ease of travel, providing it's not too cold to leave the cabin. It is in spring before breakup—a period that may last a few weeks, when the sun has melted all the snow and the land is oozing water, and skis, snowshoes, snowmachines, dogsleds, and riverboats are useless—that one's freedom of movement is severely restricted and one's mind starts to seriously wear. Trappers can get very "bushy" in spring.

There are also snowmachine problems. The most likely scenario is that a snowmachine becomes mired in overflow or bogged down in a wind-packed drift. Though Heimo carries a come-along, sometimes called a power pull, to winch his snowmachine out of deep drifts, in much of this country, a come-along is worthless; there are seldom any trees large enough for him to chain up to and crank out a 400-pound machine. Another possibility is a drive belt problem; a drive belt can break just about anytime. At 40 below or more, a whole assortment of things can go wrong. Steel can snap like kindling—a ski, perhaps; an axle; a clutch; bearings; a shaft—even the snowmachine's handlebars.

That's what happened to Heimo in mid-March 1990—things went wrong when he was driving from the cabin on the Old Crow drainage to the cabin on the upper Coleen River. It was spring and time to move again. A bush plane had already transported the girls and Edna and all of their belongings.

In an effort to let the land and its animal populations rebound from their seasonal presence and to ensure a steady supply of fur, the Korths are seminomadic, moving each spring to one of their three cabins in the Arctic National Wildlife Refuge and each summer to Fort Yukon. They do this not for a change of scenery or for recreation, as someone who escapes to a summer home, but out of necessity, employing a practice of land stewardship once c mon among small farmers in the Midwest— letting a field lie fallow. They relocate even when they feel like staying put.

Heimo's job was to bring the snowmachine overland, a journey that would take him across a 2,500-foot divide that separates the two drainages. Though Heimo had assured Edna that there was nothing to be concerned about, privately he knew that the reality was different. At the divide, southerly winds had lathed the snow into three-foot drifts, which were, for the most part, as hard as pavement. What Heimo had to watch out for were the soft spots where a heavy snowmachine could break through and become mired. Though black spruce circled the mountain at lower elevations, on top there would not be a tree in sight other than whip-thin dwarf birch and alder, so his come-along would be ineffective.

Heimo set off early in the afternoon. He brought a book of matches, his ax, his snowshoes, and an extra drive belt, just in case. At first, he traveled comfortably on a meandering creek bed, and he dreamed of the cabin on the upper Coleen, the one he always referred to as "home." He dreamed of breakup and May waterfowl hunting on the newly exposed gravel bars; of the taste of a white-fronted goose slow-boiling in a cast-iron pot; of sweet, cold river water; and of the return of the songbirds. He made it to the mountain and the dense spruce forest without incident and resisted the temptation to relax. Instead, he stood up on the machine and supported himself with his legs, as a horseback rider preparing for a log jump, and carefully maneuvered through the narrow alleys between the trees. The land was still in winter's bitter grip, and mounds of snow clung to the boughs of the black spruce trees, bending them double under their weight.

When Heimo reached the divide, the sun was shining brightly, and he stopped long enough to enjoy its light and to rest his legs and his throttle hand, which had started to cramp. He looked back at his trail and noticed how the hard-packed snow had easily supported the weight of the machine. Then he gazed off into the distance, across the radiant white tundra to the dark outline of trees that marked the Old Crow drainage, and said good-bye. He would not be back again for another three years. He pulled the hood of his parka and the wolverine ruff tightly around his head and face and gave the snowmachine some throttle.

On the far side of the divide, with the tall white spruce of the Coleen River in sight, he flushed a covey of willow ptarmigan. White as the snow that hid them, they burst from the ground clucking their disapproval. Suddenly the machine fishtailed, and Heimo struggled to keep it from going over. When it fishtailed again, he took pressure off the throttle, and the machine lurched, throwing him. Heimo landed in a sitting position with his legs extended, buried up to his chest in snow. He could only watch as the snowmachine tipped over on its side and stalled. He struggled to get out of the snow, but with nothing to hold on to, he was unable to stand up. So he rolled onto his belly, dug his arms shoulder high into the snow, and pushed. Eventually he got to his knees. Then he rocked back and forth until he was finally able to stand up. He brushed himself off and cursed his luck. Approaching the machine, he wondered if it would start again. Then he pulled the manual start, and to his surprise, the machine responded. He was fighting to muscle it back onto the trail when the handlebar snapped like a thin twig. His handlebar had broken before. In the past, though, there had been a stem to which he could attach a vise grip so he could still steer the machine. Not this time. He would have to leave the machine and come back to get it another day, when he had the tools to fix it. Heimo was fifteen miles from the Coleen cabin, and it was five in the afternoon. He knew that he had no other choice than to strap on his snowshoes, whose bindings he had remembered to repair the previous evening, and set out for the Coleen. Normally, a fifteen-mile trip would be nothing to be overly concerned about, but under the conditions it was bad—he would have to struggle through the deep snow, breaking trail for almost the entire way in the dark. And he would have to hustle. Edna would worry, so there was no way he could split up the trip into two days, walking half the distance, building a small snow shelter, and finishing the hike to the cabin the following morning.

What with Rhonda, who was four, and Krin, who was not even one yet, Edna had her hands full. It wouldn't help matters for her to have to be concerned about him, too.

Shortly after he set out, he was up to his thighs in snow, despite the snowshoes, trudging across a mountaintop that he knew few people in the 10,000-year human history of the region had ever seen. Fortunately, the wind had shifted earlier in the day and was now at his back. Once he got off the mountain and into the treeline, the snow was shallower, only knee high. Although the temperature was well below zero, the sweat was draining out of him. Ice crystals had formed on his beard, eyebrows, and eyelashes. Two hours into the hike, the sun set, and Heimo was tired and wet. He managed to stay calm, though; he had been in tough situations before.

Not long after the sun slumped below the horizon, Heimo recognized Arcturus, a red giant of a star, and he regarded it as a good omen. Three hours later, the aurora came out, too, illuminating his way. Heimo watched it build in the west, lighting the sky with its shimmering braids of color, and then slowly it vanished. By the time he reached Doghouse Creek, which flowed into the Coleen, he checked his watch again—nearly 11:00 P.M. Still five miles from the cabin, he was soaked in sweat and nearly falling over with fatigue. He knew he was in trouble. He'd broken one of the cardinal rules of the woods—never overexert.

He cleared out an area in the snow and gathered kindling from a copse of willows and chopped down a dead black spruce with his ax. The kindling and the tree were dry and when he set a match to them a fire crackled quickly. Then he pulled another spruce tree out by its roots and threw it onto the fire. Crouching down, he blew on the fire until it snapped and popped again. Once the fire was blazing, he ate two biscuits that he had brought along. Thirsty, he resorted to melting snow, holding his cupped hands as close to the fire as he could without burning them. Then he drank the few drops of water that had collected in his cupped hands. Though he was tired and drowsy, he resisted sitting down because he knew that it would be hard to get up again. Instead, he stood by the fire, hopping up and down to keep the blood flowing and stave off hypothermia, but he was still shivering. His core temperature had dropped so low that the fire failed to warm him, and he knew that he would have to keep walking to stay alive.

Heimo walked on the tundra. Though the snow was deep there, it was even deeper where it had accumulated in the creek bed. He pumped his arms and legs as if he were marching, in order to get the feeling back into his limbs. Still he was shivering. "Don't stop walking! Don't stop walking!" he repeated to himself. Since the creek ran into the Coleen above the cabin, he didn't have to worry about finding his way in the dark. He knew that he wouldn't find water, though, because the creek was frozen solid to the bottom. Once he made it to the river, there'd be water, but by that time there'd be no sense in stopping; the confluence of Doghouse Creek and the Coleen was only a half-mile from the cabin.

Heimo arrived at the cabin at 2:00 A.M. the following morning, chilled and vomiting from exhaustion. The last half-mile had seemed almost impossible. By the time he reached the cabin, Heimo was dangerously hypothermic, shivering and slurring his words. Edna helped him out of his clothes, wrapped a sleeping bag and a caribou skin blanket around him, and set him by the fire with a cup of hot tea and a bowl of moose broth. Then she led him to bed, where she held him until the following morning, when she could feel that his body temperature was finally beginning to rise. Heimo got up briefly, long enough to sip some of the soup. Then he fell asleep again. Waking in the early afternoon, he saw that Edna had crawled back in bed with him. She was nuzzled against him with Krin cradled in her arms. Rhonda slept on the other bed, snoring softly. The cabin was warm and smelled of fresh fry bread. Heimo walked to the stove and put more wood in. Slipping back into bed, he realized just how close he'd come to freezing in a snowbank like some dumb greenhorn. He kissed Edna on the forehead. Then he held Krin's tiny hand and watched her until she and Edna woke.

CHAPTER 4

The Big Woods

For Heimo, the Brooks Range represented the culmination of his boyhood desires. As soon as he landed in the mountains, he knew he was home. Some of his Wisconsin buddies might have thought that Alaska was a passing phase, but Heimo knew otherwise. John Peterson, the personable Minnesota-raised bush pilot who flew him into the Brooks Range to meet up with Keith Koontz and who remains Heimo's good friend almost thirty years later, remembers the first time he ever met Heimo. "He was in Alaska, and he was beside himself. I have a picture of him stepping off the plane. He was grinning from ear to ear. He had his Wisconsin beer weight on and he was pudgy, but, God, was he eager. He told me that he'd spent two miserable years being a factory guy, and he'd hated it. He told me he'd been drinking a lot. Then he said—get this—he said, 'I'm gonna be a mountain man.' I thought, sure as shit this guy's gotta be kidding. But then I could see that he was serious. Most guys that green don't stand a chance. You know they're going to die. But there was something about Heimo. He was going to do it."

Heimo recalls his first day in the Brooks Range. "I was singing the John Denver tune 'Rocky Mountain High' to myself," he says. "You know, 'I was born in the summer of my twenty-seventh year.' I changed the lyrics to 'I was born in the summer of my twentieth year,' 'coming home to the place I'd never been before.' "

In mid-August Heimo wrote to his friend, Jim Kryzmarcik:

> Hey Budnick Buddy,
>
>   Well I'm in Alaska and I am here to stay. . . . You wouldn't
> believe the beauty up here. This is the only place a person can
> really say is God's country. Dall sheep on the mountains, moose
> in the valleys, caribou on the tundra, ducks and geese all over,
> wolves and bear (grizzly). . . . I am definitely going to live up
> here and for good.

Heimo signed it "The Alaskan Kid" and included a P.S.: "Get a map
of Alaska and look above the Arctic Circle for Fort Yukon and I'm 150
miles north of Fort Yukon by Arctic Village."

But even while surrounded by all the beauty, Heimo was having
nightmares about going back to Wisconsin. He knew that by the end of
August, he would again be searching for a job, and he was determined
not to return. His indissoluble bond with the Alaskan landscape—the
only wilderness large enough to patch the considerable hole in his heart
and move his spirit—had already been established. It was a grand and
ultimately costly obsession.

"I was praying that I wouldn't have to go back," Heimo says. Thank-
fully, it never came to that. "Keith Koontz is really the one who got me
started in Alaska. He knew I wanted to trap, so he contacted a friend of
his, Kenny Miller, who agreed to set me up on Beaver Creek. I was
about forty miles southwest of the village of Birch Creek and seventy
miles south of Fort Yukon. I knew very little about trapping, but I knew
that I wanted to live out in the woods."

John Peterson, who flew Heimo out to the cabin, shakes his head in
disbelief and laughs now about Heimo's determination. Peterson was
doing some trapping then, too, and knew what it took. "I asked him if
he wanted a radio, and he turned me down. He said, 'No, I won't have
time for distractions. I'm gonna learn how to trap.' "

By the end of September 1975, Heimo was set up in a cabin on
Beaver Creek, and already his body had transformed to fit the country.

In two short months he had dropped nearly fifty pounds from his Wisconsin high of 240 pounds. While working for Koontz he was cooking and cleaning up after hunters, escorting them up to 6,000 feet, and then, when they got a sheep or a caribou, a moose or a bear, packing it out toting loads of over one hundred pounds. And for the first month on Beaver Creek, he was living off what he could shoot—spruce and ruffed grouse and ducks.

Beaver Creek was once the trapping territory of a Minnesota-born Swede named Iver Peterson, who trapped it until 1939. Folks in Fort Yukon called Peterson "the toughest man there ever was." It was said that sled dogs couldn't keep up with him. He was so strong and so intent on making money that during the winter months he trapped at night with a candle lantern regardless of the temperature. He was one of the country's rugged, indestructible "hard-trappers." One story goes that a trapper met up with him in the woods and noticed that he was nearly buckling under the weight of six fox skins and another half dozen frozen fox. He was on his way back to his cabin and had another seven miles to go. The trapper, who was running dogs, offered to take him home, and Iver shook his head. "This ain't weight I'm carrying," he replied, "this is money." When he was thirty-nine Peterson snowshoed into the village of Beaver, picked up his new bride, a fourteen-year-old girl named Ruth, and carried her on his back, covering the sixty miles in two days. Well into his seventies, Peterson could still cut three cords of wood a day and he could draw a map of Beaver Creek from memory that was every bit as good as a USGS topographical map.

Heimo had learned bits and pieces of Peterson's history in Fort Yukon, and he was excited to be trapping the same country. For grubstaking Heimo, Kenny Miller had worked out an arrangement—Heimo would trap, and Miller would get half the fur. Heimo was happy to do it, since it meant that his dream would become a reality. When he called his mother from the pay phone at the airport in Fort Yukon and told her that he was headed for the woods to be an Alaskan trapper, she insisted on sending him the money to buy traps. She told him that other parents had to pay for college educations, but since Heimo wasn't going to college, she and his father would gladly pay for his traps; Erich, though, still refused to talk with Heimo.

Heimo went north because of a primal urge as strong as the drive that sends the caribou each year out of their coastal calving grounds and south over the passes of the Brooks Range. Contrary to what his father believed, Heimo was not running away from reality, but confronting it head-on. Beaver Creek was to be Heimo's testing ground. Erich Korth regarded his son's decision to make his life in Alaska as a deliberate repudiation of everything he'd urged his son to believe in, and Heimo was still bitter enough to let his father think what he wanted.

From prehistory onward, the word *wilderness* has been used to define areas inimical to man. People's imaginations populated these places with all sorts of malevolent creatures. In his book *The Wooing of Earth*, Rene Dubos reports that the word *wilderness* is used nearly 300 times in the Bible. "All its meanings are derogatory," he argues.

Interestingly, Dubos points out that in the Bible, *wilderness* became associated with a place where a chosen people were tested before deliverance to the Promised Land. After having undergone what Dubos calls his "spiritual catharsis," Jesus emerged from the *wilderness* after forty days and forty nights of fasting, desolation, and grappling with the devil, and "withdrew into Galilee," fulfilling the prophesies of Isaiah.

In his influential book *Wilderness and the American Mind*, Roderick Nash examines another early reference in literature to wilderness. Of the eighth-century epic *Beowulf*, he writes, " 'wildeor' appeared in reference to savage and fantastic beasts inhabiting a dismal region of forests, crags, and cliffs. . . . The wilderness," he continues, "was conceived as a region where a person was likely to get into a disordered, confused, or 'wild' condition."

The word *panic*, as Nash asserts, originated from the terror that travelers felt when they heard strange and eerie cries in the wilderness. Assuming the cries to signify the approach of Pan, the Greek and Roman god of flocks and herds, who was portrayed as having two horns, pointed ears, and goat's legs, the travelers often became as frightened as children. Nash also writes of the semihuman Wild Man, whom people believed roamed the forests of Medieval Europe naked, covered with nothing but a thick coat of hair.

The Gwich'in of the Fort Yukon area had a version of the Medieval Wild Man—Na'in—the Brush Man. Na'in wandered the woods, though occasionally he would approach human settlements to raid fish racks and steal food and, sometimes, to kidnap people, particularly women, for companionship. Na'in rarely left a trace. Sightings were uncommon, but those who claimed to have seen him insisted that he was real.

Heimo had always been comfortable in the woods, beginning in Wisconsin's North Woods, which are small by Alaska's standards, but are big enough and wild enough even for an accomplished woodsman to lose his way. Though the woods at night still held a sense of dread for him, it didn't take long for him to conquer his fear. Like an agoraphobic willing himself to leave the house, each night Heimo forced himself to roam the woods, but he did it incrementally. At first, he wandered just outside the cabin, then a few hundred feet away, always keeping it in sight. After his first month, he was ready to really challenge himself. Each night, he walked a mile or two from the cabin, teaching himself to become comfortable with the night, fighting off the fear that came from leaving the comfort of the fire and the security of the cabin. Slowly the fear disappeared, reinforced by the empirical fact that each night he returned home unharmed.

Surprisingly, the Na'in legend never bothered him. Even as a boy he had never been afraid of ghosts and goblins and witches, and he dismissed the stories of Na'in with the same assurance. Nevertheless, he worried. Alaska was just so goddamn big.

"Can you imagine being dropped off in the middle of nowhere?" he asks. "I was a real *cheechako*" he admits, using the Alaskan euphemism for an unskilled, wet-behind-the-ears greenhorn, a tenderfoot, what the trappers of the Rocky Mountain West would have called a *mangeur de lard*, a pork eater, a man inexperienced in the mountains. "I knew about being in the woods in Wisconsin, but this was Alaska. There wasn't even a stove in the cabin. There was supposed to be someone coming downriver with a stove, but because of freeze-up, he never made it as far as the cabin, and here I was looking at winter with temperatures of 50 below. I was real scared."

Joe Dart, a University of Alaska Fairbanks professor in the Computer Sciences Department and former editor of *Alaska Trapper* magazine, says, in his still-thick Maine accent, "Lots of guys came up to do the Alaska thing. They'd seen *Sergeant Preston of the Yukon*, and they wanted to live in the woods. Most of them ended up on the pipeline." Dart, an avid woodsman and canoeist even before he arrived in Alaska, was one of those who worked the pipeline. "Alaska intimidated a lot of young men," he says. "A guy on the pipeline that I knew years ago hit the nail on the head. He said, 'Alaska is beyond human scale. The rivers are too big, the mountains are too big; it's bigger than you can grasp.' "

Heimo was so frightened that he wrote an ill-advised letter to his parents expressing his doubts about living in the bush. A few days later, when a pilot brought in what meager food supplies Heimo was able to buy while in Fort Yukon—mostly beans, macaroni, and white flour to augment the spruce and ruffed grouse and ducks he'd been eating—Heimo sent the letter out. "I wasn't thinking," Heimo says. "You can write a letter when you're in that state of mind, but you should never send it. Later I learned that Mom called the state troopers. The troopers had no way of reaching me, so they contacted the pilot, who assured them that I was okay. Okay?" Heimo scoffs. "I wasn't okay; I didn't have a goddamn stove. I had to sleep outside and build bonfires to keep warm."

Heimo had no luck shooting a bear or a moose either, and he had grown discouraged. The ducks had migrated through, leaving only grouse and rabbits, which he knew would never sustain him through the long, cold winter. So Heimo resolved to walk. He would hunt for sixteen hours a day and keep warm at the same time.

Soon enough, however, Heimo's worst fears were realized. By late September, a foot of snow had already fallen, and it kept coming, meaning that he was almost always breaking trail. And the temperature was tumbling. First 5 below, then 10 below. On October 1, Heimo woke up early, shivering in his sleeping bag, covered in a thin layer of frost. The sky was slate blue, and wind was barreling out of the north. Reluctantly,

Heimo crawled out of his bag and walked over to the cabin, where he had nailed a thermometer to a large white spruce. It read 15 below, and now Heimo knew, for certain, that he was in trouble.

Resisting the temptation to panic required all the fortitude Heimo had. He slipped on his parka, canvas mukluks from Arctic Village, wool gloves, hat and pants, and a backpack, in which he'd packed macaroni and bread enough to last him three days, and set off upriver, determined not to return until he'd killed a black bear or a moose.

He was behind the cabin, bound for a willow- and alder-choked gravel bar where he had seen moose tracks the previous week, when he discovered a collapsed cache that he had not noticed before. Lying on the ground were a few rusted traps, a torn plastic tarp, a fur stretcher, and a lynx skull. Among the mess of rotting wood, he found a sheet-metal woodstove and fifteen feet of stovepipe. Twenty-seven years later, still astounded by his discovery, Heimo says, "I thought I was dreaming. I rubbed my eyes to make sure I wasn't seeing things."

Heimo carried the stove and the pipe back to the cabin and searched for wire to seal the stovepipe shut. Then he remembered that he had brought out #2 picture wire to set rabbit snares. He wrapped it around the pipe, cut the wire and twisted the ends tightly. Shoving the pipe up through the old stovepipe hole in the roof, he attached it to the sheet-metal stove. He tore the pages out of a novel, crumpled them up, and threw them into the belly of the stove, and then lit the match, touched it to the paper, and waited to see if it would draw. Running outside the cabin, he stood and watched and his heart leapt when he saw smoke coming from the pipe. He had heat.

The Gwich'in say that the far north is where a man has room to dream. By early November, Heimo had almost exhausted the local supply of grouse and rabbits and was running dangerously low on macaroni and flour. What he was dreaming of was food. He had shot and wounded a small bullmoose in October. He tracked it late into the day but never found it, and only then did he realize that he was nearly ten miles from the cabin, too far to hike back in the dark. Instead of taking the chance of getting lost in unfamiliar country, he built a lean-to and spent the night with only a fire and the clothes on his back to keep him warm.

His efforts to bag a bear were also unsuccessful, and the local moose fled when a pack of wolves moved into the area. He thought his luck had changed when he discovered a large patch of rosehips just southeast of a big bend in the river, no more than a half-mile from the cabin. He knew that for the early Gwich'in, rosehips were a source of vitamin C, and a constant one since rosehips stay on the bush all winter long. He was craving vitamin C, and he stood right in the middle of the patch like a feeding grizzly. It was 36 below. Taking off his mittens, he picked and ate the frozen rosehips until his fingers were too cold to move. That night he awakened with the worst gastrointestinal problems of his life and spent much of the night in the outhouse in temperatures that had fallen to 45 below. Days later he was still sick and weak and unable to hunt.

By the second week of November, he knew he had to do something drastic. He had heard stories of trappers dying of hunger in their cabins, and he had already experienced two of the symptoms of serious hunger—mental fuzziness and lethargy. He was hunting and splitting wood constantly now, and he didn't have enough food to replace the calories he was burning at 30 and 40 below. But to give up, he knew, was a death sentence. He might as well take his .44 magnum and put it to his head and end it quickly. Desperately low on food, he decided to walk fifteen miles upriver where he knew that Miller had a second cabin. He hoped that perhaps he'd find a stockpile of flour or spaghetti or beans, something to carry him through the winter.

He was walking on the river, carrying a backpack and pulling a sled, loaded with his sleeping bag, his rifle and shotgun, and what remained of his food—a grouse, some flour, a few cups of macaroni, and a couple of pounds of rice—when he failed to recognize bad ice. He fell through, flung his arms out and caught himself, lucky not to have been sucked under the ice by the quick current. Soaked from the chest down, he crawled on top of the ice like a seal and only then did he realize that he'd lost his sled. Somehow his rifle and sleeping bag had fallen out of the sled before it went under, but everything else was gone, including his food. He was three miles from his cabin.

Heimo ran as fast as he could, and when he reached the cabin, he was in luck: The fire was still burning in the stove. He hung his sleeping bag near the stove to dry, and then he shed all his clothes and wrapped himself in a blanket. He sat next to the stove until late afternoon, shivering, still too cold to move more than a few feet from the heat. Even though he resisted it, one persistent thought kept entering his head—"What are my chances?"—and he was forced to contemplate what twenty-year-olds should never have to consider—death. That night, while lying in his bunk, he resolved to try to signal a plane.

The following day, he stood out on a snowy gravel bar, hoping that a plane would fly by. His odds were next to nothing. In late summer, planes in the remote Interior are common sights, carrying hunters to and from camp, but in November they are rare. Heimo sat on the gravel bar until the sun set and then returned to the cabin feeling gloomy. On day two, he repeated his vigil, but again failed to spot a plane. On day three, he was disappointed again and hungrier than he'd ever been in his life. By day four, he was sitting on the gravel bar, assessing his chances of walking out. Birch Creek was nearly forty miles, a trip that under normal circumstances he could make. But now he was weak with hunger, and he'd have to break trail the entire way. To his amazement, early in the afternoon he heard a distant engine, unmistakable in winter when sound is so clearly borne. Using his mirror, he desperately tried to get the pilot's attention, by angling it into the waning sun; but eventually the sound trailed off into silence. He found two packets of noodles that night that he'd tucked away in the loft, but they did little to assuage his hunger. Despair had set in.

The following morning, Heimo woke determined to try his luck one last time. If he failed, he would attempt to shoot a few rabbits, expending as little energy as possible, then eat and rest for a few days, hoping to get some of his strength back.

He resorted to stomping out SOS in the snow, an effort he recognized was so futile that he couldn't help laughing at himself. If he didn't get out, he would be one of the anonymous numbers, another dreamy *cheechako* who lost his life in Alaska. He cut spruce boughs and laid them in the troughs that formed the letters, hoping that a pilot might recognize the blue-green outline of the letters against the white snow. He had just finished the S and the O, when once again he heard a plane.

John Peterson, his bush pilot friend, who was trapping out of Fort Yukon, had asked a pilot who flew the Fort Yukon-to-Fairbanks run to check on Heimo. When his flight from Fort Yukon to Fairbanks was empty, the pilot made good on his promise. Using a map that Jon Peterson had given him, the pilot flew over the cabin. Heimo was carrying an armful of boughs when he spotted the plane. He dropped the boughs and "started to go crazy," jumping up and down and trying to remember the land-to-air signals that were described on the back of his hunting license. When the pilot didn't acknowledge, Heimo ran to the end of the gravel bar and frantically stomped out "Pic Me." He was beginning the U of "UP" when the pilot tipped his wings, indicating that he understood. Since he was flying a big twin-engine Grand Commander commuter plane and couldn't land, the pilot radioed John Peterson in Fort Yukon. Peterson, who'd flown Heimo in three months earlier and had developed a fondness for him, was glad to come and get Heimo. Fort Yukon was only seventy miles away, and by late afternoon, on that same day, Heimo was in town.

In Fort Yukon, Heimo sold what fur he'd managed to trap. He'd been so busy feeding himself that he'd had little time or energy for trapping, so his catch amounted to nothing more than a weasel, a few muskrats, and a half dozen marten. The Fort Yukon fur buyer only gave him $90 for his winter catch, but Heimo was so happy just to be alive that he didn't care. Reality set in a few days later. Heimo had only $100 to his name, and he had to come up with a plan. He had resolved never to return to Wisconsin, though he knew he could use the other portion of the round-trip ticket his mother had bought for him. Fort Yukon to Appleton, Wisconsin, he could do in two days, three days max. Instead, he decided to go to Fairbanks and stay with a cousin of Keith Koontz and get a job, any job, that might allow him to stay in Alaska.

In a letter to his friend Jim Kryzmarcik, written on notecards, Heimo provided more details of his first months on the river and his brush with death:

Newton,

Sorry I didn't write sooner but when you live out in the bush you don't come in contact with humans too much. I haven't seen or heard from a person. No one to talk to. The first week was hell living by myself out in the wilderness but after the first week I got used to it and now I would not want to live in town. I like living by myself in the Arctic. . . . I'm not in the bush no more because I lost everything I had. Food, axes, etc. And almost lost my life. . . . I decided to go to cabin no. 2. I got about 3 miles from the home cabin and had to cross the river. . . . I started to cross and broke through. . . . Fell in up to my chin and the current almost pulled me under the ice. I couldn't feel bottom. I don't know how I pulled my self out. So I got out and it was 44 below and I ran 3 miles back to the home cabin. Almost passed out the last half mile. I was cold and almost froze to death when I got back to the cabin. I ripped off my clothes. My skin was a real dark blue. One eyelid froze shut. My beard . . . was a solid brick of ice. I thought I'd get gangrene for sure. . . . Boy I tell you I was scared. I am very lucky I'm alive. A few days later I tried to get to the cabin again. When I got there I almost cryed. There was a great big hole in the roof. Dirt was piled up about 3 ft. on the floor, froze solid. The bed was broke. Snow was piled up in the cabin. So I had to spend the night with no roof or stove because it was too late to go back to my cabin. I spent the nite in the corner of the cabin with a fire going. The temperature 48 below. So I was awake the whole nite, dared not to sleep cause it would have been my last. Longest nite in my life. Prayed to God. I was scared I'd never get out alive. Next day I barely made it back to the home cabin. Didn't sleep for 2 days, hiked over 20 miles. Was worn out. When I got back I ate and went to bed at 4:00 p.m. Got up next day at 11:00 a.m. So now I'm in Fort Yukon. Lost all I owned and don't know what to do. But will not go back to Wis. I got this wilderness blood in me now and no way will I go back no matter how much trouble I have at first. But that's a trapper's life.

Heimo signed this letter "Heimo the Alaskan bush trapper, guide, packer, and mountain man," and included the tail feathers of one of the spruce grouse he'd shot.

Fairbanks was ground zero for the pipeline, and the city was booming and giddy. From Fairbanks, construction crews built north to Prudhoe Bay and south to Valdez. "It was crazy," Heimo remembers. "There was money wherever you looked." 2-Street, as 2nd Avenue is called, was loaded with hookers who catered to the young men who flocked to town in hopes of working hard on the pipeline and making pocketfuls of money. One thousand dollars a week was an average weekly paycheck for a pipeline worker, and consequently the hookers did well, too. In a one-block area, Heimo guessed, there were more hookers than in all of New York City. "They'd have to stand out there in their short skirts and fishnet stockings and show their stuff at 40 below," he laughs. "But business was good, and they could always duck into a building to warm up." Pimps cruised the streets of downtown in big cars, and drug dealers made their daily rounds of the bars. Fairbanks was "sin city," and ironically many people who were born and raised there welcomed the change. Greed oozed.

In Fairbanks Heimo got a letter from Keith Koontz, the hunting guide who had taken a paternal interest in him. Koontz enclosed a $500 check. "Take the money and reoutfit yourself and go back to the trapline, go to Nome and get a job, or come to St. Lawrence Island and work for me," the letter said. Though Heimo had no idea where St. Lawrence Island was, it looked to him like the beginning of another adventure.

That day he cashed the $500 check, hid $475 in his sleeping bag, took the other $25, and walked to a tavern down the street. Delighted by the turn of events, he got shit-faced drunk. He remembers a dart team at the bar whose members were wearing T-shirts that read "The Pipeline Sucks." A guy from Green Bay, Wisconsin, who'd recently come off the pipeline, was so taken with Heimo's stories that he started buying Heimo drinks, stretching Heimo's $25 to include a full night of boozing. The next morning, with a hangover to match the roaring Alaskan economy, Heimo boarded a plane for St. Lawrence Island.

* * *

St. Lawrence Island, or "Sivuqaq," the traditional Siberian Yupik name, is roughly 100 miles long and 20 miles wide, about the size of Delaware. It is a treeless, fog-ridden place of rock and lava, pummeled year-round by winds, stuck out in the middle of the abundant Bering Sea, only forty miles from Indian Point on Russia's Chukchi Peninsula, and only twenty miles from the international date line. It is farther west than the Hawaiian Islands, 120 miles west of Nome, Alaska, and until the last half century, it has remained largely isolated from the Alaskan mainland.

A map of the island shows a northern spine of 2,000-foot volcanic ridges called the Kukulgit Mountains, drained by rivers and creeks and separated by wet tundra valleys, while the south is a sea of blue lakes, inlets, and lagoons. Engulfed in cold ocean mists, which are created when cold Arctic waters collide with warm air blown up from the Pacific, St. Lawrence Island can be a chronically overcast place, except for a few short weeks every year when the island's interior breaks out in a riot of color. Larkspur, saxifrage, daisies, anemones, and a host of other flowers bloom brilliantly in the ephemeral sunshine, which is soon replaced by dense Bering Sea fog.

St. Lawrence Island was once a plateau in the Great Bering Land Bridge. Eskimo legend has it that the entire island, even the barren interior mountains, was once covered by a vast ocean. Slowly, as the island was "squeezed dry" by "Apa," the Creator, land began to emerge from the sea's black depths. "Sivuqaq" is roughly translated as "wrung out" or "squeezed dry."

"They took him in," says Keith Koontz, referring to Heimo's arrival in Savoonga, one of only two villages on the island, which was settled as a reindeer camp by herders from the island's only other village, Gambell, in 1917. Keith Koontz is a likable, well-educated, practicing Baha'i, who sometimes lets his hair grow long and talks in kind of a Texas drawl. Koontz is married to an Eskimo woman from Savoonga. "I don't know what it was about Heimo, but they loved him," Koontz continues, letting out a booming, genial belly laugh. "Heimo's a gregarious guy and he's very funny. He was curious about their culture, too, and the people of Savoonga appreciated that."

In early December, Heimo wrote his friend Jim Kryzmarcik again.

Newt,

Well I'm in Savoonga, on St. Lawrence Island only 90 miles from Siberia. . . . I couldn't go back out to the trapline. . . . So Keith loaned me $500.00 and said I could live out by him on the island. As you can figure this is an Eskimo village, still semi-primitive. 90% of the people live off the sea. . . . You wouldn't believe the size of the animals (walrus). Huge. Average weight 4,500 lbs. With pure ivory tusks 3 ft. long. . . . I really wish I had a camera. Could get some beautiful pictures.

This time Heimo signed it "Alaskan wilderness bush trapper, wilderness guide, mountain man," and "Arctic ice pack man," too.

Three and one half months later, he wrote again.

Hi Budnick Buddy,

I got a million things to tell you but there ain't enough paper in Alaska to write it all down. Eating a lot of walrus, seal, whale, fish (raw), polar bear, seaweed, birds, reindeer, and white fox even. . . . This island has no trees, all tundra. . . . Only two villages . . . and all live off the land. . . . Whaling starts in a few days. You wouldn't believe the hustle and bustle of the village. They use big boats made out of walrus hides and the frame is made of whale bones. . . . Stores, school, and everything is shut down for a few weeks when the first whale is spotted on the south side of the island. . . . The old women have tatoos on their faces and hands. . . . They [the old women] are the most wonderful people . . . if you can understand them.

Heimo helped Koontz build a house and he put in extra time at Koontz's store in return for room and board. Television hadn't come to the island yet, comic books were the craze, and Koontz's was the only place in the village that sold them. So, while tending the cash register, Heimo met nearly everyone in Savoonga, a village no larger than two city blocks, with elevated boardwalks and plywood houses whose paint had been blasted off by wind and ice storms. Most of the village's 350 people spoke English, although they preferred their native Siberian Yupik. Heimo quickly learned enough Yupik to get by, and as time passed he became friendly with the villagers. One of those to befriend Heimo was a thirty-five-year-old hunter named Herman Toolie. Herman's mother was one of the women in Savoonga to wear the traditional tattoos. Heimo remembers that she had one on her face that resembled a whale's tail.

Herman was considered Savoonga's best hunter, which made him a living connection to one of the most accomplished hunting cultures the modern world has ever known. Though Heimo was an outsider, Herman mentored him, teaching Heimo hunting skills that few white men would ever learn—how to hunt walrus, seal, and polar bear, how to read ice and the sky. Herman explained to Heimo that the sky reflected what lay below it. A hunter's ability to read a "sky map" was an essential skill, and Heimo learned the basics: Above ice the sky turned a pale white. Above open water it was dark, what the Eskimos of Savoonga called "black smoke."

Bound by ice for six months of every year, St. Lawrence Island in December resembled an ancient glacier. Heimo had never seen such an alien landscape and he was drawn to it. When he wasn't working for Koontz, he and Herman fished on the ice pack for sculpin, using hand-made Eskimo treble snag hooks of copper tubing. The sculpin, or "bull-head," as the people of Savoonga called the fish, were yellowish green and black, about ten inches long, with bloated, oversized heads. After digging a hole, Herman and Heimo would jig by hand, bouncing the hooks off the sea's bottom, nearly a hundred feet down. They would catch thirty or forty at a time. As Heimo became better acquainted with the ice and its dangers, Herman took him out seal hunting, too.

Heimo's first seal hunt was a memorable one. Herman and Heimo walked out onto the ice against a fierce northerly wind. The wet wind cut through Heimo's parka, and he remarked about how cold it was. Herman

agreed, but explained that a north wind was a blessing. Always beware of a
south wind, he told Heimo. A south wind was capable of forming a lead,
or channel of open water, between the shore-fast ice and the pack ice, setting the once immovable ice in motion and leaving unsuspecting hunters
to float to oblivion. Swimming, Heimo knew, wasn't an option once the
ice had separated. Even an expert swimmer would quickly be overcome
with hypothermia. Every other year, the village of Savoonga lost expert
hunters to the ice, which was shaped by currents, tides, and winds, and
which opened and closed capriciously under their influence. The village
accepted these deaths with equanimity. Even a grieving widow knew that
the Eskimo hunter was never more alive than when he was on the ice.

Walking was difficult, and when Herman located a lead, a channel of
water in the ice, two miles out, Heimo was glad for the rest. The ice, he
discovered, had topography, an erratic relief formed by emerging pressure ridges, high walls of ice that buckled upward. Often he and Herman
had to scale the pressure ridges, which could be fifty feet high. It was
dangerous, unpredictable climbing.

Herman and Heimo concealed themselves behind a small pressure
ridge about fifty feet from the lead. The lead—the *meghaat*—was one
hundred yards long and one hundred yards wide, the only lead in sight,
and Herman knew that this was where a seal would surface for its next
breath of air. Seals, he explained, had to come up every twenty minutes
to fill their lungs.

Before whalers introduced the rifle to St. Lawrence Island, villagers
used nets or ivory-tipped harpoons for hunting seals. If there were large
stretches of open water, allowing the seal to surface just about anywhere, hunters stood little chance of success. However, if the currents
had not broken up the ice fields, and hunters successfully located a
breathing hole or a small lead, they needed only patience.

By late afternoon, Heimo and Herman abandoned their vigil. Not a
single seal had surfaced. Back at the village, they returned to a commotion. One of the elders had shot a polar bear, which he'd dragged into
the main room of his house on a large plastic tarp. People were coming
and going, not just to see the bear, but to get their allotment of meat,
which was always divided among the extended family.

When Heimo and Herman arrived, the hunter was eager to tell them the story of his kill. It was then that Heimo learned that while he and Herman were waiting for a seal to surface in the lead, the polar bear had caught their scent downwind. It had been stalking them, the hunter said, moving slowly from pressure ridge to pressure ridge to avoid being seen. The hunter was scouting for leads when he saw the bear. He shot it only a hundred yards from where Heimo and Herman had been hunting. It was wounded and the hunter chased it and shot it again, knowing that a wounded bear could never be allowed to escape. It had to be killed and its soul released or the hunter would come to harm. Battered by the wind, neither Herman nor Heimo ever heard the shots.

Three weeks later, Heimo shot his first seal, two miles out from the village, in a fifty-foot lead. He shot it right behind the head as Herman had instructed him. "Bullet placement," Herman said. "That's the key." Herman showed him how to swing and throw the seal hook, and after many attempts, Heimo finally succeeded in hooking and retrieving the seal, a 140-pound young hair seal—*nuksuk*. Heimo learned from Herman that traditionally a hunter who'd killed a seal would melt ice in his mouth and put his mouth to the seal's to give it a drink of water. After the meat was stripped from its bones, the bones were then returned to the sea to ensure the success of future seal hunts.

Heimo left Savoonga in mid-April, vowing to return every spring.

By late April, Heimo's first spring in Alaska, he was back on Beaver Creek, thirty miles upriver from where he'd been the previous fall, tending the trapping cabin of a friend who was going to Anchorage for the summer. He had twenty-five pounds of kidney beans, a case of macaroni, and a case of canned spinach.

The cabin was tucked in the woods at the foothills of the White Mountains, not far off the banks of Beaver Creek. It was a pretty place, bathed now, in late spring, in twenty-two hours of light. Again Heimo was eating ducks—Alaskans who live in the bush are allowed to hunt waterfowl in spring—and beaver, which he learned how to gut and skin from a book he found in the cabin. At first he hunted on snowshoes, but he quickly noticed that wet snow would pile up on the decking of the snowshoes, making walking nearly impossible. He discarded the snowshoes and wore instead an old pair of waterproof but heavy military-issue bunny boots, which lasted him until the snow melted. Though he'd never liked sunglasses, they were essential now in the long light of spring. Early trappers and Athabaskan hunters rubbed soot on their eyelids and around their eyes to protect themselves from the reflection of the sun off the snow. While in Savoonga, Heimo had learned from Herman that before the introduction of sunglasses, the hunters of St. Lawrence Island had used ivory to carve round cups into which they cut small slits and tied the cups around their heads using strips of sealskin.

Heimo was still a greenhorn, and since he hadn't wintered in the Interior, he couldn't call himself a trapper yet, but he returned to Beaver Creek with a newfound sense of purpose. After his experiences on St. Lawrence Island, he was convinced that he could survive Alaska's Interior, too. Though friendly and outgoing, he didn't mind being alone. In fact, he relished it—the solitude of the woods, the self-reliance. It was like swimming or diving; a man had only himself to count on, and Heimo looked forward to the challenges. This time he would "make it."

By early May 1976, snow was melting in the mountains and overflow was rushing out of Victoria Creek into Beaver Creek, which was misnamed, because if anything it resembled a large Alaskan river. In some spots the overflow was nearly a foot deep. Underneath, the winter ice was beginning to melt away. With twenty-two hours of sun, it was only a matter of time before four-foot-thick fields of ice would come careening downstream like an avalanche.

That day came May 8. Beaver Creek had begun to break up overnight. Half a mile from the cabin, a house-sized slab of ice jammed, and the river rose, slowly at first. Never having witnessed a breakup, Heimo didn't know enough to worry. Surely, he thought, the ice jam would be washed away. Besides, he had ducks to shoot. The previous evening he had noticed a large flock of black ducks circling a tundra pond, and he needed more meat. His plan was to jump-shoot them. He would walk to the pond and then crawl across the snow on his belly, surprising them while they swam in the shallows near the pond's edge. The birds would be dripping in spring fat, and if he was lucky, he'd have enough meat for the rest of the week.

That was the plan, but when Heimo reached the pond and tried to stalk the ducks, they spooked, flying far out of range. Heimo lay on his back along the pond's steep bank among dense bushes of Labrador tea, waiting for the ducks to return. They never did. It was late afternoon when another flock of pintails discovered the pond. Heimo could see them through his binoculars, swimming contentedly on the pond's far side, five drakes and two hens. He crept out of the bushes and circled the lake. They were swimming separately, too far apart for Heimo to kill more than one with a shot, so he held off. He listened to them chatter and waited for his opportunity. Gradually, they swam closer together, and when they were in range, Heimo lifted his gun and shot three times. Four ducks lay dead in the lake. Heimo fired twice more, trying to drop one of the escaping ducks with a wing shot, but missed. He waited twenty minutes for the wind to blow the ducks closer to shore, and then he waded out and collected them. Putting them in his backpack, he began the three-mile walk back to the cabin, feeling good about the hunt.

A half-mile from the cabin, he heard a sound like a locomotive—the ice rending, struggling to free itself. The sound frightened him, and now he ran, nearly sprinting through the melting, foot-deep snow. One hundred feet from the river, he could see water pouring over the bank: flood. By the time he reached the cabin, the water was already up to the front door. What to do first? Don't panic, he reminded himself. Don't panic now.

His friend's dogs were tied to their trees, and they were terrified, howling and pulling at their chains. Heimo unleashed them and shooed them off into the woods where they'd be safe. Then he remembered the puppies. Heimo ran around the cabin, yelling and whistling for them. He stopped long enough to listen and heard them whining from where they'd hidden under the cabin. Heimo called, but they were too frightened to move. He thought about sliding under the cabin to rescue them, but it was too late now. The water was too high. Heimo ran into the cabin, grabbed his sleeping bag, and stuffed his coat pockets with packets of macaroni. He came back out, searching frantically for the canoe. "Where's the goddamn canoe?" Abandoning the idea, he pulled himself up onto the cabin's roof. Seconds later, the river rushed through the cabin's front door.

Horrified, Heimo sat on the roof and watched as the river groaned and labored and launched huge, truck-sized chunks of ice into the air. Suddenly the cabin shuddered as if it might collapse. Heimo held on to the main roof beam like a baby clutching his mother. With every blow, the cabin shook and Heimo held on tighter, knowing that if he let go and was thrown from the roof, he would probably be crushed to death.

When the ice jam broke, the river let out a resounding yawn and the water retreated as quickly as it had come, as if it were being sucked into an enormous drain. Heimo watched, unwilling to let go of his grip, as if he expected the water to return. An hour later, he warily climbed down from the cabin's roof to inspect the damage. The cabin yard looked like the scene of a battle. Huge trees had been uprooted and lay scattered around the cabin yard like corpses. Other trees had snapped like twigs. Great brown monuments of ice, looking like tanks left behind by a retreating army, lay melting in the hot sun. Miraculously, the cabin was still standing, but inside Heimo found a dune of silt four inches deep. Too tired to shovel it out, he slept that night in his bunk in the stench of the river's backwash.

After the flood, Heimo foraged for duck and goose eggs and caught pike, which had come up into the sloughs to spawn. When the pike dropped their eggs, they left the sloughs, and soon Heimo again was wondering how he'd survive the summer. He was learning that the Arctic is a sparse country, its abundance short-lived. Animals appear in great numbers for brief periods of time, and then they move on.

By late afternoon the sun was shining. Robins yodeled and tiny ruby-crowned kinglets sang vigorously. Heimo was cleaning two young ducks he'd shot on Victoria Creek. He had already plucked them both; next he'd have to gut them. He grabbed one of the ducks, made a small cut at the bottom of its breast cage, and pulled out the viscera. Leaning back, he launched them twenty feet into the river. Then he heard it— "Slurp"—the unmistakable sound of a fish rising to suck up the entrails, followed by spreading concentric circles on the river's surface. Heimo gutted the next duck. Pitching the entrails into the river again, he listened. There it was again. Arctic grayling! Beaver Creek was still turbid with spring runoff, but there was no doubt now, grayling were in the river. He hadn't expected them until midsummer.

Heimo ran to the cabin to get his rod, tied on a spinner, and threw the lure into a deep pool. Instantly, he felt the strike. He set the hook, reeled in the fish, grabbed it and banged the back of its head on a rock. When it went limp, he tossed the fish onto the ground behind him. He cast again. Boom, another grayling hit. After a long, icebound winter, the fish were ravenous.

Despite the grayling, by late June Heimo was craving fat again and losing weight. He knew now that he needed more than fish and the occasional duck. He'd have to shoot a bear. Beaver Creek was supposed to be black bear country, but Heimo had never seen anything but tracks and scat. Deciding that he'd have to look farther away from the cabin, one morning he headed up Beaver Creek to one of the side creeks with gear and food enough to last him for three days. He couldn't paddle against the river's current. And he'd need the boat to bring back the meat. Attaching a rope to its bow and stern, he walked with the loop along the bank of the river, straining to hold the rope in just the right place so that the canoe would stay out of the shallows and track into the current in the river's deeper water, a technique called "lining," which Heimo was not accomplished at. He was making steady progress until he reached a cutbank where the rush of water had carved out a deep cavern. Heimo didn't know enough to beware of cutbanks, and sure enough the bank collapsed under his weight with a sudden whoosh of sand and dirt.

Heimo heard it happening, grabbed for a nearby tree, and held on. Six feet of cutbank hit the canoe, which tipped and then, amazingly, righted itself. Heimo scrambled down the bank and waded into the water to recover his canoe. His camping gear was wet, but worst of all, his bear rifle, his .444 Marlin, had fallen out. Fortunately, he'd had enough sense to tie everything else down. Searching the bottom of the muddy river with his hands, he realized that the rifle was gone for good. He cursed himself for his stupidity and paddled back down the river to the cabin.

A few days after this mishap, still determined to get a bear, he packed the canoe again with gear and loaded his shotgun with lead slugs. Downriver he shot not one, but two black bears. He gutted and skinned them and then lined the canoe up Beaver Creek, moving cautiously from gravel bar to gravel bar. Heimo had learned that the way to line a boat on a river with cutbanks was to avoid them entirely. Instead, he walked from gravel bar to gravel bar and paddled the short distance between them. With a canoe full of meat, this was a balancing act. He used only one rope, with one end tied to the bow and one end tied to the stern, and he held the rope so it formed something of a V. When he pulled the rope too tightly, the canoe would tack toward the shallow water and ground out. When he grasped it too loosely, the bow would pull out into the fast current. Gradually, he got to where he could line almost entirely by feel. He reached the cabin by evening and butchered the bears under the nearly constant sun. He made most of the meat into jerky (called "drymeat" in Alaska) so it wouldn't spoil in the summer heat, and was able to feed himself and the dogs for five days on the fresh meat.

That summer was his first in Alaska, and as Heimo readily admits, he made every mistake there was to make. Nothing came easy. Yet his good spirits were not diminished. Near the end of July, he wrote his friend again.

> Jammie,
>
> Wish you could be here. Mountains all around. Nobody for 100 or so miles. You wouldn't believe the mosquitoes up here in the Arctic. 17.65 million of them just flying around my head. Bug spray is useless. You just have to suffer. The summer is no time for sleep. The sun never sets.

This time Heimo followed his name with "seal hunter," "wilderness scout," and now "subsistence hunter," too.

CHAPTER 5

On the Coleen

In early June 1978, Heimo came to the Coleen River. He had wintered over in the Chandalar River country for two years and could now call himself a trapper, the real thing: "Heimo Korth—Guide of the North" and now "Trapper of the North," too. Best of all, he was on his own, tied to no one. Keith Koontz and Kenny Miller had given him his start, but when Heimo came to the Coleen, he was a free trapper. John Peterson, who flew Heimo out, remembers that he "looked like a full-fledged mountain man." Peterson shakes his head in disbelief at the image. "Man, he had hair down to the middle of his back—he hadn't cut it since he left home—a full beard, and a sealskin headband from Savoonga with an eagle feather in it. And he was wearing the same belt that he had when he first came up in 1975. He'd cut out new notches. He was so fit by that time, there were ten inches of leather hanging below his waist."

Paul Herbert, a Fort Yukon Gwich'in who was born on the Porcupine River shortly after World War II and grew up in the woods trapping and hunting, says, "Heimo came up from Wisconsin and he didn't know jack shit about livin' in the toolies. Most of the guys didn't make it. But Heimo was a tough son of a bitch. He was hard core and he learned and pretty soon he knew more about living out there than me or anybody else in Fort Yukon."

Where Your Creek meets the middle fork of the Chandalar River, forty miles southwest of the Gwich'in village of Arctic Village, is mountain country. But it is a "hungry" country, too. Although Heimo was tending nearly eighty miles of line and over 150 traps and snares, all on foot, his fur take amounted to nothing more than a few wolves, three or four wolverines, and some fox—hardly enough to pay for his meager supplies. But it wasn't for a lack of effort.

Each morning Heimo woke at 5:00 A.M. When he had success on his trapline, he worked on fur for two hours before breakfast. Otherwise, he cut wood. Once every two weeks, he would take a towel bath, heating water in a large pot on the woodstove, waiting until it nearly boiled, then using a towel and a bar of soap to scrub off two weeks of sweat, grease, and grime. And sometimes he would make medicine bags out of small pieces of fur, which he would later sell in Fort Yukon; or he'd patch holes in his clothes using the tanned skins from the ground squirrels he sometimes ate to conserve his food supply. He'd also reserve his mornings for writing letters.

> Jammie,
>
> Well trappin' hasn't been spectacular. . . . As of today I got 2 wolves, 2 wolverine, 2 red fox, and one ermine. Boy them wolverines are mean sons a bitches, strong too. I'd rather try to fight off 3 wolves than one wolverine. . . . There's always something bad about every life and trapping is no exception. It is the fleas on wolverines. Terrible. First one I caught I skinned him out then started to flesh him. About an hour later my head, beard, eyebrows, and armpits were loaded with fleas. I was itching like hell. . . . So I took a million baths. Threw the clothes outside to freeze, finally got all the fleas off of me. . . . I shot a moose. . . . The caribou never came. In caribou country you don't shoot a moose unless you are absolutely, positively sure the caribou aren't coming. . . . Oh also I haven't seen the sun since the beginning of November. 21 hours of night on my trapline here in the Brooks Range.

In closing, he drew his friend a map of Alaska, showing him where his trapline was, noting the prominent reference points.

A few months later, Heimo wrote his good friend again.

Allo Jammy,

My catch is almost exactly the same as the first part of the season. It was a hard year for snow. The deep snow pushed the fur out of the mountains where I am. This summer I'm going to take a piece of plastic (10 x10) . . . and my rifle and walk all over the Brooks Range. . . . By your address it sounds like it's a pretty high class apt. you're living in . . . I sometimes sleep in a lean-to at −70 just to catch one fox.

On his typical day, by 8:00 A.M., after eating a breakfast of boiled Dall sheep or moose steaks and drinking the broth for vitamins, he'd check his line, sometimes walking more than twenty miles in a single day. He wouldn't return to the cabin until late in the afternoon. Upon his return, he'd first load up the stove with wood. After a full day without heat, the cabin would be almost as cold as the outside. After stoking the fire, he'd go out and cut meat for his supper. The meals never changed—fried or boiled steaks, a can of spinach, and bannock—but they were enough to keep him fortified. After supper, he'd read for an hour, usually science fiction and spy novels, lying under a caribou skin for warmth, often submitting to sleep with the book still in his hands.

What would be drudgery for almost anyone else was freedom for Heimo. "I loved it," he says. "I was trapping for myself, and I was in the mountains, and I was strong." John Peterson adds, "Very few people could have done it—same food, no radio, no company, nothing. And it's a helluva lot of work. But Heimo didn't need much."

If his friend from Camp Mecan had any doubts about Heimo's intention to remain in Alaska, Heimo put those doubts to rest with a letter he sent from Fort Yukon in late spring.

Jim,

I just got back . . . from Savoonga. I was out there for 2 months. I went whaling with the Eskimos. You asked me if I liked it up here. To put it plain I would die before I would live down there again. I could never have a job again, 8 to 5. Can't wait to get out to my home.

While in Chandalar country, Heimo's bush education continued. He was tested time and again, but with every test, Heimo became more accomplished, and by the summer of his first year on the Chandalar, he had come to believe in his own abilities. He could survive the extreme cold, the months without sun, the isolation, and with a little luck, perhaps the mishaps, too. Whatever didn't kill him served to make him stronger.

Twenty-four years later, Heimo recalls an incident on the Chandalar and laughs at the irony of the situation. It was a hot summer evening without even the suggestion of a breeze, and the air whirred with the sound of mosquitoes. Heimo sat outside by a smudge fire he'd made of green willow branches, which gave off enough smoke to keep most of the mosquitoes away. He was sipping a cup of tea when he saw two figures coming up from the river. Had the light been worse, he would have grabbed his gun, thinking that his smoke rack had attracted two hungry grizzlies. For the last three days, he'd been smoking what remained of his winter meat supply. But he could clearly make out these two forms. There were two people walking toward him. "Evening," he shouted when they were within one hundred feet of the fire. They returned his greeting. They were poling a raft to a cabin fifty miles downstream—a husband and wife team and two dogs—where they were eager to begin their wilderness experiment, a year in the woods.

Heimo hadn't seen another human being in nearly two months, and he was glad for the company. Heimo recalls, "They were nice people. They pitched their tent in my cabin yard for a few days, and I fed them. We ate sheep, pike, lots of drymeat, and, of course, canned spinach, too," he chuckles. It turns out that the woman had spent part of her childhood in the bush. She told Heimo about it one night while sitting around the smudge fire. She'd also done an epic river trip in the Canadian Arctic with her mother, who wrote a book about the experience, and now, she said, she and her husband were going to try their hand at bush life. They'd spent one winter in a bush cabin, but she confessed that she was concerned that she might not have what it took to stay. The woman asked a lot of questions: Was it hard, did it get lonely, that kind of thing. Heimo confessed that he couldn't wait to get to town, that he needed a break and was looking forward to seeing people, to drinking a beer, to taking a shower. The kicker for Heimo was that before they left she walked up to him and told him that she didn't think that he'd last in the woods. " 'You don't have what it takes to make it in the bush,' " Heimo recalls her telling him. "At the time, that really chafed me," he says. "Here, she eats my food, asks me a lot of questions about what it's like to live out here, and then she insults me. I was ticked. I laugh about it now. She's living in Arizona or somewhere."

A year later, Heimo was bound for Fort Yukon, hoping to reverse his fortunes. In the late 1970s, according to longtime trapper and fur buyer Dean Wilson, "The fur market was hotter than a pistol." Heimo knew that at the rate he'd been going he couldn't hold out much longer. His fur take had been so small that he could barely scrape together enough money to outfit himself with food, much less buy new traps to add to the four dozen traps his mother had bought him so he could extend his lines. If he didn't find good fur country soon, Heimo feared, the woman's prophecy would turn out to be correct.

Paul Jagow, a New York City-born trapper who came into the country in the late 1970s and still lives for six months a year with his family on the Porcupine River, sheds some light on Heimo's situation. "You can be a romantic about living in the bush," he says. "I am. But it's important to pursue something economically, too. You really don't know a place until you have to make money there. Hikers may love the land, but they're only passing through. Trapping is a small part of the experience, but it's an essential part. It binds you to the land. And cash is a part of the rural economy; it has been for a hundred years. Besides, the winters can get terribly long, and you have to keep busy to stay sane."

Near the end of his stay on the Chandalar, Heimo contemplated calling home and asking for money, but that idea didn't last long. By the time he landed in Fort Yukon, he had already dismissed it. Another option was to go to one of Alaska's end-of-the-road bush villages, such as Circle or Central or Eagle, but none of those places had ever appealed to him. They were frontier towns, sure, but they weren't the wilderness. Finally, there was Fairbanks. But if he took a wage-paying job in Fairbanks, he thought, he might as well just go home where he had friends and family. So Heimo came to Fort Yukon asking a lot of questions.

He inquired among the locals about a new trapping territory. Initially, he had his sights set on the Yukon Flats, a 10,000-square-mile chunk of lowland, larger than Lake Erie, made up of swamp and bog and 36,000 lakes and muskeg ponds. The Yukon Flats were lynx country, and at $200 a pelt, Heimo was eager to start trapping lynx. But the answers he got were hardly encouraging. With fur prices as high as they were, other trappers had already staked out much of the Flats, which were closer to Fort Yukon and could be reached by river, and Heimo knew that trappers, like miners, were not the type of people to take kindly to another man's intrusion. They wouldn't have any hesitation about taking the law into their own hands. Hence he stayed clear of the Yukon Flats.

Then he heard the name that would figure prominently in the rest of his life—the Coleen—pronounced alternately "CO-leen" (long *o*) or Col-EEN (short *o*)—a French word, some said, meaning "little hills," because of the hills that could be found at the river's mouth. Heimo first heard about the Coleen River from an old Fort Yukon Indian who told him that there was fur to be had there. Much of the Coleen, the man said, had only been nominally trapped. Native hunters and trappers never had the tradition of going into the country with supplies. Before the 1940s, when the Bureau of Indian Affairs began building schools in bush villages, enticing peripatetic Native families to abandon their year-round wanderings, small Native groups came through, smearing themselves in summer with muskrat grease or an ointment of moose tallow or lard to fend off the mosquitoes. In winter they traveled with birch-bark baskets or hardened moose-skin sacks containing hot coals for the next fire. But they were always moving, so they never hunted or trapped the river heavily.

When a trapper friend, who'd just arrived in Fort Yukon to sell his winter catch, told Heimo that the Coleen area was indeed rich with fur, confirming the old Indian's report, Heimo was already imagining the river. The friend was trapping on the middle Coleen, and he invited Heimo to trap above him. It was better to have someone he knew trapping in his territory than a stranger. That was all Heimo needed. Like Jim Bridger, he had a "hankerin' to see more of the country" anyway, and he quickly made preparations to leave Fort Yukon for the Coleen River.

Heimo bought supplies and arranged for a bush flight. Just when he thought he'd attended to everything, he realized that he was missing maps. The Coleen was unfamiliar country, and he'd need them. Heimo searched Fort Yukon for the maps and discovered that a friend of his who also had his sights set on the Coleen owned the only set in town. The friend, however, didn't have the money to outfit himself, and he wasn't about to go out into the country for ten months without supplies. Realizing that Heimo had the jump on him, the friend offered to sell Heimo the set. His asking price—more than ten times what it was worth. Heimo was down to his last $40, but he bought the maps anyway, and he was good-natured about his friend's banditry. One-upmanship was a trapping tradition. It didn't matter anyway—Heimo was bound for the Coleen River. "I would have spent my last dime on those maps," Heimo says. "I couldn't wait to get out there."

The Coleen River is a clear, ice-hearted river, one of several major rivers of northeast Alaska helping to drain an area as large as the state of Texas. It is also remote. Its headwaters lie 160 miles above the Arctic Circle. Heimo's nearest neighbors would be the trapper friend who had told him about the Coleen—he lived fifty-five miles downriver—and a small group of Athabaskans who were trapping at the river's mouth where it met the Porcupine River, one hundred miles downriver.

Heimo discovered that the area where he would be on the Coleen was once the upper reaches of the trapping territory of Ed Owens, a legendary miner-trapper from Hanging Gulch, Oklahoma, who came to the Coleen in the early 1900s and died there in the 1960s. Owens always said that he was "born a prospector." He trapped only enough to make money to finance his mining forays, always certain that one day he would strike it rich. Between trapping and mining, Owens and his wife found the time to raise a family, and a number of the area creeks still bear the names of his daughters.

Owens was a large man of prodigious strength. Folks in Fort Yukon claimed that he could dance and drink all night and snowshoe forty miles the following day. In the 1920s the country was a web of well-used trails, which made the walking easier; breaking trail would have been impossible even for a man of Owens's stamina. Nevertheless, forty miles in a day was a feat of nearly incredible proportions.

Owens was as surly as he was strong. Miners and trappers knew not to get too close to Ed Owens's country. Rumor had it that one particularly brazen trapper insisted on venturing into his area, ignoring others' advice to stay away. One day the trapper just disappeared. Some say that Owens discovered tracks near his trapline and followed them to an abandoned line cabin. There, Owens found the trespasser and promptly shot him.

Abel Tritt, an Arctic Village Gwich'in elder who had befriended Heimo while Heimo was on the Chandalar, was in Fort Yukon at the time Heimo was preparing to head out for the Coleen. Abel had heard of Heimo's intention to trap on the upper part of the river and was eager to tell Heimo what he knew.

In 1919, when Abel was only seven, his family left the Chandalar River country in February at 40 below, setting off for the Old Crow drainage, a grueling trip of 150 miles. When they reached the Coleen River, they ran into a small herd of caribou, and Abel's father shot a large bull. They arrived in the Old Crow Flats country in mid-March and trapped muskrat until late spring. Then they walked to the village of Old Crow, where they shot more caribou. Fashioning caribou skin boats supported by green willow frames, they floated down the Porcupine to Fort Yukon, where they traded skins for supplies. In late June, they walked the 160 miles back to the Chandalar.

Abel's story captured Heimo's imagination, particularly the part about Abel's father shooting the caribou on the Coleen. Both his trapper friend and an old Fort Yukon Indian told Heimo that caribou commonly traveled through the Coleen River country in July and August en route to their wintering grounds in the Ogilvie Mountains of Canada's Yukon Territory. In May and June, he was told, they often came again, roaming back to their coastal plain calving area. But this was the first Heimo heard of caribou along the Coleen in early spring. This was good news, and he knew that Abel Tritt was not a man who took liberties with the truth. If Abel Tritt said there were caribou on the Coleen in spring, there were caribou.

When Heimo left Fort Yukon for the Coleen River in June 1978, he was laying down roots that would bind him to Alaska forever. Beaver Creek and the Chandalar were temporary stopping points, acts in an adventurous play. He had sworn the day he left that he'd never return to Wisconsin. But before he came to the Coleen, Heimo still had his doubts—could he really make it in the Alaskan wilderness?

The Coleen River changed all that. Though Heimo had never considered himself a spiritual pilgrim, the Coleen saved him. On Beaver Creek and the Chandalar, he was staying in friends' cabins. On the Coleen River he would build his own. It would be the first real home he had since leaving Wisconsin, and he was filled with hope. He could not know then that the river he loved one day would turn on him.

That first summer on the Coleen, Heimo enjoyed the company of his thirteen-year-old brother, Tom. Tom was fascinated by his oldest brother's life and had been dreaming of this trip since Heimo told him that he'd welcome a visit.

Tom had almost two months free for the trip. He would have to return to Wisconsin in early August before school began, and Heimo would leave to guide for Keith Koontz. In that time, there was much work to be done and country to see.

Tom was the first family member to visit Heimo in the three years since he left home. It was a big responsibility, caring for his thirteen-year-old brother; Irene Korth made sure Heimo understood that. But Tom was enough like Heimo that she knew she couldn't refuse to allow him to visit. Tom had been only ten, nothing more than a kid, when Heimo left home, and he admired his older brother.

According to Heimo, Tom's relationship with Erich Korth was much closer than his own had been. Heimo wonders if his father had mellowed, if as the youngest child of the family Tom had been spared the outbursts, the beatings. Perhaps Erich Korth had changed his expectations since Heimo left home. Maybe Tom had been allowed to grow up at his own pace with his own dreams. Could it be that Erich Korth had learned something from his relationship with his older son, that he was aware of the mistakes he'd made with Heimo and was determined to make good with his youngest son?

Still, when Tom came to visit, Heimo regarded him as his personal project. He was eager to play the role of the big brother. Because Erich Korth had never introduced Heimo to the woods, Heimo assumed that Tom was similarly impoverished. Heimo had seven weeks to introduce his brother to the woods, and not just any woods, but Alaska, the granddaddy of them all.

A bush pilot flew in the two of them and all their provisions in late June, but the pilot had a hard time finding a place to land. Fortunately, he was flying a floatplane. After surveying the area that Heimo had pinpointed on the map, he located a lake a mile and a half from the river. Heimo had hoped that he'd be able to land on the river, but it was still dangerously high with runoff and the pilot was concerned about hitting a submerged log. Heimo knew what that meant: The pilot would land on a lake, and he and Tom would have to pack in all their provisions to the river. Fortunately, Heimo didn't have much. In addition to the food, he'd brought out a chain saw, a tent, sleeping bags, an ax, spikes, and nails for building a cabin. Still, lugging the supplies from the drop-off site to the river would require many trips.

It took Heimo and his brother Tom the better part of two days to lug everything to the river. In winter with snow cover, the trip would have been a less arduous one, but in early June, with water flooding the land and a maze of muskeg, like an obstacle course, sucking at their boots and tripping them when they weren't careful, it proved to be exhausting. Tom worked without complaining, but at thirteen he hardly had the strength to carry heavy loads.

Once they had packed in all the provisions, Heimo and Tom walked

up the river, searching for a suitable place to build a cabin. They didn't
have to look hard. After only a quarter of a mile, Heimo discovered a
sizable stand of timber. His only problem was that it was on a large island. Wading the river wasn't an option, since the river was high and
still roiling with spring runoff. So Heimo had to make a decision—did
they wait, biding their time until the river played itself out, or did they
attempt a crossing? Heimo didn't deliberate long. He was eager to get
on with his life. They would risk a crossing. He and Tom would fashion
a raft and pole across.

Using his chain saw, Heimo toppled four white spruce trees. Then
he cleared out an area and built a smudge fire, coaxing the fire with dry
black spruce to keep it fueled, adding green willow boughs for smoke.
Heimo sectioned the trees into ten logs, each ten-feet long. Tom
limbed them with an ax. Because of the swarms of mosquitoes, newly
hatched and hungry, they worked as near to the fire as they could.
When either of them strayed from the fire, though, the mosquitoes
were relentless, and Heimo worried that Tom might not be able to
hold up.

In addition to the mosquitoes and wondering if he was working Tom
too hard, Heimo had another concern—meat. Though he'd flown in
food, it was not enough to carry him and Tom for more than a few
weeks. He'd wanted to bring in more, but he was low on money and
could only buy the essentials—flour, oatmeal, spinach, noodles, and tea.
He knew that soon he'd need to kill a caribou.

After their first day of work, Tom and Heimo sat outside their tent
near the smudge fire. They were sticky with sweat and reeked of wood
smoke. After a supper of noodles and a can of spinach each, Tom
crawled into the tent and fell almost instantly to sleep. Heimo sat by the
fire and fretted. Did he dare risk the river crossing? Would he be able to
shoot a caribou or a bear? In July there would be grayling, but now the
river was too muddy for grayling—they were lying in the feeder creeks
waiting for the river to clear up.

That night, sitting by the fire, listening to Tom snore in the tent,
Heimo chain-smoked, lighting a second cigarette before he snuffed out
the one he was smoking. He was dragging on a fresh cigarette, pulling

in deeply and filling his lungs with smoke, when he saw movement on the riverbank. Though it was 11 P.M., it was broad daylight. There it was again, in the willows ten feet from the river's edge. He was certain this time. His 300 Winchester Magnum rifle was leaning on a log next to him. Slowly he grabbed it, brought it up to his shoulder, and sighted it in on the bushes. He pressed his cheek against the stock of the gun and watched. When the animal appeared, Heimo's heart jumped—a big bull caribou. The pregnant cows, followed by their yearling calves, had come through earlier. He and Tom had found their tracks and beaten trails leading to the river.

The bull emerged from the willows and stopped at the riverbank, anxious about the crossing. Heimo knew he'd have to take him soon. In the water the bull would be an easy target, but Heimo would never recover the meat. Heimo sighted in on the bull's neck. He took a deep breath and blew out half the air, then held it. Slowly he pulled back on the trigger. The shot sounded and the caribou's legs buckled. Tom stormed out of the tent and discovered Heimo dancing in front of the fire. They would have meat for the summer.

Under the midnight sun, Heimo gutted the caribou and then showed Tom how to build a smoke rack. With temperatures certain to reach the eighties, Heimo knew that the meat would not keep for long. They would have to smoke most of it and subsist on drymeat until the grayling returned to the river. Heimo cut the caribou into strips and salted them in a mixing bowl of clear creek water from an upriver stream while Tom gathered dead willow sticks. After the meat had salted for thirty minutes, Tom slid the sticks through the strips of meat and then placed the sticks on the rack over a fire. Working steadily in the light of the Alaskan summer night, they cut and hung the entire caribou by early the next morning.

A few days later, they finished the raft. Near a slow spot in the river, Heimo found a place from which to launch it. They loaded their gear, and ten minutes later Heimo pushed off from the bank with his long pole, casting his and Tom's lot with the hard-running river.

It was exhilarating, at first, the wild tug of the current. Using the eight-foot poles, Heimo and Tom managed to guide the raft safely into the middle of the river. Everything was going well; the raft was holding up. Thirty more feet and the riverbank would be theirs. Heimo went to plant his pole to steer the raft around a large deadhead log protruding from the water's surface when he realized that something was seriously wrong. He stuck his pole in again and tried to push off. He felt nothing but water. Stay calm, he thought, it's just a deep hole. He tried again, removing his pole and digging it in on the other side of the raft, stabbing at the water, searching in vain for the river bottom. Tom was lunging frantically, too.

Heimo knew they were in serious trouble; the water was deeper than their poles were long. Without the poles, they had no way to maneuver the raft in the fast current. They were at the mercy of the river. The current whipped them downstream. Then Heimo saw it—a large white spruce tree, its roots pulled from the ground, the main portion of its trunk dangling over the river. "Sweeper!" he yelled. The next thing he knew the sweeper caught him in the hips and threw him into the water. He made a swipe for the raft, but missed and was dragged under by the current. He fought back to the water's surface and fumbled again for a handhold. This time he grabbed one of the logs, but all he could do was hold on. He didn't have the strength to pull himself up. Tom was poling and screaming, and the water was cold and Heimo was tiring. Just once, he thought; I have to try to get on the raft. Heimo threw a leg up and fell back into the water. He threw a leg over the raft again and wrestled his upper body onto the logs. He was retching now, throwing up river water. Though he managed to pull himself to the middle of the raft, he was too weak to help Tom.

When the current slowed, Heimo was aware enough to realize that it might be their only chance. He struggled to his feet and shouted to Tom, "Pole, pole like hell!" This time Tom struck bottom. Tom poled the raft closer to the riverbank, and then Heimo saw his opportunity— he jumped back into the river. It was only waist deep, and he leaned into the raft and pushed while Tom poled. When they reached shallower water, Heimo grabbed the bow rope and scrambled out of the river and up the bank. The current was tugging at the raft, but he was able to wrap the rope around the trunk of a large tree. He tied it off and then ran into the river to get Tom. Lifting Tom from the raft, he carried him to the bank. Then he rescued the supplies. Ten minutes later, after he had hauled everything to the riverbank, he took inventory. They'd lost only a .22 rifle and a fishing pole.

Heimo recalls the incident with horror. "Here my mother trusts me with my thirteen-year-old brother and I almost get him killed," he says. "It was a dumb *cheechako* thing to do. I should've just waited for the water to go down. I was sick for three days after that. After I got everything out of the raft, it started to rain. We built a big fire, but it still took me three days to stop shivering."

When Heimo finally recovered, he knew that their work had just begun. He and Tom had a cabin to build, and now that he had his strength back, he worked like a man possessed. He and Tom spent three days cutting and limbing trees for the cabin walls. Heimo wanted the cabin to be a sturdy one—Keith Koontz had taught him that—and he was fortunate that the upper Coleen River had one of the northernmost outposts of white spruce in the polar north. When they finished cutting logs, there were forty of them, each one ten to twelve inches in diameter. Heimo then used his ax to smooth out flat surfaces so that they would fit together tightly when laid on top of each other. Then he carved out saddle notches near the ends of each log, reminding himself to lay the notches down so that water would not be able to collect in the grooves and weaken the walls. Though he tried to match the logs as closely as possible, there was little uniformity, and many of them didn't fit as snugly as he had hoped. The spaces between them would have to be chinked with lots of moss.

Two weeks after they'd begun the project, Heimo and Tom confronted their biggest challenge yet—they had to set the cross member. The cross member had to run widthwise, perpendicular to the roof poles. Since it had to support not only the weight of the moss, but also the poles and the three feet of snow that would collect during the winter, it was very large and heavy. Heimo and Tom rolled the log to the corner of the cabin, where they both lifted up one end and propped it up on the cabin wall. Then they struggled to lift the other end. The log was so big they could not get the cross member higher than their waists. They tried several times and wore themselves out in the process. Frustrated, Heimo insisted they take a break.

Sitting against the cabin wall, wiping the sweat from his face with a handkerchief, Heimo came up with an idea. He grabbed his chain saw and walked over to where he'd cut the wall logs and cut a large tree stump off at its base. Heimo hoped that he and Tom could lift the end of the log high enough to rest it on the stump. If they were able to do that, and if Tom could hold it in place, then maybe, just maybe, Heimo could squat underneath and power it up, using his leg strength. They tried twice and failed. On their third attempt, they got it on top of the stump, but the log rolled off before Heimo could get underneath it. Then on their fourth attempt, they did it. Tom was able to balance the log long enough for Heimo to get underneath and lift. Heimo was standing now and Tom jumped in to help. At the count of three they both jerked the log over their heads and pushed it, so that the log was suspended between the cabin's south and east walls. Although they'd gotten the cross member up, their job was far from being over. The log was balanced precariously, and it wouldn't take much to upset that balance. If the log fell, they'd have to begin again.

Heimo climbed and straddled the wall. His job was to muscle the cross member to the north wall and then roll it into place. There was little Tom could do now but watch and hope that cross member didn't tumble back, that Heimo didn't take a bad fall. Half an hour later, Heimo finally got the cross member set. Though it was hardly noon, both Heimo and Tom were worn out from the effort. Rest wasn't an option, though. They needed to lay the roof poles.

Setting the roof poles, which were green and heavy, proved to be even more difficult than lugging and lifting the wall logs. It took all the strength that Heimo and Tom had to hoist the roof poles and roll them into place. By early evening, they'd set all forty roof poles. They went to bed that night without supper and woke early the following morning with hunger gnawing at their bellies. Heimo knew they needed a good meal to keep their strength, so he fried up caribou steaks and made bannock, using flour, powdered milk, water, and baking powder.

After breakfast, they went to collect moss for the roof. The roof would have four layers: the poles and then a layer of insulating moss, followed by a big plastic sheet of Visqueen, which in turn would be covered with another layer of moss. Heimo had hoped that moss would be easy to find, but finding it in the woods, gathering it, loading it onto the tarp, and lugging the tarp to the cabin took them a good portion of the day. It was evening when they finally put the finishing touches on the roof, smothering the Visqueen in a six-inch blanket of moss.

The entire project had taken them nearly a month. Looking at the cabin, Heimo knew that it was not a thing of beauty. It had a flat roof and a five-and-a-half-foot ceiling, but Heimo was willing to sacrifice comfort for function. He deliberately built the roof a full six inches shorter than he stood. In winter, at 50 below, when the heat of the stove was trapped in the cabin, he would be grateful. Thinking back, Heimo laughs that the only time he was ever able to extend his six-foot frame was when he was sleeping.

Heimo and Tom rested and fished for two days, and then they walked five miles upriver, near the mouth of Marten Creek, and built a flat-roofed line cabin. Though it was smaller than the first, only ten by ten, and roughly constructed, that cabin took a full week to build. The line cabin was an essential trapper's trick. It allowed the trapper to expand the size of his trapline. For Heimo, it meant that he could trap farther upriver and also lay out side lines, confident that if he were too tired to make it back to the main cabin, or if he got caught in rough weather, he could always overnight at the line cabin. Ideally, he would have built one even farther north, fifteen or so miles upriver instead of only five, but he'd already pushed Tom to his limits. Though Tom was stronger than most thirteen-year-olds, a five-mile walk through muskeg, carrying a full load of gear, was about all he could muster.

In mid-July, two days after they finished building the line cabin, Heimo and Tom woke and realized that there had been a hard freeze. Ponds had frosted over in the night, and although Heimo was worried, because he hadn't even begun to cut firewood, he was seduced by the weather. The sun shone brilliantly and the freeze had come with its own blessing; the bugs that had menaced them for a month and a half were gone. Heimo would cut wood when he returned in September. For the last two weeks before the plane came to get them, Heimo and Tom fished and explored up and down the river, living completely in the moment, the way young men and boys can.

CHAPTER 6

Spring

Kirk Sweetsir tips the wings of the plane, waving good-bye, bush pilot style. Heimo and I wave back and wait until the plane has disappeared and we can only hear the far-off buzz of the Cessna 180 engine.

Heimo turns to me, sniffing at the air. "You smell like town," he says.

"And you look like a ski bunny," I say, retaliating. Heimo has shaved off his winter beard, though he still wears his sideburns long in modified muttonchops, and his face is now deeply tanned as if he's spent the two and a half months since I last saw him skiing the slopes of Aspen. "You'll look the same way when you leave here," he says. "Tan from the neck up with rings around your eyes from your sunglasses. You did bring a pair, didn't you? You're gonna need 'em."

I look around. The land is luminously white, and I can't imagine how it can ever be spring. A month past the vernal equinox, and the temperature is still 5 below. The black spruce labor under the weight of snow and the frosted willows tremble in the raw breeze, producing a strange musical sound, like a jazz drummer lightly brushing his snare drum. We are still in the grips of winter, but the shadows are gone. The polar world has tilted toward light—for the last month, the Korths have been gaining more than ten minutes of sunlight each day—and the sun is shining as if it is another season. I lift my face to it. Though it offers little warmth, it is dazzling, and I have to shade my eyes.

119

The sound of Kirk's plane trails off into nothing.

In the last half century, the bush plane has dramatically changed the Alaskan landscape, unlocking the door to a wilderness whose sheer breadth would otherwise be unapproachable. Cubs, single-engine Otters, Beavers, and tail-dragging Cessnas like Kirk's, fifty-year-old planes that have been rebuilt by resourceful pilots, are standard fare in the Alaskan bush. By some accounts, these "flying coffins," as Alaskans with a flair for black comedy call the bush planes, have been a gift to those eager to experience Alaska. By others, the bush plane has been a great spoiler, rendering areas that were nearly unreachable within the grasp of anyone with a pilot's license or any Tom, Dick, Harry, Susan, or Jane with enough money to hire one. The prevalence of planes in the bush is sometimes alarming, particularly during the summer backpacking, floating, and big-game hunting seasons, when pilots take advantage of the midnight sun and hustle like big-city cab drivers, running clients to and from the farthest points on the map.

The plane has been a mixed blessing for the Korths. Sounding like Daniel Boone, who moved with his family from western Virginia to Missouri because he needed "elbow room," Heimo says, "The Old Crow cabin is unreachable by water and almost impossible to get to by land, which is just the way I want it." The plane, in other words, has made their life in the bush possible. It allows them their isolation. It is also their connection to the world outside. Friends who own planes bring in supplies, food, and mail, and shuttle the Korths from one cabin to another in spring and from the bush to Fort Yukon and back again every summer. Without the help of good friends, the Korths would be hard-pressed to live the way they do. On the other hand, the plane also poses a threat to their lifestyle, allowing hunters, backpackers, and river floaters access to Alaska's most remote wilderness areas, including the Coleen River and the Old Crow drainage.

"That's Bear Mountain," Heimo says, slipping on his sunglasses and pointing north at a massive peak. "And way over there," he continues, gesturing to the southeast, "those are what we named the Strangle-woman Mountains." The scene is that of a minimalist painting: the mountains, snow-covered and white, set starkly against a robin's-egg-blue sky, the peregrinations of the icy Coleen River outlined by the dark trunks of tall white spruce trees.

"It's beautiful," I say, putting on my own sunglasses. "Yeah," Heimo agrees. "I love it here at the upper cabin, especially in spring."

Heimo and Edna have been "springing out" at one of their three cabins ever since they were married, twenty years ago. "Springing out" is an old-time bush term meaning to spend spring in the bush all the way until after breakup and only then to head for town. Rhonda and Krin have been "springing out" all their lives. They know nothing else.

Spring is a joyous time in the bush, but waiting for breakup can be tough psychologically. There's a sense of eagerness, an anticipation that builds, that begins to weigh on a person. Everybody is excited to get to town and wonders when breakup will come. When the timing is perfect, breakup happens around mid-May, a week or two after the songbirds and ducks and geese have appeared. However, sometimes breakup is late; it can stretch into early June. When that happens, even the most stable psyches are challenged.

When the Korths leave their cabin for town, they head to Fort Yukon. They've been going there for six weeks of "town life" every summer, replicating the historic movement of families out of the woods. Town was always part of the cycle of bush life. Fred Thomas, Heimo's good friend and the traveling companion of Edward Hoagland in his story "Up the Black to the Chalkyitsik," recalls, "Families came out in early June to sell their furs, to visit friends, and to stock up on supplies. Sometimes the men would hire themselves out for summer labor. Then in August, they'd load up their boats and head back up the rivers for home."

We load my gear into the sled, but before going upriver, Heimo quizzes me. "Can you figure out where the Old Crow cabin is?" he asks. I don't balk. Instead I point confidently in the direction of some rounded, glacial hills, feeling like Heimo's sister Angie might have when she tried to name tracks in the woods near their childhood home. "Over there," I say. Heimo follows my outstretched finger, roughly northeast. "Not bad," he replies, moving my arm six inches to the north, like a piano teacher readjusting a student's hands. "Twenty miles that way," he says.

We pull up to the cabin, and I admire Heimo's woodpile. He's already cut, split, and stacked nine cords of spruce wood for the following winter. "I was hoping that you left some of that work for me," I tell him, and then I bound to the door and stomp my feet—remembering my winter lesson—to announce that I am coming in.

Inside the cabin, the girls are hard at work finishing up their studies for the day. Rhonda is clutching her pencil and staring at a long algebra equation, and Krin is working on her spelling. "Meteorology," I hear her say as I walk in. Edna is sitting in front of the cabin's only window tending her plants—an apple, a pear tree, and watermelon seeds. She's placed the plants and seeds in a large plastic bowl filled with dirt. Next to the bowl is an avocado pit soaking in a glass jar half full of water.

Edna rises and hugs me, and the girls smile mischievously. "Uh-oh," I say. "What are they up to, Edna?" "You know them," she answers, looking at the girls, who are giggling over their notebooks. "They've been plotting. They have a whole month of pranks in store for you." "Ah, fresh meat," I say. "I should have known."

Heimo walks in and catches the tail end of our conversation. "Jeez," he says, "you're not even gonna give him a chance to get settled in, are you?" Rhonda and Krin both drop their pencils and beam. "No way!" they shout. "Don't worry," I say to Heimo, who is scowling. "I know what to expect from the Merry Pranksters." On my winter trip, the girls so tormented me with their practical jokes that I'd taken to calling them the "Merry Pranksters." This time, by the looks of it, they are determined to outdo themselves.

I walk out to the sled, grab my gear, and lug it to the orange Arctic oven tent, which Heimo has pitched in an opening near the outdoor fire pit about fifty feet from the cabin. There is a sign taped to the tent, decorated in bold black letters: "Welcome to Another Nightmare." I pull the sign from the tent and turn to see who is watching me. Rhonda and Krin dive through the cabin door, and Edna jumps back from the cabin window. I set down my bags to unzip the tent's rain fly and I realize that I can't find the zipper. For a moment I am puzzled. Have I forgotten how to get into the tent, my home away from home? Then I realize—another prank. I walk around the tent and discover that the girls have rearranged the rain fly so that its door is at the back. I unclip it and twist it to the front.

I enter the tent warily. What next? Before I know it, I am tangled in something. I throw open the tent door and rain fly to let the light in, and then I know. The girls have strung a spider's web of invisible nylon thread throughout the tent. It is wound around my neck and arms and legs. I can hear wild laughter coming from the cabin. I have fallen into their trap like an unsuspecting marten, and the girls are cackling loud enough for me to hear.

Before heading back to the cabin for dinner, I set up my cot and stove, slip in my stovepipe, and notice that the girls have stuffed it with tinfoil. It is a fortunate discovery. A clogged stovepipe would have smoked me out five minutes after I started the fire. It isn't dangerous, but it would have made things uncomfortable on my first night back in the bush since late January. Fishing the tinfoil out of the pipe, I imagine the girls' glee had the prank succeeded—me retiring to my tent for the night and then rushing out, coughing and cursing and barefoot, into the subzero temperatures and a foot of snow.

"Heimo, Edna," I say, kicking the snow from my boots before ducking into the doorway "Your girls are a bunch of incorrigible mischief makers." Krin sweeps the cabin floor, and Rhonda is getting the plates and silverware ready for supper. Both answer in unison with mock innocence, "Who, us?" They are listening to Sir Arthur Conan Doyle's *The Hound of the Baskervilles*, their favorite tape, so they reply in their best English accents. "Yes, you," I say. "Mischief makers, just like their father," Edna interjects. "That's where they get it."

"Shhh," Heimo says. "I want to hear this." He turns up the sound on the tape player, and he and Rhonda and Krin anticipate Dr. Watson's next line: "In those hours of darkness when the powers of evil are exalted . . ."

Edna announces that the food will be a little late—lentils with caribou hocks and beaver tail—so I take a seat on a bucket near the door and listen along to *The Hound of the Baskervilles*. The beaver tail is lying on the woodstove.

While we wait for the lentils and the beaver tail, I look around the cabin. Heimo had told me its dimensions, fourteen feet by fourteen feet. It is four feet wider than the Old Crow cabin and only two feet shorter, but for some reason it looks considerably smaller, perhaps because it is even more cluttered, though the clutter is tasteful. In many ways, the Korths consider this, their upper Coleen cabin, to be their home cabin, and Edna has decorated with that in mind. Edna, not Heimo, has built three attractive tables and a corner shelf unit, using slender spruce logs with the bark still attached. The corner shelf contains books, photographs, tapes, and knickknacks, and on one of the tables, she has built a rack to store spices. In the kitchen area, she's hung colorful wallpaper, depicting fruits and flowers. Above the wallpaper, using plastic milk crates, she's erected shelves for the plates, dishes, bowls, cups, and utensils. She's decorated the log walls with shelves, too, and family photographs, and the girls' drawings. Edna notices me admiring the drawings from my side of the cabin and takes them down. "Here," she says, handing them to me. "What do you think?"

The girls, I know, love to draw, but on my first visit they were reluctant to let me see any of their work. Edna tried to show me some of it, but when they caught her, they invariably grabbed it away from her and hid it. Maybe now they are more comfortable with me, or perhaps they're too preoccupied to notice. In any case, neither of them object. On one sheet of paper, Krin has drawn a horned puffin and managed to capture the large, odd-shaped bill. On another, she's drawn a raven, large and black, and she's endowed it with something of the raven's roguishness. Rhonda has drawn a picture of an angelic-looking child, black hair, round face, full lips. She catches me looking at it, but rather than demanding it back, she hands me a photograph. "That's Krin when she was little," she says. "I tried to copy it."

"They're good artists, aren't they?" Edna asks. "Like their mother," I reply. On my first trip, Edna made a pair of Eskimo slippers for my four-year-old daughter, using moose and caribou hide the color of walnut, spiky, short-haired strips of sealskin, and small pieces of lynx and wolf fur, both a mottled gray. On the top of the shoes, she added a white background of beadwork accented by intricately beaded red, yellow, and blue flowers. The slippers were works of art.

The thick reptilelike skin of the twelve-inch beaver tail is bubbling on the woodstove. Heimo rises from a camping chair and peels the skin off the tail with a fork, revealing a semi solid slab of fat. "You're gonna try it when it's done, aren't you?" Heimo asks, challenging me. He holds the tail suspended over a plate. Large drops of fat fall from it like juice from an orange that's been cut in half. "Wouldn't miss it for the world," I say, and grimace. "It's rich," Heimo warns. "I wouldn't eat too much of it or you'll be awful sick." Then he adds, "The PETA people would love the image of you eating beaver tail. I'm a member of PETA, you know. People for the Eating of Tasty Animals, that is."

Then he wraps the tail in tinfoil and sets it back on the stove. Twenty minutes later, Edna peels the foil back, peeks at the tail, and pokes at it gingerly with a fork. "Done," she says. "Turn off that tape. Dinner's ready."

Heimo hands me a large bowl of green lentils, which includes a sizeable bone, and a piece of beaver tail about the size of a hamburger patty. I try the beaver tail first, and they all watch and wait for my reaction. It is richer than anything I have ever eaten. It tastes like the drippings of southern fried chicken. Imagine removing the chicken from a cast-iron skillet and using a fork to scrape off what remains—skin, fat, and Crisco. Dip the fork in a bowl of melted butter, and you have beaver tail. "So, what do you think?" Heimo asks enthusiastically. "Just wait until we have pickled beaver's feet." At that, he grabs the two feet from a bowl and holds them for me to see. They look as big as diving fins. "We boil them and then we pickle them in onion and vinegar. They're delicious."

I finish my lentils and ask for a second helping. Though I've enjoyed the beaver tail, I've had enough. It is now sitting in my stomach like a giant sponge. "There's lots," Heimo says, ladling lentils into my bowl. "Eat more." "Stop," I say, slowly pulling my bowl away so he doesn't dump a ladleful onto the floor. I knew better than to listen to Heimo. I've never witnessed anyone with such an insatiable appetite. He burns a lot of calories, that is true, but there is no accounting for his ability to eat. Heimo eats like a wolf, bingeing when he can, as if preparing himself for a time of scarcity. Next to him, I look like a child playing with his food.

I finish my meal first and then I watch as Heimo and Krin clean their

caribou bones, using their jackknives to trim away the gristle and cartilage. Though I am loath to waste food, I look prodigal next to them. It's
a basic rule up here: You can use God's name in vain when the snow has
destroyed your trail or a lynx has stolen a marten from your poleset or
the mosquitoes are murderous or it's so goddamn cold that you don't
want to leave the cabin. But it's sinful to waste anything, especially food.

When Heimo and Krin finish with their jackknives, they gnaw on the
bones as if they might never again see another meal, as if the ducks and
geese on which they depend for spring food have ceased their spring
migration to the Arctic nesting grounds. Finally, they dig their knife
blades into the bones to winnow out the marrow. "I love the marrow,"
Heimo says. Then he looks at me. "You eat like a white man. We eat like
Natives. You leave the best parts. Natives would never do that. They
utilize the whole animal."

"Give me back my bone," I say, knowing that Rhonda has already
cleared my plate.

When Heimo finally finishes his bone, he plops it onto his plate, and
it looks as if it has been bleached by the sun and then polished. There
isn't a scrap of cartilage remaining. Rhonda, who is cleaning up the
dishes, takes the bone and ducks out the cabin door. Then she winds up
and tosses it into the bushes thirty feet from the cabin.

She pokes her head in through the door, smiling at me.

"Your bone's out there, too, if you still want it."

Next day, we have a lunch of Edna's sourdough bread and honey—early
white trappers and miners regarded sourdough as one of their most
prized possessions, hence the epithet "sourdough" to describe someone
who makes his living in the bush. Then Heimo helps me collect water at
the spring behind the cabin. This morning I woke up with stomach pains
and promptly reconsidered my decision to drink the water right out of
the Coleen, as the Korths do, because the river has beaver. Heimo has
taken four beaver this spring, but he left a family and a few others—
"seed," he calls them—as breeding stock for next year. I am determined
now to use the spring to guard against giardia, sometimes called "beaver
fever." Giardias are parasitic protozoans that live in beaver feces—though

all mammals can be infected—and are transmitted through unfiltered water. Though the Korths sometimes use the spring, they prefer the water in the river and seem to have built up a resistance to the parasite based on a long-term, low-level exposure. In fact, according to a Fairbanks parasitologist, they could probably drink heavily contaminated water now without becoming infected. I, on the other hand, have no such resistance, and I've heard enough giardia horror stories—intestinal pain, cramping, diarrhea—to feel sufficiently chastened. The last thing I want to do is spend my spring trip running to and from the outhouse.

What passes for an outhouse at the upper Coleen cabin is nothing more than a three-foot hole in the ground over which Heimo has erected a kind of toilet. The toilet has four legs like a table. Where the top should be, Heimo has built a sort of seat, nothing more than a V formed by two pieces of wood with the open end of the V facing forward. It is primitive, but it works, though each and every time I visit I wonder just how the contraption will withstand my 225-pound frame. Last winter, Heimo told me the story of a fledgling Fort Yukon trapper who once fell into an outhouse hole and forever after was known by the name of "Shitslinger," and I am not eager to see just how creative Heimo, Edna, and the girls can be in the event that I take a similar spill. One good thing about the outhouse is that it has a degree of privacy. In preparation for my visit—more to ensure the privacy of Edna and the girls—Heimo tied up a large green plastic tarp in front of the hole. The outhouse is open on three sides, though the side facing the cabin is shielded. In comparison to the Old Crow setup this is practically luxurious. Along the Old Crow, the permafrost—a layer of permanently frozen ground, which farther north in the High Arctic extends nearly 2,000 feet down—is so near the surface that it's impossible to dig an outhouse hole. The outhouse there was the frozen creek bed. Everyone selected a spot in the snow, squatted, and then covered it up like a cat. Heimo's reasoning was that when the spring floods came, they would wash away the shit, diluting the presence of human feces in the water, as Heimo said, to something like "parts per billion." Toilet paper wasn't discarded. In keeping with the no-waste ethic, Heimo encouraged me to bring it back and use it as firestarter.

On the way to the spring, it occurs to me that I should probably ask Heimo about grizzlies. I should have inquired yesterday, when I arrived, but I didn't want to give him the impression that I was overly anxious, though it would have been an entirely reasonable question. The Interior abounds with tales of *Ursus arctos horribilis*, one of the largest carnivores left on the planet. Although grizzlies aren't really a worry in winter, the most chilling tale I've heard concerns the "winter" or "ice" bear, an animal that would sooner eat than sleep. While most bears den up for four to five months to wait out the worst of the weather in a state akin to sleep, where their heart rate drops to as few as eight beats per minute, the ice bear is forced by hunger to leave the comfort of its den and go out in search of food. After emerging from its den, it finds water as quickly as it can and submerges itself in it, forming a thick coat of insulating ice on top of its fur and fat. The ice bear is not only unafraid of the human scent, some people say it is attracted to it. Worst of all, its ice coat makes the bear impervious to bullets. But for all the ferocity of the stories, the ice bear is largely the stuff of legend. Yet once heard, it is as hard to wrest the ice bear from the imagination as it is for a boy or girl to escape night terrors after listening, for the first time, to the ghost story "The Man with the Golden Arm" around a campfire.

Krin and Rhonda are creeping through the trees behind us, like spies. They overhear my question and immediately launch into an impersonation of Dorothy in *The Wizard of Oz*. " 'Lions and tigers and bears, oh my!' " they shout. " 'Lions and tigers and bears, oh my!' " They dash behind a makeshift rack containing perhaps a hundred leghold traps and dozens of snares, which Heimo has pulled for the year, and cower as if being charged by an attacking grizzly. Heimo is more serious. "Some of the males are out of their dens by now," he says, "so you should be careful when walking around, especially upriver. I wouldn't worry too much about coming back here to the spring, but maybe you should carry a gun just in case." He pauses. "I'd hate to be the one to deliver the bad news to your wife and mother." He hoots, not at all reluctant to laugh at his own joke.

I decide right then that I will take a shotgun with me whenever I visit the spring, "just in case." I had a scare the previous summer while backpacking with a friend, north of here, near the Canadian border, and I am not about to take any chances.

It was morning, and my buddy Burns and I had just finished breakfast. I was repacking my pack while Burns went off into some willows to relieve himself. Minutes later, I saw him coming back. Ten feet from the campsite he suddenly stopped. "What's going on?" I asked. He didn't answer immediately, and when he did he nearly whispered—"Turn around." I turned around slowly, sensing the tension in his voice, and there was a 600-pound, honey-humped boar grizzly fifty yards away, walking right at us. Though my first instinct was to run, I held my ground. There was nowhere to run. There wasn't a climbable tree within fifty miles.

Six hundred pounds is big, yet the barren-lands grizzly of northern Alaska is only half as large as its coastal bear cousin, which dines on fish aplenty instead of roots, berries, and ground squirrels. Burns and I tried to keep calm and do as we'd been told. We locked arms to look larger and more imposing and started talking to the bear. We didn't shout, but we spoke loud enough for him to hear, in confident, casual tones. "Howdy, bear," we said. "We're right here, big fella. Sorry to be camped out on your creek. Just passin' through." But the bear waddled toward us, as if he hadn't heard a word. "Run if it's a moose, stand if it's a bear." The closer he got, the more the mantra fast-tracked through my head.

The distance was shrinking, forty yards, then thirty. We'd been hoping to see a grizzly—from a safe distance—but this didn't qualify. There's something about staring a bear in the face that makes a person immediately aware of his place in the food chain. My heart was pounding as I watched him amble down our side of the creek, seemingly unaware of, or indifferent to, our presence. It was dead calm and there was always the possibility that he hadn't winded us yet. So I kept talking at him, while Burns grabbed a pot and banged on it with a soupspoon, but still the bear didn't stop. Finally, as a last resort, I grabbed my pistol, a Ruger .44 Magnum double-action revolver. "Should I shoot one into the air?" I asked Burns. "It might scare him off." Burns stopped banging on the pot. "Just hold on a moment," he said.

When the bear was thirty feet away, he crossed to the other side of the four-foot wide creek and stood on his hind legs, sniffing at the air, nostrils quivering, the first sign that he had noticed us, and a good sign, too. If he'd wanted to attack, he would have been slobbering. His ears would have been cocked back, and his head hung low, swinging back and forth. He would have been "woofing," too. Nevertheless, I could hear him breathe and that was enough to make every nerve ending in my body tingle with a fear-inspired electricity. After a minute or so, he settled back down on all fours. Remembering the words of a hiking guide who made his living taking city folk into the Alaskan wilds, I kept the gun zeroed in on his shoulder anyway. "Break him down," the guide had told me. "I carry a sawed-off shotgun with slugs when I'm taking clients out. If you're going to shoot a grizzly with a .44 Magnum, you have to break him down. Go for the shoulders first." I held the gun as steady as possible, wondering how even a .44 Magnum could damage that magnificently muscular shoulder. All the while, Burns and I kept talking to him. "Just be on your way now, big boy, and we'll be on ours."

The grizzly sniffed at the air again, and then he crossed back to our side of the small creek and lazily wandered around us, giving us a wide berth. He was almost gracious about it. Nevertheless, we'd heard enough about the treachery of grizzlies not to be lulled into complacency by his apparent generosity. I kept the gun on him and Burns kept talking. Only when there were one hundred yards between us, and the bear was happily digging for roots in the tundra, did we allow ourselves to think that perhaps we wouldn't be mauled.

The truth of the matter is that a .44 Magnum offers a false sense of security. A grizzly can move quicker than Warren Sapp on a Sunday afternoon, covering fifteen yards in just over a second. It takes a steady hand and a rapid succession of shots from someone very comfortable with a .44 Magnum to bring down a charging bear. Heimo carries a .44 for protection against bears, but he knows how to handle the gun. He would stand a chance against a rushing, ill-intentioned grizzly; I wouldn't.

An old trapper was the first to break the news to me about the fecklessness of a .44 Magnum in the hands of someone who isn't accustomed to shooting one. We'd been talking about bears, and he'd asked me if I'd ever run into a grizzly. Why, sure I had, I told him, just the summer before. He was close, I said. "Were you carrying a gun?" he drawled. "Heck, yeah," I told him with some bluster. "I was carrying a .44 Magnum." "Psst," he said, winking and bending close to me, as if he were ready to share a secret. I was all ears. "Next time you're carrying that .44 of yours, be sure to file off the sight." "File off the sight?" I asked him, thoroughly perplexed. "Hell, yeah," he said, repeating the advice. "File off the sight." I looked at him, waiting for his words of wisdom. He let the anticipation build. "That way," he said, drawing in a deep breath, "when a grizzly shoves that gun up your ass, it won't hurt so goddamn much."

Still, the most persistent fallacy of Alaska is that there's a hungry bear hiding in every thicket just waiting to devour you. The truth is that grizzlies in the Interior have a range of one hundred square miles. Unless you know where to find them and what to look for, you're lucky to spot a pigeon-toed track much less a real bear. Yet the primal fear one feels when hiking in grizzly country persists. A fresh pile of spoor or the sight of an excavated hill where a grizzly has torn up everything to get at roots or a squirrel is sure to raise the hair on the back of the human neck.

Heimo has already been out to wake me—at 6:30 sharp, as he has for the last week. But I'd just put a fresh log in the stove, and I was seduced into sleeping for another hour by the womblike warmth of the tent.

This time it is Krin who appears. Heimo or Edna has sent her out to get me, and she isn't happy about it. "Breakfast," she says with a growl. "Wake up." Then I hear her run off through the snow. The sharp "thump" of the spring-loaded cabin door closing tells me that she is now inside and that it is safe for me to come out and take my morning pee. In winter I kept a plastic jug next to my cot, which I used as a pee bottle to avoid having to go outside. But spring is a whole other story. In spring I look forward to my morning pee and to boring a deep hole into the snowbank behind my tent.

At the cabin door I kick the snow off my feet to something of a Scottish jig rhythm. I perfected the step while on the Old Crow, but since no one has picked up on it, I do it largely for my own amusement.

The others have already eaten their breakfast, but they've left behind a large bowl of oatmeal for me. "Oatmeal or no meal," I say, smothering it in honey and sitting down on a chair, a large tree trunk to which Edna has nailed a comfortable cushion.

Heimo is paging through a book I gave him the previous evening—E. C. Pielou's *A Naturalist's Guide to the Arctic*. He points to the photo of the walruses on the book's front cover and makes a hoarse barking sound like a dog with kennel cough. "*Ayvuq*," he says. "Walrus. They call walrus *ayvuq* on St. Lawrence Island." Edna corrects him. "*Au-vuq*," she says, only her pronunciation is more guttural.

"We used to hunt them when I was in Savoonga," continues Heimo. "You had to shoot them six inches behind the eye. It was the only place. The rest was solid blubber. Sometimes we'd hunt them in a fog. We couldn't see them until we were almost on top of them, but you could hear the cows barking, and you could smell them. God, the stink, you wouldn't believe it."

Edna is sitting on their sleeping platform and Heimo is lying in her arms while he tells the story. Even after twenty years of marriage, and enough tragedy to break up any relationship, there is an easy intimacy between them. Edna grabs Heimo's belly and then rubs it. At forty-seven, Heimo is remarkably fit, so Edna grabs what she can. "More here than there used to be," she says, teasing him. "Where?" Heimo asks, perhaps wondering if the push-ups and sit-ups he does four times a week are working. "Right here," Edna responds, latching onto as much skin as she can. "Ouch," Heimo yelps, and then bends his head back and kisses Edna on the underside of her chin.

The girls are doing freewriting exercises and don't seem at all distracted by their parents' antics. "Finished," Krin says, and hands me her story. Rhonda is still hard at work on hers, twirling her hair with her free hand, concentrating. This is dangerous territory; I am to tell Krin what I think of her writing. Krin, who is at work on a diarylike book called *On the Banks of the Coleen*, writes of an owl trying to make its way through swirling snow. I read silently. When I'm through with Krin's story, Rhonda hands me hers. Rhonda writes of walking on a trail through a copse of willows—bear country. Though she has her 30.30 rifle, a gift from Fred Thomas, which she's carried since she was ten, she is feeling uneasy. Aside from the occasional misspellings and grammatical mistakes, they are both good pieces of writing, detailed and evocative, and I tell them that. If they are pleased by my comments, though, it doesn't show. Without a word, they take back their stories and continue writing.

In spring, life here on the banks of the Coleen slows down. In winter, it was get up and go and try to get as much done as possible while there was still light. But in spring the light is nearly endless, and the Korths adjust their days to accommodate a new tempo. Trapping is over. Heimo has limited out on beaver. Though the wolf season is still open, their pelts are so mangy that Heimo is content to let them be. Most mornings, we just sit around and casually, or not so casually, visit.

The girls call Heimo "The Reverend" because of his propensity for polemic. I refer to him as "The Puzzle." He once expressed delight when I called his friend Keith Koontz, the hunting guide, a puzzle, but Heimo embodies many of the same contradictions. He is a gun-toting, park-hating, anti-animal-rights trapper with a soft side. Though he makes his living off the land, hunting and trapping, taking from it, he cares about it deeply. Fran Mauer, a widely respected biologist and a twenty-eight-year veteran of the U.S. Fish and Wildlife Service, says, "I admire Heimo's relationship to the land. He's very respectful of the land and the lifestyle. He's matured and he's deepened since he first came into the country." Don Ross, former assistant manager of the Arctic National Wildlife Refuge and pilot for the Refuge, concurs with Mauer. "Heimo's the only full-time trapper left in the refuge who's still living off the land. Most of the others have fallen by the wayside. He traps sustainably, and he has great regard for the land. I appreciate his love for the place and a lifestyle that is vanishing."

Except for his family, the land is the thing Heimo loves the most, and he translates that love into a knowledge of the natural world that is nothing short of astounding. Though Heimo never made it through high school while he was in Appleton, during his first year on the Coleen River, he decided that a diploma was something important to him. He studied at night, after checking his lines, and completed his diploma through the high school in Fort Yukon in May 1980. His grammar is still often rough and unpolished, but what he lacks in such skills, he more than makes up for with his knowledge of the Arctic. He could teach a college course in Arctic ecology or natural history. As for his family, he hugs and kisses his girls and tells them he loves them at least a dozen times a day. "My mom loved us up," he says, "and I try to do the same with Rhonda and Krin." Like many teenagers, they sometimes bristle at his affection, but more often than not, they return his tendernesses—an unexpected hug, a kiss on the cheek before bed.

Although Heimo has been called a pioneer, he strenuously rejects the notion. He does not see himself as the advance guard of a civilization certain of its own righteousness. He is not committed to inspiring acolytes or finding a new route to the Promised Land, either. Nor is he an evangelical proponent of some life-changing back-to-nature doctrine—to hell with spreading the gospel. He has no interest in reviving America's moribund frontier spirit. In fact, the fewer people he sees out in the country, the better, though if you push him he'll admit that there's some power in numbers; in other words, he wishes there were a few more trappers helping him to carry on the wilderness tradition, albeit at a safe hundred-mile distance. His is not an ascetic experiment, either. Though he has been living in the remote bush for almost three decades, he was alone for only six of them, and those six years were enough. Six years alone in the Alaskan bush will undo almost any man. "The mind needs people," Heimo says. "I craved people. Nobody's a wolverine. A wolverine is a strict loner."

In the mornings, lingering after breakfast, Heimo rails against waste, excess, consumerism, comfort, and the softness of American society like a dyed-in-the-wool environmentalist reformer, yet he has little patience with the movement itself. Cambridge-educated bush pilot Kirk Sweetsir understands Heimo's distaste for environmentalists and a brand of environmentalism that doesn't appreciate his presence on the land. "They are all too blatant about their bourgeois intellectual tourism, and it is just too trivializing of his world for Heimo to stomach them," he says.

Heimo believes that environmentalists (and Democrats, too) are out to eradicate his way of life. They're antiguns and antitrapping. He calls most environmentalist do-gooders "greenies," practically spitting the word, though he and the environmental movement have more in common than he'd like to admit—the Arctic National Wildlife Refuge, for one. Heimo does not want it developed under any circumstances, and he is emphatic in his defense. With the impending state budget crisis (Alaska's Constitutional Budget Reserve, a $1.9 billion savings, will be exhausted by 2004), his is an unpopular opinion in Alaska these days. Oil royalties mean money for the state. Oil's enthusiastic champion is Frank Murkowski, Alaska's former prodevelopment senator and now its newly elected governor. In his State of the State address, Murkowski made it clear how he intends to solve Alaska's impending budget debacle. "Ladies and gentlemen," he said in his address in Juneau on January 23, 2003, "in a single word, it's oil." Meanwhile pro-oil legislators are seeking to exempt pipeline permits from court challenges initiated by environmental groups and authorized under the National Environmental Protection Act.

Oil, it seems, *is* the only answer in Alaska. Although the cupboard is nearly bare, Governor Murkowski and most of the state's oil advocates refuse to discuss an income tax as a possible solution to the imminent deficit pinch. Taxes are for liberal Eastern states like Connecticut and "Taxachusetts," but not for Alaska. Some suggest that this attitude reflects a crude and suspect form of frontierism, a deal sealed with the "Alaskan handshake," hand held out and palm turned upward—taxes bad, oil extraction good. Reading Donald Worster, who is an environmental historian critical of the United States's exploitative history, one might be tempted to draw comparisons between Worster's arid West and Alaska today. Worster writes: "The hydraulic society of the West is . . . increasingly a coersive, monolithic, and heirarchical system, ruled by a power elite based on the ownership of capital and expertise." Worster points out that despite the West's image as a region of hardy, antigovernment individualists, corporate control of water actually has subverted, and continues to jeopardize, small-scale democracy and individual freedom. The same might be said of Alaska today, where a rhetoric of frontier individualism often bumps up against an economic reality of ongoing and monumental fiscal shortfalls (nearly $1 billion in 2002). Since 80 percent of the state's revenues come from taxes and royalties on oil and gas—*Anchorage Daily News* columnist Mike Doogan jokes that "There's nothing more Alaskan than having an eye for a fast buck"—it's probably safe to assume that despite the regulation of the industry, big oil wields a corresponding influence over Alaska's internal affairs.

Edna leans back to turn on the radio for the morning weather report, but the radio responds with nothing but static. "Shut that thing off," Heimo grumbles. Heimo is mad—they haven't been able to get a clear message for nearly a month. Actually, what he's really ticked off about is that the station has decided to drop its report for the southern foothills of the eastern Brooks Range—upper Coleen River country.

Heimo's anger passes quickly, and then he nuzzles his face against Edna's cheek. Edna shrieks. "You need a shave," she says, pushing him away. "Do that again, and you'll be sleeping in the cache tonight."

Sending Heimo to the cache for the night is Edna's favorite threat. Wives in the Lower Forty-eight might threaten their husbands with an evening in the doghouse, but that has little currency up here. The cache is a threat Edna can make good on since the Korths have two of them.

The cache—French for "hiding place"—is a fixture in the Alaskan bush, where animals, particularly marauding bears, can threaten anything within reach. The Korths store everything they don't want torn apart or eaten—the canoe, food supplies, decoys, skis, snowshoes, clothes, etc.—in the cache. The cache is a freestanding tree-fortlike structure built on four sturdy spruce legs. The Korths have built wooden ladders to each of their two caches under the assumption that even surprisingly agile and intelligent grizzlies can't climb ladders. One cache is open-air and two-tiered with coffee cans wrapped around its legs to discourage squirrels and marten. The top tier is nearly twenty-five feet off the ground. The other cache is built like a fortress with thick log walls. It stands about fifteen feet off the ground. An animal would have to be plenty smart to get inside.

"Whose turn is it to do the dishes?" Edna asks. Krin responds immediately, "It's Rhonda's. I did them last night." "Heck you did," Rhonda replies. "I did." The girls bicker, and finally Edna settles the matter. "Krin, you'll get the water, and Rhonda, you'll do the dishes." Rhonda grumbles.

Fighting over who is going to do the dishes is a scene that takes place almost on a daily basis. I could set my watch by it. The girls are best of friends, but when it comes time to do the dishes, they are ready to do battle. It doesn't make sense to me, since hauling the water seems the harder of the two jobs, but the girls fight about it as if doing the dishes were the worst of all possible fates.

Heimo asks me to escort Krin to the river. "Take my shotgun," he says. Heimo spotted fresh bear tracks two days ago on the island that separates the river's two channels, and he's not taking any chances. He hands me the gun and four shells, two slugs and two buckshot.

Unlike the creek at the Old Crow cabin, the Coleen doesn't freeze to the bottom, so getting water is hard work, but not the undertaking it was on the Old Crow. The water hole is a quarter-mile walk upriver to where Heimo has chopped an opening in the ice. The current rushes below, occasionally slopping over the edges of the hole. Staring down at the river, I realize just how indifferent the natural world is to our presence. If the ice were to break, I'd be gone in a second, swept a hundred miles downriver to where the Coleen dumps into the Porcupine River—"kissin' the ice from the bottom side," I've heard it called. Not a pleasant thought, but nothing to obsess over either, though the danger is real, particularly as breakup approaches and the ice is getting thinner and weaker.

Krin finishes tying her shoe and joins me at the hole. "It's safe," I say, to which she says nothing. Krin and Rhonda are sometimes a puzzling pair. With me they are alternately mischievous and sweet, guarded, unfriendly, and sullen. Their inconsistency is what gets to me, since their moods seem to have almost nothing to do with my behavior. Sometimes it's simply my being here that seems to bother them. I try to put their attitudes into perspective. I am an outsider—they see very few visitors—and as far as they're concerned I am the biggest rube ever plopped down in the Arctic. I invade their lives for a month at a time and then subject them to my ineptitude, photographs, and meddlesome questions.

Krin kneels beside the hole and dips the five-pound bucket into the river. Then she gets to her feet and struggles to lift the bucket to her shoulder. At five-feet nine inches, she really has to hoist it. "May I help you with that?" I ask her, and she glares at me and starts to walk back to the cabin. "C'mon, Krin," I say, "let me give you a hand." "I'm not a weakling," she replies, and doubles her pace. The last thing she needs is my help.

"Five more to go," Heimo says. "This is number seventy-nine." Heimo gestures toward a pile of spruce poles. There are eighty-four of them in all—Heimo has numbered them—trunks of dead trees, which Heimo cut down and hauled to the river before I arrived. The cabin's pole roof is eighteen years old, and Heimo's intention is to replace it with these new poles.

For the last three days, Heimo and I have been using a drawknife to peel the bark off the poles, because bark makes the inside of a cabin look like a dark cellar, and because it contributes to rot, and Heimo wants a roof that will last at least another eighteen years, preferably more. "I'm not going anywhere," he says. "Edna and I will grow old out here, and then when it comes time, she and the girls can scatter my ashes over the upper Coleen." Peeling poles is not exactly grueling work, but it takes time and requires some arm strength. Alone Heimo can do ten a day. Together we've almost doubled that. Heimo does the ends of the poles, which require some finesse, and I do the rest.

I am standing in a pile of peelings, straddling one of the poles, working on a knot, and cursing it for resisting my attempts to shave it. "Hold on," Heimo says, and chips it out using the ax. "Now, go over it again with the knife." Getting every bur is essential to ensuring a waterproof roof, since one of the roof's four layers will be a sheet of Visqueen. A hole in the Visqueen spells trouble once the mid-August rains arrive. In other words, you can't be careful enough.

Though it is May 6, the temperature last night dropped to 15 below. I lay awake in my tent listening to the river ice snap in the cold like the sharp crack of a small-caliber rifle. Sometimes the ice sounded like a chorus of crickets. But now, at the river, in the early afternoon, the sun spills everywhere, and the temperature has risen to the low forties, and the ice is silent though slushy.

I am working in a long-sleeved micro fleece shirt, and I am dripping sweat. Perched on a tree beside us, Heimo has a small tape player with a bird tape in it. He's preparing for the spring songbird migration. He listens to the bird's song and before the man on the tape identifies it, Heimo announces its name: "ruby-crowned kinglet, varied thrush, American robin, rusty blackbird, Bohemian waxwing, dark-eyed junco, American wigeon, red-necked grebe, trumpeter swan." Heimo doesn't miss a song. "I like birding more than just about anything."

For nearly the last week, Heimo, Edna, and the girls, who have inherited their father's love of ornithology, have been awaiting the return of spring's birds. They have been watching the sky, listening for the faintest song, but spring has been slow to progress and the winter birds are all we see and hear—boreal chickadees, gray jays, pine grosbeaks.

In spring, when the snow in the cabin yard still registers eight inches on the snow stick and nighttime temperatures still fall below 0, life on the Coleen River can take on a quality resembling drudgery. The Korths have had enough of the cold and the snow. So they wait moodily for the announcement of winter's end, for the first signs of spring: the golden eagles followed by snow buntings, and then the ruby-crowned kinglets; hatches of caddis flies and mosquitoes on which the birds depend for food; willow buds, which show up like small miracles of color among the shrub's bare, nearly white branches; a hint of overflow coming down from Bear Mountain; the first patches of open ground. Then suddenly, spring snaps, the dramatic quickening begins, and it seems as if the entire bird world is following the Coleen River corridor north. The ice moves out with a great roaring. The river carves out new channels at will, defying the land to hold it back. Trees are torn from their roots as if they were nothing more than weeds.

"I can hardly wait," Heimo says as I put the finishing touches on our second-to-last pole. I know enough now not to ask what he's waiting for; in fact, I have the spring bug myself. "C'mon, spring," I say, tossing the finished pole onto the pile. Just then, I catch Krin out of the corner of my eye doing a flying leap from the river's bank down onto the pile of spruce shavings. And it's no mere hop. It's a jump of at least six feet. She lands on her feet, stumbles a little, but doesn't fall. Heimo just shakes his head. "Don't you have schoolwork?" he asks. Krin ignores him. She picks a young willow bud and chews it and then skates out onto the ice in her boots. "I've got cabin fever," she finally replies, skating back to us. "You always have cabin fever," Heimo says, dropping the drawknife, and wrapping his arms around her. "My crazy Krin." "Tigger," I correct him quietly, but Krin hears and scowls at me.

I call Krin "Tigger," though rarely to her face, because at thirteen she imagines herself too old for affectionate nicknames. Like Tigger, Krin bounces wherever she goes, and she's utterly fearless about it. If she's been splitting wood and wants to go into the cabin, she doesn't walk around the pile; she's tall for her age, so she backs up, gets a running start, and leaps over, stretching her athletic five-foot nine-inch frame as far as it will go. If she's going to get something out of the high cache and encounters a fallen tree, she simply jumps it. If she goes to church in Fort Yukon during the summer, she arrives fifteen minutes late in order to make what she calls a "grand entrance," and then bounds down the aisle to the front pew, sitting as far from Edna and Rhonda as she can get.

Heimo peels the ends of our last pole. "I'll be glad to have this over with," he says. "Why don't I just finish this one?" I don't object. Instead I walk back to the cabin to get a box for the shavings. They'll be good fire starters for my stove. At the cabin yard, Rhonda is sitting on a bench outside, taking a break from her studies. She points to a hawk owl, clinging to the top branch of a nearby white spruce. "He's a curious fella," she says. "He's been watching me." Then she gets up and walks over to a small spruce tree and scrapes off some pitch with her index finger. She sits back down next to me and shows me a small cut on the top of her hand, near her thumb. "I did it with the bow saw," she says, rubbing the pitch into the cut. "I thought I heard a Bohemian waxwing and I got excited. It doesn't hurt too bad though. Serves me right. I wasn't paying attention because I was thinking about running to the cabin to get Mom. Bohemian waxwings are a sure sign of spring. If I saw a Bohemian waxwing we wouldn't be out here much longer. We'd be getting off the river, for sure."

* * *

Everyone is getting antsy. For days I've watched the girls walk in and out of the cabin ten times an hour, unable to concentrate on their studies. They're supposed to do four to five hours of work a day, but the year is winding down. Rhonda is sick of algebra. Krin just wants the birds to come.

Rhonda and Krin are part of the Alaska Gateway Correspondence School out of Tok, Alaska. Every year, just before they leave Fort Yukon for the bush, they are sent a year's supply of study materials. They're required by the state to take the basic subjects: writing, math, U.S. history and government, and science. They're able to send out their work with the occasional pilot, who, in turn, sends it to Tok. The lessons are graded by their correspondence teacher and then mailed to Fort Yukon. Sometimes a pilot will pick up the Korths' mail and bring it out for them. They get months of mail at a time. The girls then have a chance to look over their many graded lessons. It's a difficult way to learn. They have no direct contact with their teacher. Although they are naturally bright, verbal, and inquisitive, I cannot help but think that their education occasionally suffers from this arrangement, particularly as they get older and the lessons get tougher, too hard for either Heimo or Edna to lend any appreciable help.

Even Edna needs a break. All year long she's tried to guide the girls' studies as best she can, given her own limited education; she never finished high school. She's struggled with many of the lessons herself. But this time of year, like the girls, she just wants it all to be over. The Korths have been in the bush since July, and Edna is eager to get to Fort Yukon, where she has a summer flower garden and a handful of close friends. "Occasionally a pilot will pay us a visit out here," she says. "But they're always men. They're nice, but they talk to Heimo."

Dawn Jagow, whose family—husband, Paul, and two children—spends part of the year in the bush, understands Edna's sentiments. "I know how hard it must be for her. On the river, we get visitors, but they're almost always men, too. I make tea and back off most of the time. For a woman the hardest part is not having anyone to share your feelings with. It really becomes apparent to me when we come to town and I realize how much I've missed my friends. On the river, I read a lot and I have conversations in my head with my friends. But I've never found a substitute for the lack of friends. The bush is very much a man's world. But it's my home, and I consider myself lucky to live like this."

The girls are eager to get to town, too. They want to see their friends, talk about new CDs, watch videos, play computer games, read music magazines, drink Mountain Dews and Cokes, and maybe dye their hair and meet boys. They have big plans for summer, and when they talk about them, it's difficult for me to remember that they grew up out here rather than in some suburb of Milwaukee or Chicago. Krin used to be a big fan of pop icon Britney Spears, but now she leans toward Pink, Lil Bow Wow, and Lil' Kim. Rhonda likes to write rap lyrics, incorporating messages of racial tolerance, which, if nothing else, is testament to the power and pervasiveness of the modern media machine. But more than anything else they want friends. They want to grow up like normal kids—"Like Dad did," Rhonda points out.

Rhonda, Krin, and I are walking one of the river's many braids looking for bare ground. We are out collecting Indian potato, a carrotlike tuber found along the river's cutbanks. The girls each carry a pick, our digging tools, and I tote the shotgun. "Just hanging out with people our own age," Rhonda continues, "it's something we've hardly had a chance to do. It was always get into town and get back out as quickly as we could. A month and a half goes so fast. We'd just get to know people again and it'd be time to come back out to the cabin. Plus, Dad's so protective of us when we're in Fort Yukon. He likes us to stay around the cabin, so he can keep an eye on us.

"Why do we live like this?" she continues. "It's a question I've asked myself so many times. There really is no answer; we just do. Daddy and Mom chose to live this way. Daddy loves it, and Mom does too, I think. Besides, Dad's done it for so long, I don't know what else he'd want to do, or could do. It's all he knows now."

The temperature is in the low 50s today—it hasn't reached 50 since early September—and Rhonda is wearing an Adidas sweatsuit and a red bandana and would look more like a New York City rapper than a wilderness girl if it weren't for her hip boots. Catch her in Fort Yukon in

June, and it'd be easy to think she'd never spent a day in the bush. I know otherwise. In the last half hour, Rhonda has pointed out to me mink, porcupine, wolverine, and snowshoe hare tracks, and a small pile of fox scat. Both she and Krin have carried knives and matches since they were five. Familiarity with knives and fire-building skills are essential in the bush, and Heimo and Edna reasoned that it was better to teach the girls when they were young, which was a good thing because when she was eight Rhonda was called upon to use them in an emergency.

It was mid-September 1994, and Heimo hadn't shot a moose yet; in fact, he hadn't even seen one. Hoping that his luck would change, he and Rhonda, who barely came up to his ribs, set off in the canoe downriver to explore a slough where Heimo had found moose in the past. The weather had turned cold, and ice was beginning to run in the river. They tied off the boat at the mouth of the slough and walked the bank. Heimo stopped occasionally to cow call, hoping to lure in a bull moose eager to mate. When he saw movement in the willows, he paused. An animal revealed itself, but it wasn't a bull moose. It was a caribou, a bull leading five other bulls and a small herd of cows. The Korths needed meat, and the prospects of getting a moose were getting slimmer every day, so Heimo snapped off four shots and dropped three of the bulls. He and Rhonda cut them up and then they walked back to get the canoe. They loaded the meat and paddled to the river. When they reached the river and got out of the canoe, Heimo was grateful that they were only two miles from the cabin. Three caribou made for a heavy load, and Heimo knew that lining the canoe wasn't going to be easy.

Heimo and Rhonda were walking a gravel bar. Heimo struggled to keep the canoe's bow out of the whirling eddies and tracking into the current. Suddenly the boat took off sideways and water spilled over the gunwales. Then the boat turned over, dumping everything—the caribou meat, Heimo's rifle, his binoculars, a backpack. Heimo waded into the river to rescue what he could. The water was shockingly cold. He grabbed his backpack, turned and yelled for Rhonda to build a big fire. Ten minutes later, when Heimo returned to the gravel bar, having saved his gun and binoculars, his backpack, and, miraculously, much of the meat, too, Rhonda had the fire roaring.

"I love the isolation sometimes, but I miss talking with people my age," Rhonda continues. "Ten and a half months is too long. I wish we could spend more time in town. I like being able to just walk down to the store. Everything here is hard. I'll always live in Alaska, I think, but I don't know if I'll want to live out here," she adds, and then interrupts herself to show me a bush of soapberries, which, she tells me, grizzlies are fond of. "I worry about this area though," she says, picking up her train of thought. "I worry that one day they'll discover oil or gold or something." Krin chimes in and startles me. Sometimes getting Krin to talk is like prying information out of a hostile witness. "I like the peace and quiet," she says, "but I miss my friends." Krin confesses that she'd like to live somewhere else when she grows up—"Hawaii or Europe," she says. Then, with coaxing from Rhonda, she tells me about the only real friend she's ever had, a girl named Zane. It was the summer of 2000, and Heimo was commercial fishing. He was worried about Edna and the girls being in Fort Yukon alone, so instead they rented a cabin in Circle Hot Springs. Krin met Zane during her first week in Circle, and for nearly two months, the two of them were inseparable.

The girls are suddenly silent, as if each feels that she has said too much. We are walking along a side slough, and they run ahead of me. "This is where we had our bunny snares in winter," Rhonda shouts back to me. Krin isn't paying attention. She scales the riverbank and walks out into the tundra, where the snow has melted enough to reveal the vegetation underneath. "Low-bush cranberries," she yells. Rhonda and I join her, and I eat the berries like a foraging grizzly. They are thawing now and are filled with sweetness. Krin has been watching me. "What's the matter?" she says. "Haven't you ever had cranberries in spring before?"

Rhonda and Krin walk ahead, leaving me with the berries. I graze for a few more minutes and then catch up to them, stopping briefly to inspect a willow bush and rub the soft rabbit fur of its young buds. Rhonda shouts to me, "On the way home, we'll pick some of the leaves for a salad. They're really tender."

The girls have found the perfect south-facing cutbank. The snow is completely gone. "Daddy likes to get down on his hands and knees and smell the ground in spring," Rhonda says, grabbing her pick and digging into the bank. Neither Rhonda nor Krin swings her pick with any force. Rather they hold their picks near the head and scratch at the dirt, digging gently like a woodcarver using a gouge to shape the features of a human face. Krin sets her pick aside and brushes away the dirt and roots to get at the main tuber of an Indian potato. She snaps it off. "Here," she says, handing it to me. "Wash it off in the puddle." I do as I'm instructed and then bite into it. It tastes starchy, like raw corn. "What do you think?" Rhonda asks, but doesn't wait for my reply. "In fall we collect them in gunnysacks and set them outside to freeze. Then in winter, we'll fry them up."

Breakup is behind schedule, and even the geese have been slow to come. Heimo is puzzled. "I just can't figure it out. We should be seeing flock after flock by now."

Heimo and I are sitting in a makeshift driftwood goose blind, covered up to our waists in a white sheet, swatting at the first mosquitoes of the year. They're fat, slow "bombers," and they're easy to exterminate. We have six decoys—four feeders and two sentinels—dug into the ice near the edge of the river channel. Though the advance of spring seems to have stalled, a five-foot-wide lead has formed in the middle of the river, where the ice has melted from the nearly constant sun. For the past two days the wind has come out of the north, bringing cold air out of the polar regions, and the temperature hasn't climbed above the low forties. Heimo says he can feel it switching to the south though—good news. That will bring warm air. With twenty-one hours of full-on sun, it won't take long for the snow and ice to melt, for this country to sprout new spring streams everywhere. Water will trickle and ooze out of every mountain, hill, and hump. If the wind does not shift, however, we could be locked in winter's vise for another month. Earlier in the day Heimo and Edna were talking about the winter of 1992-1993, when the snow that fell on September 9 didn't melt until early June 1993. "God," Heimo said, "I hope that doesn't happen this year. I love to spring out here, but I don't want to be here until mid-June."

The girls tell me that Heimo gets like this every year, a little irritable, they say, impatient to get to town. By mid-May, he is often just as eager as the girls are for a change of pace. This year he is more anxious than usual. He thinks it's going to be a good year for muskrats, and he's hoping to get out by the third week in May, so that he won't miss the season. In late spring he and Fred Thomas go "ratting" together in the lakes around Fort Yukon; with .22s, they shoot muskrats for the meat, which Heimo likes fried, and for the skins, which bring an average of $2.50. Heimo is also thinking about the king salmon run. He and Fred set and tend fifty feet of gill net on the Yukon River once the run starts. But it isn't just the ratting and the king salmon. Heimo likes to chum around with Fred, who, though he is nearly forty years older than Heimo, is still his best friend in town. Then there's Heimo's daily four-mile jog and his occasional indulgence—an ice-cold Coke from the Alaska Commercial Company store, which everyone calls the AC.

At this rate, however, unless the weather takes a dramatic turn, Heimo will surely miss the ratting season. As spring advances, things get tricky for the bush pilots. There's usually a two-week period when a plane can't get in or out, when there's too little snow to land on skis and too much snow to land on wheels on the gravel bars.

Adding insult to injury, the annual spring migration of geese and ducks back to their Arctic nesting grounds is late, and this time of year the Korths depend on waterfowl for food.

Meat is an essential part of the bush diet. Though the Korths bring in provisions—black beans, peas, pinto beans, lentils, canned corn, green beans, spinach, rice, soups, spaghetti noodles, oatmeal, powdered milk, coffee, spices, butter, honey, sugar, and flour—these items are expensive, and the Korths buy only enough to supplement a main meal of meat, though Heimo does admit that their menu has grown more exotic over the years.

In spring when the temperature is consistently above thirty-two, the Korths cut up what's left of their caribou for drymeat. Yesterday, Rhonda took the last hindquarter of caribou out of the small snow shelter that she had built to keep it fresh, and we made drymeat. It was a family project. Heimo cut the caribou into long, thin strips, following the grain of the meat, and then he put the strips into a bowl filled with

Heimo Korth with the day's catch of Arctic char,
Kongakut River, 2002.

Heimo in town to sell fur, 1979.

Walrus skinboats at Savoonga, 1978.

Edna, Coleen, Millie, and Heimo in the lower cabin, 1982.

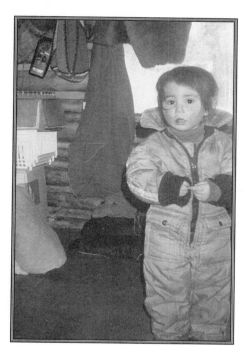

Coleen Korth, April 1984.

Krin with snowshoe hares and grouse, 1993.

Rhonda playing cowboys on a wolverine carcass, 1993.

The main cabin and its new mossy roof.

NOTICE
This cabin is permitted
for year-round use to
Heimo Korth and his
family by the U.S. Fish
and Wildlife Service,
Arctic National Wildlife
Refuge.

Unauthorized use is
prohibited except during
an emergency.

The Korth family's right to live in the
Arctic National Wildlife Refuge ends with Krin.

Krin sawing
caribou steaks.

A break during sledding—44 degrees below zero.

Krin and Rhonda Korth.

Heimo and Edna Korth.

The final frontiersman hunting caribou.

salt water. Krin used her knife to sharpen the dry willow sticks, which served as skewers, handed them to me, and then I impaled the strips, fat end down. Rhonda dug a hole in the middle of the smoke rack and built a fire in the hole with dry cottonwood. Afterward, she joined me. The job took a full afternoon, but when we finished, the smoke rack held nearly seventy willow sticks, all dripping with five to six fresh caribou strips. Rhonda covered the rack with a plastic tarp, and Heimo reminded her that she'd need to tend the fire for the next two days. Rhonda shot him a look of disgust, as if to say, "Yeah, I know, Dad. I've only done this every spring since I was a little girl."

Yesterday morning, Krin and Heimo each shot a goose, Krin's first. They were the only two geese they saw all day. I helped Heimo pluck them. One was a good-sized Canada and the other was a speckle-belly. Both were "rolling in fat," as Heimo likes to say. We saved the livers, gizzards, and hearts, which Edna fried up later while the geese were boiling. Heimo kept the wings, too. He'll use them for bait once the trapping season begins. He is still upset with himself though. He and Krin had shot females. "I don't like to shoot nesters," he explained while we were plucking them. "Usually we'll only take the males."

In 1918, the United States and Canada enacted the Migratory Bird Treaty Act, which prevents the hunting of waterfowl between March 10 and September 1. In doing so, Congress failed to adequately consider the fact that Alaskans who live in the bush often depend on waterfowl for their spring and summer meat. For years the U.S. Fish and Wildlife Service, which is charged with implementing the statute, turned a benevolent blind eye to this practice, choosing instead to enforce other aspects of the act. But now an amendment to the Migratory Bird Treaty Act allows for the spring harvest of waterfowl by rural residents, legalizing a hundred-year-old tradition.

Spring waterfowl hunting is a practice that doesn't go unnoticed by urban waterfowl hunters who feel that they're being shortchanged. Subsistence, in general, is a prickly issue in Alaska, pitting urban users against rural users, a controversy that often manifests itself as a Native/non-Native divide. The Alaska Federation of Natives insists that a subsistence preference is needed to protect village lifestyles and economies, and it takes issue with Fairbanks hunters who regard taking a moose every fall as their inalienable right. Urban hunters retaliate, accusing Natives of shooting indiscriminately and not observing game laws. Plus, urban hunters are quick to point out that they have the Alaska state constitution on their side.

Tracking the history of the disagreement is messy. Alaska's state constitution guarantees equal access for all residents to all natural resources; however, federal legislation awarded rural residents priority use of fish and game. So a conflict was born between federal law, which guarantees a "rural priority," and the state constitution. After twenty-plus years of controversy, the federal government prevailed and since 1990 has managed wildlife on all federal lands in Alaska.

Back at the goose blind, it is late afternoon when we finally abandon our hunt. The day has been a bust except for the brief visit of an immature rough-legged hawk, which displayed an interest in our decoys and the sound of a ruby-crowned kinglet singing in the distance. Heimo was almost beside himself with joy when he heard that. He closed his eyes as if listening to Enya. "Such a little bird with such a big song."

We slosh through the overflow in our hip boots like two little boys, splashing and running, but by the time we reach the river's main channel, Heimo is serious. "We'll have to be careful here. This time of year, the ice changes every second." We walk tentatively. Weak ice spells danger, so we avoid the telltale gray spots. "Look for the dark blue ice; that's the best," Heimo says, as I try to ignore the strange, unnerving moan of the ice under my feet.

Edna, Krin, and Rhonda are waiting for us on the riverbank. "Nothing today, huh," Edna says. "Nothing," Heimo replies. "Not a thing."

It has been decided; we will leave this weekend, Saturday, May 18, or Sunday, depending upon the weather. Yesterday a plane flew over. The pilot, it turned out, was a friend of the Korths. Months before, Heimo had made arrangements with him to pick us up, and he was flying over, scouting, checking on the weather conditions and the gravel bars. Using the handheld aircraft radio, Heimo talked with him and asked how things looked from the air. The pilot advised him to get out before the melting started and the river rose. If that happened, he said, we'd be on the river for at least another two to three weeks. That was all Heimo needed to hear. The two of them discussed a date and time, and Heimo said that we'd be ready.

When I got the news that we'd be leaving early, I wasn't disappointed. The prospect of springing out and not getting off the river until early to mid June, wasn't one I was looking forward to. I had a family to go home to, my wife was six months pregnant with our second child, and I had already been gone for a long time. She needed my help, and my daughter missed her daddy.

"Springing out" has been the final act in a yearly cycle repeated thousands of times over the last one hundred years, a tradition that is kept alive by the few remaining families that still call the Alaskan wilderness their home. For the Korths it means the end of nearly a year of hunting, trapping, cutting and splitting wood, cooking on a woodstove, sewing and patching clothes, schoolwork, hauling ice and water, and doing the dishes.

For the last two weeks, they've been wondering: When will breakup come? When will we get off the river? Everyone has been looking forward to town. But now that the date is set, there is much work to be done—too much. The snowmachines have to be put away on three-foot-high platforms in case of flooding. But first Heimo has to run all the gas out of the tanks and carburetors and take out the spark plugs and put two-cycle oil in the cylinders. The house has to be cleaned and packed up, too. Clothes, boots, parkas, guns, ammunition, food, pots and pans need to be stored in the cache or in sealed 55-gallon drums. Finally, Heimo has to varmint- and grizzly-proof the cabin, screwing the door shut and boarding up the windows.

Edna grabs a box and starts putting clothes in it.

The girls roll their eyes and grumble, "Not yet, Mom."

Heimo pulls on his boots and starts to lace them up. "Forget the work," he mumbles. "How about some hockey?"

"No way," Edna answers. "We got lots of work to do."

"C'mon, Mom," Heimo says, "we can start tomorrow."

Edna continues packing clothes into the box, then she looks at

Heimo and smiles as if she is up to no good. Rhonda and Krin are already running for the river.

Ten minutes later all five of us are on the ice, ready to play our favorite game—hockey, played in boots instead of on skates—for what will be the last time this year. The ice is dark blue and as smooth as a pane of glass, but the warm-up that Heimo felt when we were hunting is now a reality. The wind is out of the south; the temperature is pushing the high 40s. By tomorrow night the river ice will be full of slush, splattered with small ponds of water and very dangerous.

Rhonda sets the puck—a round plug of cottonwood coated in ice—between Heimo and me, and we simulate a ferocious hockey face-off, using our boots as sticks. Heimo pushes me to win the puck and is advancing toward our goal unimpeded until I catch him, tripping him with a hook slide. While he's down I jump on him, giving Rhonda just enough time to steal the puck. "So you're going to play that way, eh?" Krin says, making a beeline for Rhonda. I give Heimo one last push before I rush down the ice, moving my arms and legs as if I am cross-country skiing. Rhonda and Krin are battling for the puck. I slide in and take it away. Rushing toward Edna, I am dribbling the puck, struggling not to lose it, while still trying to escape Heimo, who is gaining on me. Edna crouches down in front of the goal. She has no intention of letting me score. Ten feet away, I decide to take it all the way in instead of stopping and shooting. Suddenly Krin catches me blindside with an NFL hit and sends me flying in the air toward Edna. I hit Edna at the ankles with an inadvertent cross-body block. Edna falls over me and then up-ends Heimo, who has been chasing the play. Krin jumps on Heimo, and Rhonda flops onto Krin. It's one big pileup, and we are all laughing too hard to even think about moving. Then Heimo hears something. "Shhh," he says, as a small flock of Canada geese flies overhead. "Shhh." Heimo points his index finger to the blue sky. "Blam," he says. "Blam."

CHAPTER 7

Back-to-Nature Boys

In 1975, when Heimo Korth left Wisconsin, leaving behind everything and everybody he knew, he was answering a universally familiar call—the yearning to escape home. When he went to Alaska, he put a uniquely American spin on the theme of escape. Mythologies are relevant to all countries, and in America none has been more enduring than the notion that in wilderness a person can escape the reins and restrictions of an insipid and often corrupt society and re-create himself in the boundlessness of the natural world.

Daniel Boone, America's protowoodsman, escaped his father's brutal beatings by fleeing periodically to the woods. By the time he was in his midteens, he was already known as one of the most accomplished woodsmen in the Pennsylvania wilderness. The first of all the mountain men, John Colter, left Virginia for Kentucky in 1803 to join Lewis and Clark's Corps of Discovery. Nearly three years later, when the expedition was on its way back St. Louis, Colter parted ways with Lewis and Clark and returned to the wilderness that he loved. Jim Bridger was bonded to a blacksmith in St. Louis, Missouri. When his five years were nearly up, a notice appeared in the *Missouri Republican:* Major Andrew Henry and Colonel William Ashley needed "one hundred young men" to join their Rocky Mountain Fur Company and its 1822 expedition to the headwaters of the Missouri River. At the age of eighteen, Bridger signed on and became the most famous of all the Rocky Mountain trapper-explorers.

In America, the belief that wilderness can serve as an antidote to civilization, as a place of freedom and personal renewal, gave birth to a new and revolutionary literature, an authentically American narrative. When Henry David Thoreau escaped Concord and retired to Walden Pond to lead by example and live as an anchorite in the woods, demanding that people start their lives anew, he was not only passing judgment on the society of Concord, he was consciously enacting a peculiarly American story. When young American men, and women, both real and fictional, left home, they escaped to the wilderness to lose and, subsequently, find themselves. Ernest Hemingway's Nick Adams returns home from the war and seeks refuge in the woods of Michigan's Upper Peninsula. A.B. Guthrie's Boone Caudill takes off for the Wild West after having it out with his father. Molly Gloss's Lydia Sanderson heads to the Oregon frontier following the death of her husband. Hoping to escape the "damp, drizzly November" in his soul, Herman Melville's Ishmael flees Manhattan and then New Bedford and goes not to the woods but to another wilderness—the sea.

Gertrude Stein said, "In the United States, there is more space where nobody is, than where anybody is. That is what makes America what it is." The poet Charles Olson echoed her words: "I take Space to be the central fact to man born in America. I spell it large because it comes large here. It is geography at bottom, a hell of a wide land from the beginning!" Though both Stein and Olson wrote decades after Frederick Jackson Turner eulogized the frontier (a word he often used interchangeably with "wilderness,") in his epoch-making thesis *The Significance of the Frontier in American History*, the frontier metaphor was still a vital, psychic force, one that, even today, continues to determine America's national identity, its sense of history, and its vision of the future.

But by the time Mark Twain wrote of the mystical Mississippi and a young, bedraggled boy's dream to escape the cruelties of his drunken and abusive father, "Pap Finn," Miss Watson and the Widow Douglas, and later Aunt Sally and her attempts to "sivilize" him, there was little "Territory" left to "light out for." Much of America had been tamed. The free lands of the West, as Turner declared them in 1893, were "exhausted."

But the frontier myth persisted, given new life by what remained—Alaska, a new world waiting to be discovered, an uncharted land that lay not west, but far to the northwest, a figurative frontier-wilderness, as well as the final material embodiment of American "Space."

When Heimo Korth came to Alaska, he wasn't the only one. Other young men, and also women, eager to leave home, clinging to a dream of seeing what remained of the American wilderness, came, too. The young men of Heimo's generation who headed to Alaska with the intention of immersing themselves in nature were cut from a different cloth than those they left behind. Some of them, like Heimo, had suffered at the hands of brutal, imperious fathers. However, they were not simply injured souls hoping to lick their wounds where no one would notice. Nor were they casual adventurers who just strolled into the bush or profiteers hoping to make money in the fur or oil boom. As a group, they were bright, wild, some of them bruised, for sure, vigorous young men with a sense of urgency and vision. Like the mountain men who came before them, they had the "ha'r of the b'ar" in them. They'd been influenced by experiences in the Boy Scouts; the Woodcraft wilderness tradition and its emphasis on trapping, hunting, guiding, and living off the land; Daniel Boone biographies and tales of the early mountain men; A. R. Harding's series on trapping; *Fur-Fish-Game* magazine, *Outdoor Life, Field & Stream*; the television show *Sergeant Preston of the Yukon*; Jack London, Henry David Thoreau, James Fenimore Cooper, Robert Service, Ernest Hemingway. No airily platonic mama's boys, they were determined to subject themselves to the rigors of living by their wits in the wild. What they could not abide was a life of routine, predictability, and quiet resignation. They were what John McPhee called "white Indians," embodiments of a forgotten frontier spirit, intent on reclaiming the basic virtues and skills of an earlier era. Yet each one of them went to the woods to create his own version of the dream, knowing full well that loneliness and isolation were part of the deal.

Like Heimo, some of the wilderness men—and women—who came to Alaska in the 1970s had the good fortune to fall in with an old sourdough who knew the ropes and took a notion to helping them out, pointing them in the right direction. Others just picked a spot on the map, jumped off, and hoped they didn't get shot by some pissed-off old-timer like Ed Owens. For some, finding their way to the woods wasn't quite as easy. They took temporary jobs—on the pipeline, even—hoping to make enough money to outfit themselves. Others tried, failed, brushed themselves off, and tried again. An overwhelming majority who made it to the woods lived in trespass in a state where trespass is a time-honored tradition. They built cabins, hunted, and ran traplines on land that had always been held loosely in federal trust, and many of them grew, as Jack London once said, "magnificently strong."

Ron Long, a respected Fairbanks trapper and fur buyer who's helped his share of young men get their start in the woods, says in an Oklahoma drawl, "I called 'em woods hippies. They were real back-to-nature boys. There was money to be made, but more than anything, these guys came out for the experience of being in the woods."

Young men were coming to Alaska as they hadn't since the turn-of-the-century gold rush years or the 1920s and 1930s, when fur prices soared. Those who arrived hoping to make a quick buck far outnumbered the young men who came to the woods with the intention of settling there. Simply put, a commitment to a life in the woods was just too hard to be attractive to more than a handful of the most earnest young people. Most of the back-to-nature boys had no illusions about cashing in big. Their motivations were very different. They were there to put down roots, to become Alaskans, to learn to live off, and love, the land. Money was important to them only insofar as it enabled them to carry out their dream. And they didn't need much. Four thousand dollars a year was enough for most of them to live on.

Paul Jagow is a self-described "river rat." When he dreamed of settling in Alaska's Interior, he knew that he had to be on a big river—somewhere that was both remote and infused with the Native culture he admired. So he simply unfolded a map, studied it, and said, "This is it. This is where I'm going to live."

Paul Jagow grew up on the Lower East Side of Manhattan. He went

THE FINAL FRONTIERSMAN   155

to Friends Seminary in New York City from first grade on and later enrolled at the University of Pennsylvania, where he studied anthropology. After graduating, he landed on a commune in northern Maine and then, in the late spring of 1974, he came to Alaska. "I'd made it to the Maine woods," he says, "but pretty soon I was dreaming of the real woods—Alaska."

He arrived with a Klepper folding kayak, linen sails, leeboards, and 300 pounds of gear. By June he was paddling north along Behm Canal between mainland Alaska and Revillagigedo Island. "Greedy for the wind," he built a boom, but when a storm hit, he knew he was in trouble. He made a break for shore, running with the wind. The boom broke and the kayak rolled. He straddled the kayak's hull and paddled it upside down to land. Although he had saved himself and recovered his gun and some fishing equipment, he'd lost all of his food and much of his gear. He lived off the land for the next six weeks, foraging for wild plants and berries and fishing for snapper, halibut, and flounder. His luck changed when he ran into some hunters from New Jersey and flew out with them.

For the next three years, Paul worked on the pipeline. The money was just too good to pass up. And then one day he walked away from it all—literally walked, 200 miles. He left the Prudhoe Bay complex and headed south in the general direction of Arctic Village. Half a year later, after a trip back home to New York, he came back to Alaska, outfitted himself with a twenty-foot, flat-bottomed riverboat, food, supplies, and a dog team, and motored up the river of his dreams, a greenhorn in America's last great wilderness.

He taught himself how to trap and skin animals, using anthropologist Richard Nelson's book *Hunters of the Northern Forest*. It became his how-to bible. And he lived by Thoreau's economic model: "Self-sufficiency is preferable to social organization; the least commerce with others is best; consume only what you produce." It was a good, rewarding, but lonely life.

In 1993, after being more or less on his own for a decade and a half, Paul married Dawn, a woman from the Bronx, who had been handling dogs for a musher in Fairbanks, where they met. When Paul described his life on the river, Dawn decided to accompany him and give it a try. There they fell in love.

The Jagows have two children now, a seven-year-old girl, Joanna, and a boy, Charlie, who's nine. They have struck a balance between life in the bush and life in town; they spend part of the year on the river—July through January—and the remainder in Fairbanks.

Despite the fact that he no longer lives in the bush year-round, Paul is still in love with the land and the bush lifestyle. "You really have to enjoy being out there," he says, attempting to explain why he and his family haven't left for good. "On top of all the other problems, it's become a disaster economically with the low fur prices and the new export regulations and fees. It's harder than ever now to make a living."

Seven years after the communist government confiscated his family's farm, Alex Tarnai fled Hungary. First he went to Yugoslavia and then he jumped the border to Austria. A year later, he went to the American embassy in Vienna and requested asylum.

At the age of twenty-three, Alex was living in New York City and making frequent forays into New England's backcountry to camp, hunt, and canoe. But it was a visit to an Upper East Side bookstore, where he purchased a tattered copy of Roald Amundsen's *North West Passage* that would change the course of his life. He read it cover to cover, and after finishing it, he bought a large map of Alaska, laid it out on his apartment floor, and pored over it, searching for a place "at the end of the earth." Two years later, after receiving his citizenship, he was heading north up the Alaska-Canada Highway (the Alcan) bound for Alaska, determined to make his dream a reality.

By late May 1977, after a season in the high country around the Tyone and Maclaren Rivers, north of the town of Glennallen, he was bound for the Nowitna, the river he'd been imagining since he scoured the map of Alaska in his Manhattan apartment. The Nowitna was a big, beautiful river that carved out a canyon between steep, densely wooded, 2,000-foot hills. At the one hundred-mile mark, he encountered a Mormon family. In the four years that they had been there, they'd seen an occasional group of floaters, but never anyone who intended to make his life in the woods. Alex assured them that he'd keep his distance, so he went another eighty miles upriver, near the Big Mud River. It wasn't the end of the earth, but it was close—150 miles from the nearest village.

For three years, Alex lived in a tent. He insulated the tent with moss and outfitted it with furniture he made—a bed, a bench, shelves, a table, a chair, and a woodstove. He didn't even have a radio. "The last thing I wanted to do was to bring civilization with me," he says now. Besides, he had a small collection of books—Hemingway, Mailer, Capote, Jack London, and Robert Service.

Alex grew accustomed to the loneliness, and other than occasional trips to Fairbanks and the village of Tanana and summers in town, he steered clear of people and romantic involvements. That is, until the summer of 1995, when he was studying for his Coast Guard license in Fairbanks, and friends set him up on a date. Nancy, his date, was an attractive, charming, adventurous woman from Alabama who'd come to Alaska with her son, Ethan, a child from a previous marriage, on a whim. Nancy was immediately attracted to Alex. He was a modern-day frontiersman, the real deal. He was civilized, too. He could use a knife and a fork and quote Robert Service—"Have you ever been out in the great alone?"

Nancy's dream had always been to live in the woods, but shortly after marrying Alex, she realized that the loneliness and isolation were more than she'd bargained for, so they moved into a house that Alex had bought in the small village of Tanana. Alex had his pilot's license, so sometimes they flew out to the cabin on the Nowitna. Often he went out on his own, trapping for three days and then returning to Tanana. In 2000, the Tarnais moved to Fairbanks permanently so that Ethan and little Alexander, who was born in 1996, could get a better education and Nancy could pursue a career as a reporter with the *Fairbanks Daily News-Miner*. Today Alex flies back and forth between Fairbanks and the Nowitna for a portion of the trapping season.

Though he no longer lives in the wilderness full-time, Alex still remembers the romantic notions that impelled him to spend a good chunk of his life far from the embrace of civilization. "When I came to Alaska," he says, "I just went to the woods. That was real freedom."

* * *

Randy Brown came to Alaska from New Mexico at the age of seventeen in 1975. "It was a deep-seated dream," he says. "I wanted to build a cabin and live out in the woods. I wanted adventure."

When Randy arrived in Alaska, he hoped to begin his life in the bush immediately, but soon discovered that someone else had already claimed the spot where he planned to build his cabin and trap. No problem, he thought, I'll just move downriver ten miles or so. Randy was operating as if he were still in New Mexico, where ten miles of separation was a good stretch of country. But this was Alaska. Randy was informed that he'd have to multiply that number by five, and at fifty miles, he might still be too close.

Disappointed, Randy returned to Eagle, wondering what to do next. After several decades of low prices, fur demand was suddenly at an all-time high, and the country was full of people. Lynx brought as much as $600 a pelt, raw wolf skins $200, and wolverine $250. That winter, a friend mentioned that he needed help with his trapline, building a new cabin, hauling meat, and cutting firewood, and he asked Randy if he'd be interested in giving him a hand. It was a stroke of luck. Randy had found a mentor.

The following year, filled with confidence and a new set of skills, Randy struck out for the Kandik River with a friend. The Kandik was a remote river that fed into the Yukon from the north, halfway between Eagle and the town of Circle. He and his friend, Little John, met up with three others on the river, and together they lined their canoes upriver for sixty miles, a long, arduous journey that took them a full week. "It was hard," Randy says with a laugh. "But we were young and tough."

That winter, sixty miles upriver at Indian Grave Creek, Randy burned through the food supply he'd brought from Eagle. He was down to beans when he and his friend, who was thirty miles downriver at Johnson Gorge, teamed up and shot a moose. The moose tided them over while they slowly acclimated to the country and learned to hunt and trap.

For four years Randy lived alone, then, in 1981, he married. In Karen

Kallen, a schoolteacher whom he met in Fairbanks, he found a woman who loved the woods. Karen had grown up in the sprawling suburbs of New Jersey, and as a young girl, she'd dreamed of living off the land. In 1981, they were married at the mouth of the Nation River. For their honeymoon, they went back up the Kandik River and built the cabin they'd call home for the next decade.

Randy has fond memories of their years on the river. Every so often, there'd be a big river gathering, when all the families along the Yukon and its tributaries would meet for three days of festivities. They'd congregate at the mouth of the Nation River, fifty miles downstream from Eagle. People would come in their riverboats with their familes and dogs. "It was a sight," Randy remembers. "Twenty people, including young kids, dogs, homebrew, endless storytelling, a sauna, and waterskiing."

Though Randy never imagined he'd leave the bush, he and Karen and their two boys, Gabriel and Jed, came out in 1991 and moved to Fairbanks. "It was hard," Randy says. "My whole identity, for more than fifteen years, was living in the woods." Randy went back to school at the age of thirty-three and got a degree in biology. Later he finished his master's degree in fisheries, and today he works for the U.S. Fish and Wildlife Service in Fairbanks.

In Bovey, Minnesota, just twenty-five miles west of Hibbing, there were two things that boys cared about when Stu Pechek was growing up: music and the outdoors. Hibbing was the hometown of Bob Dylan, and it was hard not to get caught up in the allegorical implications of his fame—a hometown hero who hit it big. Stu played trumpet in a band. When he wasn't practicing, he was traipsing around the forest hunting, fishing, and canoeing.

"I loved the North Woods," says Stu, "but I always knew that there was something bigger and better out there."

After graduating from the University of Minnesota in 1974, Stu took a job with the Forest Service in Alaska. A few months later he was back in Minnesota again, but feeling antsy. Outside of working in the local iron-ore mines, there wasn't much happening in Bovey, so he took off for Alaska again, winding up in Fairbanks. "It was 1975," Stu remembers. "There were cowboys from Oklahoma and Texas with hundred-dollar bills falling out of their pockets and hookers everywhere."

Stu put in his own three-year stint working as a construction surveyor on the pipeline to pay off college loans, and then he got fed up and quit. In Arctic Village, while waiting for a bush plane to take him into the Brooks Range for a backpacking trip, he met up with a trapper by the name of Richard Hayden. Hayden offered to help Stu out if he was serious about trapping. But Stu had other commitments. He'd already arranged to spend the winter of 1979-1980 trapping out of a wall tent near Lake Clark on the Alaska Peninsula. After the season, Stu returned to Fairbanks and discovered a letter from Hayden inviting him to come north. The letter said he could take over a cabin of his at Grayling Lake, near the East Fork of the Sheenjek River. Stu jumped at the chance. Grayling Lake was the Arctic—raw wilderness.

Though Hayden eventually gave Stu five of his reject dogs, and Stu learned to mush, initially he checked his traps by snowshoe with the help of his lone dog, Melozi. Stu used Melozi to pull a sled, but when the snow was deep and the sled weighted down with fur, Stu harnessed himself in, too. He wore a Kelty metal-frame backpack with a bridle of nylon rope and a brass snap at the end, which he attached to the trailing rope on Melozi's harness. He still remembers that feeling of returning home at the end of the day, thoroughly exhausted—the sensation that he was the last man left on earth.

Stu trapped steadily until 1990, when he decided that he'd had enough. He loved the bush, but he missed traveling, people, female companionship, books, a daily newspaper. So many people had burnt out on the bush. Bored by the repetition, by the loss of the sense of discovery that fueled the experience and made the hardships tolerable, they pulled up stakes and vowed never to return. Stu was determined not to let that happen to him.

Today Stu is the prototypal Alaskan. He's done it all—commercial fisherman, surveyor, pilot, trapper, freelance writer-photographer, and even politician. In 1998 he made an unsuccessful run for Congress, emphasizing his real-life Alaskan experiences and the promise of fresh ideas. Recently he took a job as a land resource manager for the Alaska Department of Natural Resources in Fairbanks. He's had his own plane since 1990, and he's been back to Grayling Lake for a month at a crack, but it's never been long enough, so he still dreams of one day returning for a winter or two. Though he and his longtime girlfriend, Marta McWhorter, have decided to tie the knot, neither of them has any illusions about Stu's ability to stay away from the trapline. It's simply what he loves.

On July 4, 1974, Lynette Roberts and Steve Ulvi left Oregon for Alaska with less than $100 between them in a 1951 Dodge pickup that Steve had overhauled for the trip. Steve's younger brother, Dana, and two friends joined them. Three sat up front in the truck's cab, while the other two rode in the bed of the truck.

For Steve, heading for Alaska was part of a complicated rebellion, fueled by counterculture ideals, revulsion at the rampant taming of the Lower Forty-eight, a burgeoning environmentalism, a need for wild country, a belief in the values of self-reliance and simplicity, and a reaction to the bankruptcy of American culture.

Lynette, on the other hand, hardly knew where Alaska was. She had no firm plan to do much of anything; she was taking life one day at a time. She wasn't the outdoors type either. But one thing was for certain, if Steve was going to Alaska, she was going, too.

Their destination was the Wood-Tikchik Lakes area north of Dillingham. At McCay's Hardware in Anchorage, someone informed them that if they really wanted elbow room, they should go to the Interior. So they turned back east, hit the Taylor Highway, and drove into Eagle.

"Hey, how the hell ya doin'?" The friendly voice of Sarge Waller was the first one they heard when they arrived in town. They told Waller of their intentions to homestead along the Nation River. Waller responded that the Nation had been a blank spot on the map until that very day. He had just returned from taking two couples there.

Steve, Lynette, and Dana eventually settled on a place twelve miles upriver from Eagle, about a quarter of a mile from the Canadian border.

It was Native land and they had a letter of nonobjection from the Han Gwich'in chief of Eagle Village.

The three of them lined Grumman canoes upriver and worked feverishly to build a cabin before winter. But simplicity was their goal, so even with winter approaching fast, they worked with axes, handsaws, bucksaws, chisels, gouges, and sledgehammers. They used candles for light and moss for toilet paper.

That first year was tough. It was brutally cold, and they were broke, eating nothing but pancakes, beans, and oatmeal every day. By the spring of 1975, Lynette was fed up. She was homesick for Oregon, determined to make some money, and tired of her support role. She left the river, but got only as far as Tok, Alaska, where she picked up a job as a waitress for two weeks. Steve never expected her to return, but return she did. "The country had already gotten into my blood," Lynette says. Steve and Lynette were married the following fall.

It took three years until they felt really rooted. They raised rabbits, made their own clothes, built their own dogsleds, and canned much of their food for winter—vegetables, ducks, salmon. They also had a big garden, fertilized with fish guts, two plastic greenhouses, fish wheels, and gillnets. And by 1977, they had a daughter, too. Lena was the first child born to a member of the Yukon's growing river community, a universe of people that stretched 163 miles downriver to Circle and ninety-two miles upriver to Dawson in the Yukon Territory.

It was after the birth of Lena that Lynette became completely committed to the lifestyle. While Steve was off with Dana, hunting or exploring new trapping territory, Lynette hauled wood, drove the dog team, washed clothes and diapers in cold water with a hand scrub board, gathered berries, shot a bear in the yard with Lena on her hip.

By 1979, when Eli, their second child, was born, Steve had exorcised much of his wanderlust. "Lynette was the grounding influence," he says. "Settling in became far more important to me than being what I call a country eater, the guy who always has to go over the next mountain. Lynette created a home, and I learned the importance of family."

* * *

For those who came to Alaska's Interior, Eagle and Fort Yukon were the primary jumping-off spots. Of the two, Fort Yukon was more closely associated with the fur trade.

In 1847, Alexander Murray of the Hudson's Bay Company followed a river route down the Porcupine pioneered by John Bell, a company predecessor, and founded Fort "Youcon," the first Hudson's Bay Company trading post in Alaska. Considering Murray's initial impression of the Youcon, it's a bit surprising that he chose it as a site. Writing in his journal, Murray said, "As I sat smoking my pipe, and my face besmeared with tobacco juice to keep at bay the d---d mosquitoes still hovering in clouds around me, my first impressions of the Youcon were anything but favourable. I never saw an uglier river, everywhere low banks, apparently lately overflowed, with lakes and swamps behind, the trees too small for building, the water abominably dirty and the current furious." Nevertheless, Fort Youcon lay in the middle of one of the richest fur-trapping areas in all of North America, and Murray knew that. Following the establishment of the Hudson's Bay post, the British and the Russians on the lower Youcon competed for the trading allegiances of the Natives until both were forced out after America acquired Alaska in 1867. Just over thirty years later, the U.S. Congress amended the Customs Acts of 1868 and 1879 to allow non-Natives to trap, too, setting the stage for a tradition of white trappers coming into the country.

From the very beginning, Natives didn't know what to make of the white man's tradition of going to the woods alone. Joe Carroll, a Fort Yukon Native, whose father, Jimmy Carroll, was a trapper turned fur buyer and store owner, witnessed the wilderness revival of the 1970s and called the young men who went out into the country on their own "queer ducks." Ron Long, whose wife, Elaine, is Gwich'in, explains, "You have to understand. It's a difference in cultures. Most of these guys went off without wives or families. A Native would never do that. The Natives regarded that as weird and antisocial." In his book *Main Currents in American Thought*, Vernon Louis Parrington expands on Ron Long's observation, putting the bewilderment of the Natives into perspective. He writes, "For the Indian the wilderness was home, the locus of the tribe that was the center of his metaphysical universe as well as his social existence. The white hunter was an alien, paradoxically achieving a sense of relation to the world through an ordeal of profound physical, moral, and psychological isolation from society. His destiny was personal rather than tribal; his moral obligation was only to himself. . . ."

Many of the young men who came to Fort Yukon and Eagle were impelled by a very different cultural ideal than the one Natives knew and understood—one that celebrated the struggles of the heroic individual alone in the woods. Nevertheless, many of the white newcomers, including Heimo, eventually established friendships that tied them to the Native community, and the Natives, for the most part, came to respect them. Paul Herbert, a Fort Yukon Native who was a young man when Heimo and others like him gathered in Fort Yukon before heading out to the woods, says, "Hell, yeah, I admired them, trying to make a living out there." Still there was occasional resentment, particularly among some of the young Natives, newly empowered by the Native claims victory, who regarded going to the woods as their cultural and historical prerogative and who viewed the intrusion of the young white men as a form of cultural poaching.

Yet as early as the late 1970s, Richard Caulfield noticed that it was this generation of young white men who were keeping alive the ancient Native traditions. In his 1979 study "Subsistence Use In and Around the Proposed Yukon-Charley National Rivers," Caulfield noticed that it was the white woods hippies who were intent on learning the traditional Native skills and leading a subsistence lifestyle, while many of the young Native men seemed uninterested. This trend, which Caulfield noticed in and around the Eagle area, was also characteristic of what had occurred in Fort Yukon, where many Natives had already been lured out of the bush and their seasonal cycles by the presence of village schools and government aid.

Though our culture romanticizes the simple, lonely life of the woodsman, the reality of isolation for many of the back-to-nature boys was sometimes in stark contrast to the myth. David Schlesinger floated into Fort Yukon from Whitehorse on a raft he'd built himself and headed out into the country. "The sheer space is awesome," he says. "You look around and say, 'Okay, this is my country. That forest is my kitchen and these 300 square miles are my living room.' It's great, but after a while, it can really get to you. You can't imagine how lonely it can be."

Ron Bennett, who trapped the Yukon Flats on and off for fourteen years, says, confirming David Schlesinger's impressions, "It was a lonely, hard-luck life, so goddamn reclusive. Looking back, it's hard not to think that it was a colossal waste of time. I have a saying—the only guy dumber than a fisherman is a trapper. There wasn't a day that went by that I didn't wish a woman would appear from the woods." Every year Bennett would come out of the bush for the summer and every year he'd promise himself that he wouldn't go back out to the trapline. Yet, come August, he'd get the itch again, the same itch that had brought him to Alaska in the first place. "I was maladjusted," he says. "I should've been out chasing chicks, but there was just something about going back out to the woods." During the summers, when he was off the trapline, that's exactly what he would do—chase women. When August came around and it was time to head back out, he and the rest of the trappers would plead with their summer girlfriends to join them. "The smart ones said no, " Bennett tells me. "But occasionally one of us would convince a gal to come out. She'd hang around for a while, and then she'd leave and never look back. It takes a pretty unusual woman to tough it out in the woods."

John Peterson, who at one time or another flew in most of the trappers who used Fort Yukon as their base, adds some perspective to the plight of the male trappers. "They were all hot to hang out in Fort Yukon and find a woman," he laughs. "Most of them had come to the conclusion that they couldn't be out there alone. But finding a woman to live with any one of them guys, especially out there, was a real chore."

Lynette Roberts, who lived with her husband, Steve Ulvi, and two children on the Yukon, above Eagle, was one of those unusually tough women who thrived in the bush despite its hardships. "The most lonely thing for me was the lack of female companionship," she explains. "It's hard to find female energy in the bush. It's a real yang experience. And after I had Lena [her first child], I really felt the isolation. Although she was my sidekick, my companion, what I missed most was not being able to share that experience of motherhood with anyone else. The bush though is no place for shrinking violets. It demands an emotional sturdiness. Structure is also very important; you need that. I settled into a rhythm—teaching the kids, tending the garden, canning, checking the fishnets, raising rabbits, hauling wood. All of that gave great purpose to my life."

"The key to living out there," says Karen Kallen-Brown, who lived on the Kandik River with her husband, Randy Brown, and their two sons, "is keeping busy. I don't think I ever felt lonely," she says. "I don't know that I ever had the time, between homeschooling and the trapline. Of course, we homeschooled the boys, and I organized the program. It was a very creative program—individualized education can be so good—and we worked hard at it. But I was never willing to just stay at home. We ran the trapline together. Randy put in the trails and laid the traps early in the season, but after that we checked them as a family. We also traveled as a family. Trips into Eagle took us anywhere from a week to twelve days."

Nancy Tarnai, who spent time in the bush with her husband, Alex Tarnai, says, "It's a beautiful world out there. I always had it in the back of my mind that I wanted to live like that, and I tried it for a while, but it turned out that I couldn't do it. It's really, really isolated, and there's no one else. When we were first married, I got mad at Alex one night. I left the cabin and started walking down the river. It was nighttime, in the dead of winter, and I was scared. I came back to the cabin an hour later. Alex asked what I had planned to do, and I told him that my intention was to walk to town. Then I asked him how far town was. 'A hundred fifty miles,' he said, nearly laughing. Not long after, we moved to the village, to Tanana. I really took to village life. I felt a part of something. In the village we lived without running water and, of course, heated with wood. But it wasn't the bush. There are not many women who can live out there."

Heimo remembers that some of the Fort Yukon trappers, unable to convince their girlfriends to join them but eager for female companionship anyway, even resorted to taking out personal ads in national magazines. "Never go to the woods without a skirt," Tommy Carroll, Joe's brother, told them, and they took his advice to heart. One of them put an ad in *Mother Earth News*. "He knew hippie chicks would be interested in coming out to the Alaskan wilderness," Heimo says—and received a sackful of letters, literally. Many of the women even included photographs. Heimo helped his trapper friend sort through the letters and remembers that they usually fell into four categories: nuts writing ten-page confessionals, starting with "Some people think I'm weird . . ."; wives trying to escape their husbands (those letters were destroyed immediately); divorced women with kids (those letters were also thrown out); and single women looking for adventure. The trapper read the letters for days, narrowing his list down to a dozen letters and photographs, until he chose a young woman who seemed to have what it took to make it in the woods. It helped that she had included a picture of herself. "She was very good-looking," Heimo recalls. The trapper burned the rest of the letters, and only after they'd been reduced to ash did he realize that the woman he'd chosen had forgotten to include her return address.

Though men like Ron Bennett, David Schlesinger, and Heimo learned how to deal with the loneliness, others didn't fair as well. Those who didn't were usually the ones who'd gone to the woods on a whim or come only for the romance of it, guys who loved the idea of being in the bush but weren't willing to put in the hard work of learning the country, hunting, trapping, cutting and splitting wood, hauling water. Those were the guys who froze to death or were eaten by bears or, as Heimo says, the ones who "put the boots to themselves"—who took their own lives. There was one—nobody seems to remember his name—on some lakes near Rapid River, who came out in March, the story goes, to photograph ducks and to have some kind of religious experience. He intended to stay for only the spring and summer. Rather than hunt or trap, he was going to live off of canned vegetables. Six months later, when he didn't show up in town, the state troopers went out to investigate. They flew overhead and he crawled out of his tent and waved. Assuming he was okay, they flew off. Only he wasn't. He was low on food and waved out of joy at being discovered. A few months later a friend got worried about him and sent the troopers back out. They discovered him dead. He'd shot himself because he was too weak to move. The troopers found him frozen to his cot. The mice had burrowed holes into his body. They also came across a diary, which paints a predictable picture. After two months, he was lonely and getting stir-crazy. Since he hadn't planned to hunt, there was little reason for him to explore the country other than to satisfy his curiosity and sense of adventure and get his photographs. At first he hiked a lot, but he was covering the same terrain, and that got old fast. When he finally realized that he wanted to hunt to keep his mind off of his isolation and that he needed to—his food was running out—it was too late; he'd already pitched most of his shotgun shells into the lake. By mid-November, starving and desperate, he had only one choice, and that's when he decided to "put the boots to himself."

"Wilderness," Roderick Nash says in *Wilderness and the American Mind*, "appealed to those bored or disgusted with man and his works. . . . The solitude and total freedom of the wilderness created a perfect setting for either melancholy or exultation." Nash gets part of it right. The appeal of the woods for guys like Heimo Korth and the others is undeniable. It allowed them to shake society's dust from their feet. But in his second sentence, Nash makes a misstep. He should have written that "wilderness created a perfect setting for both melancholy *and* exultation," for even the most mentally stable of the wilderness men were subject to vagaries of mood, vacillating between moments of joy and despair. If they were lucky, very lucky, and they worked hard at it, they could achieve a kind of emotional equanimity that allowed them to enjoy highs—celebrating the return of the sun, a clean kill, spring warm-up, a snared wolverine—and ride out the inevitable lows.

And the lows were inevitable, particularly in early December, when many of the trappers could hardly wait to come to town to sell furs, and just after breakup, when they would be getting ready to leave the bush for the summer. They could barely contain themselves, and when they'd get to town, they'd pop, trying to cram in as much craziness as they could. They were like cowboys coming in after a cattle drive, like sailors on leave, like fishermen who'd been out on the water too long. They lived hard out on the trapline, and they lived just as hard when they came to town, particularly the Fort Yukon bunch. However, contrary to what one might think, the first order of business was neither booze nor women. "A shower," Heimo says, as if he can't quite believe it himself. "A shower was worth more than gold." Sometimes a trapper would head for Fairbanks, bypassing the shower. One, in particular, had a reputation for heading straight for the roughest bar—in the days of the pipeline a guy could take his pick—where he would provoke fights just to blow off steam. He was a small man and would invairably be on the losing end of the beating, but that didn't stop him. But the others would remain in Fort Yukon, rushing to the base's locker room (everyone called Fort Yukon's Air Force radar site "the base") as if a shower were necessary to sustain both body and soul. Only after their showers would they think about getting drunk. Then they would stampede the liquor store, where they'd buy cases of Olympia beer—"Oly pop," "Athabaskan champagne"—which they'd sometimes haul back to a friend's cabin in wheelbarrows.

Richard Carroll, Jr., another member of the Fort Yukon Carroll clan, says that the trappers like Heimo were just following a tried-and-true tradition. "The trappers would come to town," he says, "and they'd have one hell of a vicious party. They'd try to outsmart the fur buyers by getting them drunk, but it always backfired."

The trappers wouldn't stop drinking until the beer was gone. Then all of them—trappers, their Native buddies, Native women, non-Native women, and sometimes fur buyers, too, who at that time still made buying trips to the remote villages—loaded into the "meat wagon," a big flatbed truck with wooden slats that the small airport used to transport luggage. They'd drive the mile of dirt roads to the base's bar, where they would drink more. When the temperatures plunged to 50 and 60 below, this could be dangerous fun. The trappers and their friends often drank until they passed out. If a guy passed out in the meat wagon, someone would have to remember to haul him indoors. And someone would always have to have the presence of mind to light the woodstove. The following day, nursing crippling hangovers, the trappers would walk up to the AC and buy a set of new "town clothes," after which they'd begin the business of haggling with the fur buyers.

* * *

The summer gatherings unfolded much the same as the Christmas get-togethers—a week's revelry and then they'd settle down to serious business. Some would go commercial fishing, others would work construction, those who had dog teams to feed would prepare for fish camp, where they'd need to catch 1,500 salmon to sustain their teams through the year. In his early years, after returning in June from St. Lawrence Island, where he spent the spring months walrus and seal hunting and whaling with the Eskimos, Heimo stuck around Fort Yukon. There he'd do odd jobs for cash, tending the register at the AC Store, doing the bookings for Yukon Air Service, and working small construction jobs. But mostly he spent his time on the river.

Working the river with the likes of Fred Thomas and his brother Harry and Paul Herbert, natives who knew the river as well as most people know their backyards, learning how to set gillnets, build fish wheels, read the river's currents, and cut up salmon, was a dream come true for Heimo. When he first came to Alaska, Heimo envisioned that he'd be a river rat, living in the woods but in close proximity to the Yukon or the Porcupine. He surrendered that dream as soon as he laid his eyes on the Coleen River. A month and a half on the Yukon wasn't long, but it was enough to satisfy his desire to take part in the lifestyle of those who lived on a big, historic river. That month and a half also bound him to the community and people of Fort Yukon. Acceptance in Fort Yukon didn't come easily. It was an insular place in which outsiders were viewed with considerable suspicion, particularly young men who looked like Heimo—full beard, dark hair down to the middle of his back, a sealskin headband with an eagle feather stuck in it. Who was he pretending to be anyway—an Indian?

The image, of course, was part of the wilderness myth that Heimo was both participating in and perpetuating. The trappers of the Rocky Mountain West more closely resembled the Indians than they did the Missouri farmers or the city folk of St. Louis. A woodsman was supposed to look wild, rugged, and often altogether uncivilized. It underscored his triumphal escape, his emancipation from the galling restrictions and pretext that ruled the lives of the people he'd left behind. Roger Kaye, who as an U.S. Fish and Wildlife planner-pilot, had occasion to meet many of the men who took to the woods in the 1970s. "Almost all the young men who came to Alaska arrived with this idea about the woods firmly embedded in their minds," he says. "The big knife, the clothes, the log cabin—they were all symbols of the wilderness, symbols of their new lives as trappers and woodsmen."

If some of the people of Fort Yukon intitially greeted Heimo with mistrust, many of them soon had a change of heart. His openness, his curiosity, his eagerness to learn about their culture were disarming, and he had the same effect on the Natives of Fort Yukon as he had on the people of Savoonga. By the time he brought Edna, his fiancée, to town in the summer of 1981, many were eager to see the woman that Heimo Korth would marry.

CHAPTER 8

Hunting the Ice Whale

In the Korths' relatively spacious one-room cabin in Fort Yukon, there is a framed photograph on the wall above the kitchen table of Heimo at the helm of an Eskimo walrus hide skinboat, an *angyaq*. The sail is up, stretched tight by a stiff wind. Though the photograph doesn't show that detail, it clearly captures Heimo gripping the tiller, with a full beard that gives him the look of Ahab and his long, dark hair flowing wildly behind him. Heimo is staring straight ahead, as if searching the distant ice for a navigable lead or a great whale. The sky is ominously gray, heavy with fog and mist.

The photo occupies a prominent space on the wall next to a photographic homage to the Korths' first daughter, Coleen. It is one of Heimo's favorite photos, if only because his time on St. Lawrence Island, to this day, strikes him as nothing short of serendipity. What was a kid from Wisconsin doing hunting with the Eskimos of the Bering Sea? Surely when Heimo was a boy, dreaming of Canada's Northwest Territories and Alaska, he never imagined a place like St. Lawrence Island—an island encircled, as far as the eye could see, by, depending upon the season, either ocean or ice. His imagination, after all, had been conditioned by Wisconsin's North Woods, by small, hidden lakes surrounded by remnant white pine, and by 300-year-old hemlock, paper birch, red and sugar maples disregarded by rapacious turn-of-the-century loggers.

St. Lawrence Island is a place devoid of trees—entirely. When Heimo arrived just after Thanksgiving in November 1975, having barely survived his first three months on Beaver Creek, there were elders still living in Savoonga who had never in their lives been off the island. Consequently, they had never seen a tree. Asian currents deposited prodigious heaps of driftwood on the island's shores, but this was as close to a tree as many of the village's older residents had ever come.

Herman Toolie, Heimo's Eskimo teacher, taught Heimo to respect the wilderness of ice that stretched to the North Pole for its stark and simple beauty and its impersonal cruelty, and Heimo was an attentive student who adapted quickly to the demands of his temporary home. He loved the elemental challenge of hunting on the ice even though the failure to notice a faint change in the direction of wind could result in death. Above everything else, Herman told him, a hunter has to be acutely aware. He has to become a predator. Nothing should escape his notice—not a track, a sound, or flash of color in the distance. The final component to the hunt, Herman said, is the shot. When the animal is near, the most important rule, the only one, is bullet placement. Place the bullet where the head meets the neck.

Like Herman, Heimo had the heart of a hunter, but he was also drawn to the Siberian Yupik people. After months of isolation on the trapline, Heimo relished the easy intimacy of Savoonga's 350 residents. Though the village was in the midst of cataclysmic changes—television and telephone would come to the island by the late 1970s—Heimo discovered a people continuing the traditions and living by the rhythms that had defined the lives of their people for thousands of years.

St. Lawrence Islanders form one clan of the nine-clan Siberian Yupik people that populate Siberia, called Ungazik, and the two modern-day villages of Savoonga and Gambell. Centuries ago, the Eskimos of St. Lawrence Island, who called themselves the "Real People," lived according to clan in semisubterranean homes called "nenglus," along the shore, and subsisted on whales, walrus, seal, polar bear, fish, water birds, and eggs, and trapped arctic fox and polar bear for fur. The roofs of these nenglus were built of sod stabilized inside by the jawbones and rib bones of whales. The walls were made from what was available—driftwood and whale bones. Contrary to popular myth, Alaskan Eskimos never lived in snow houses. In the Canadian Arctic and Archipelago, however, people lived in snow houses on the shore ice for nine months a year and in animal skin shelters during the summer. Elsewhere—Labrador and west and northwest Greenland, for instance—the snow house was used only as a temporary shelter.

The first European to come upon St. Lawrence Island was the Dane Vitus Bering, who sailed in the service of the Russian crown. Bering christened the island St. Lawrence when he sighted it on August 21, 1728, the Feast of St. Lawrence. Bering was searching for the geographical link between America and Siberia and would have discovered a cultural, linguistic, and ancestral link, too, had the St. Lawrence Islanders come out to greet him and his crew. The Eskimos of "Sivuqaq" had traded with the Siberians of the Chukchi Peninsula for centuries before Bering arrived, sailing their skinboats, or *angyaqs*, which were capable of carrying thirty people back and forth over the forty miles that separated the island from the mountainous Russian mainland. Instead the Eskimos fled into the Kukulgit Mountains when they spotted his unfamiliar vessel. Bering writes: "We located this island, which we named St. Lawrence, in honor of the day, and found on it a few huts but no people, although I twice sent the midshipman to look for them." Unimpressed by what he saw, Bering moved on.

The Russian Otto von Kotzebue was the next European, or *laluramka* (literally, "people from the bearded clan"), to explore the island—in 1816—but he was similarly unmoved. Judging its commercial potential to be almost nothing, he, too, sailed on, leaving the island to its isolation until American whalers discovered in the waters off the island one of the last great populations of bowhead whales, or *aghvook*.

Both fashion and necessity fueled the pursuit of the bowhead. Baleen from the bowhead's jawbone was used to produce a fiberglasslike material that was used in upholstery, umbrellas, women's skirt hoops and corset stays, and carriage wheels and springs, and whale blubber provided lighting oil for a booming population. A bowhead was worth its weight in gold, $10,000 per whale. In the second half of the nineteenth century, whalers rushed north—they would leave Hawaii in spring and follow the melting ice pack—and the western Arctic became the country's most profitable whaling grounds and the scene of colossal butchery. In a forty-year period, more than 3,000 voyages were made.

The whalers soon discovered that the islanders were enthusiastic traders. The whalers traded rifles, shotguns, whaling guns, gunpowder and ammunition, tobacco, matches, molasses, and whiskey for walrus ivory, baleen, fur, and women. When the bottom dropped out of the whale oil market, whalers headhunted, taking only the bowhead jawbones, and leaving their headless corpses to rot in the sea. Whalers also killed hundreds of thousands of walrus for their skin, blubber, and ivory tusks. The two mammals revered by the Eskimos of St. Lawrence Island, on which they had depended for thousands of years for food, shelter, and clothing, were quickly disappearing from their waters. By the mid-1870s, disease (flu, measles, syphilis), famine, drunkenness, and a rash of bad weather conspired against the islanders. Between 1878 and 1880, St. Lawrence Island lost two-thirds of its population, leaving all but two of its eight original villages—Gambell and Pugughileq (Southwest Cape)—completely decimated. On an island for which the sea had always provided, the period came to be known as the Great Starvation. Accessible game was scarce and once-heroic hunters sold their seal nets and hunting guns for alcohol. Historian Dorothy Jean Ray, in her book *The Eskimos of Bering Strait, 1650–1898*, claims that the Eskimos "drank excessively from the first sip of liquor." She writes that they enjoyed it as a stimulant and also used it as a temporary escape from the strict behavioral codes that governed Eskimo life. Even the hunters who abstained from alcohol met with disaster. They were thwarted by fierce winds, which prevented them from reaching their hunting grounds by foot or by boat. Many died of exposure attempting to find food. Some took chances on thin ice and fell through and drowned. When a hunter did successfully kill an animal, he was often too weak with hunger and disease to carry it home. People were forced to boil and eat their walrus tents and eat their dogs and skin ropes. Only 300 islanders remained by 1890. By the early 1900s, when the price of baleen climbed so high that steel carriage springs were being used instead of baleen the whalers fled the Arctic in search of new waters, the bowhead numbers having been reduced to 3,000, one-tenth of its prewhaling population.

By the time Heimo reached St. Lawrence Island in early December 1975, the Bering Sea had rebounded, and Heimo was hunting regularly on the pack ice with Herman Toolie. Despite Herman's expertise, venturing far out onto the ice was always a calculated gamble. In March 1977, that gamble nearly cost Heimo and Herman their lives.

Heimo and Herman were two miles out on the ice. They'd each shot young bearded seals and were dragging the one hundred-pound animals behind them when Herman signaled for Heimo to stop. "Wait!" Herman said, and Heimo knew immediately that something was wrong. Herman yelled, *"Ohook!* Hurry. Black smoke. Open water." Then Herman began to sprint, his eight-foot hunting stick in one hand and the rope, which was tied through a hole cut into the seal's jaw, in the other. Heimo followed, but he was unable to keep up. Herman was small and agile, and he was used to navigating the uneven ice. A quarter of a mile from shore, Heimo discovered Herman waiting for him. The south wind had broken up the shore-fast ice. Their only hope was to jump.

Heimo clutched his hunting stick and his rope and shadowed Herman. Herman jumped from ice floe to ice floe, and Heimo followed. But Herman quickly outdistanced him. Negotiating the ice floes was something Herman had done since he was a young boy. It was how the boys of the village challenged each other—like Heimo and his friends jumping trains. It was a game of courage and balance. Where the shore-fast ice split into small floes, the boys hopped from one floe to another to see which of them was the bravest, the most sure-footed.

As Heimo neared the shore, he shuddered when he saw the open water that separated the sheets of ice. Concentrate, he thought to himself. Left, right, left, then drive the knee and spring. It was as if he were diving back in high school again. Herman, who had already made it safely onto the shore-fast ice, saw the floes parting and shouted to Heimo, *"Ohook! Ohook!"* Heimo made one jump and then another. Before he knew it, he was in the water, the weight of the seal nearly dragging him under. He struggled onto the floe, clawing at the ice for a grip. Then he lay on his belly, trying to catch his breath. He didn't have the strength for another jump. He couldn't make it. "Heimo!" Herman yelled. "Hurry." Heimo fought to get to his knees, and then he stood. Hand over hand, he tugged at the seal rope until he pulled the seal onto the ice floe. Herman was still shouting for him to hurry. Heimo could see it, too. If he waited any longer, the floe would be too far from the shore-fast ice for him to make it.

Heimo had only one more jump to make. He ran across the ice floe and hurled himself into the air. He hit the shore-fast ice, but the seal rope snapped taut and yanked him back into the water. Terrifed, Heimo struggled to reach Herman's outstretched hand. "Leave the seal," Herman screamed, but Heimo didn't hear a word. When Herman finally pulled Heimo onto the ice, to safety, Heimo's rifle was still slung across his shoulder and he still clung to the seal rope. In his panic he'd forgotten to let go.

Whaling was as dangerous as hunting on the pack ice, but still Heimo was eager for the experience. He was a cat with nine lives and had a growing sense that this was all part of his destiny.

The only problem was that on St. Lawrence Island men went whaling in family groups, and outsiders were not welcome. By March 1978, Heimo had given up all hope of ever seeing a bowhead hunt firsthand. He might have been welcome on Herman Toolie's brother's boat, but that boat was already full. The chance of making it onto another crew was almost nil.

One night, while almost every family in Savoonga was glued to its television set, Heimo was out walking. Television had come to the island only recently, and the entire village was obsessed with *The Six Million Dollar Man*, which the people called the *Bionic Man*. For Heimo, who didn't enjoy TV, the arrival of television was a curse. "People stopped visiting," he says. "It was hard to get them away from it. They watched for the sake of watching even though many of them didn't understand a word."

Nathan Noongwook was out walking that night, too. Nathan was the captain of a whaling boat. When he was a boy, his father told him how the whale hunt was once preceded by a period called *Eghqwaaq*, when villagers held ceremonies and sang songs of entreaty, asking Apa to ensure their hunting success. St. Lawrence Islanders no longer held the ceremonies though, so Nathan was out, while everyone else huddled around a televison set, engaged in his own private conversation with God.

Heimo and Nathan exchanged greetings. Nathan mentioned that he was short a man on his whaling crew, and with the season approaching, he was willing to break with tradition. He asked Heimo if he would like to join his crew. Nathan explained that he would be nothing more than a paddler and a float thrower—after striking the whale, hunters threw out plastic buoys to keep the whale from diving and to slow its flight. Both responsibilitites, however, were essential. In 1978, the International Whaling Commission, concerned about dwindling bowhead whale populations, took over management of the Eskimo bowhead whale hunt and decided to cancel it. When the Barrow, Alaska, Eskimos protested and staged a hunt, other Eskimo communities followed suit. The IWC eventually conceded, setting kill and strike limits for each village. The Eskimos bridled at the quota. They argued, but to no avail, that the impact of their hunting was insignificant. To miss only one strike now could be the difference between a season's success and failure. Nathan explained this to Heimo. Heimo was hardly listening though. He could hardly believe his good fortune.

Pursuing an animal that can reach sixty feet long and sixty tons in weight in a boat made of walrus hide is perhaps the world's most dangerous endeavor. The hunt begins unremarkably. Using binoculars, hunters glass the open water, waiting to catch sight of a blow. Sometimes they sit for days, napping or busying themselves drinking tea, telling stories, and playing cards. But after a whale is sighted breaking the surface of the water and the "Puhhh!" is heard, the unmistakable expulsion of air, the men fly into action. They board the *angyaqs*. If the wind is right, they immediately hoist the sail. If the wind is poor, they paddle vigorously, but silently, in order not to spook the whale.

Once in pursuit, the success of the hunt, at least until the boat is vir-

tually on top of the whale, is entirely up to the captain. He has to nego-
tiate the menacing ice floes and follow the leads, which are at times
miles wide and at others are nothing more than narrow channels, while
still trying to keep the whale in sight. It is a feat of maneuvering a constantly changing course that puts a captain's skills to their ultimate test.
What a captain also has to do is keep his bearings, even far out at sea,
when the fog rolls in, so he can eventually make it back to land. Com-
passes are nearly useless, since a captain is changing course too often to
take frequent readings. Out at sea, a captain reads the wind and the currents. Apart from these guides, he relies on years of experience and an
intuitive understanding of where the island lies.

To encounter a bowhead whale is to learn what fear is. Using its huge
head, reinforced with cartilage, as a battering ram, it is able to plow a
path through thick pack ice. Yet in order for the striker to make his
throw, the captain must be able to maneuver his *angyaq* within fifteen
feet of the beast. At that distance, the whale looks as big as a battleship.
You can feel it move through the water, see the whale's shiny black skin,
smell it, and practically choke on its stink. A mere flick of its tail can
crush a boat, sending the entire crew plunging into icy waters and to a
near-certain death.

At fifteen feet, the striker stands poised in front of the boat, holding
tightly to the harpoon bomb lance gun that hasn't changed since Captain Ebenezer Pierce invented it in the late 1800s. Prior to the harpoon
bomb lance gun, or darting gun, which is equipped with a fifteen-inch,
pencil-shaped brass bomb packed with dynamite, Eskimo whalers used
ivory-or slate-tipped harpoons. Once the whale was harpooned, sealskin floats were used to keep it near the surface of the water so it could
be harpooned again and again until, eventually, it bled to death. But
with the darting gun Eskimo hunters could harpoon the whale while
simultaneously shooting it with a dynamite bomb.

When the village of Savoonga was established as a reindeer camp, no
one thought about its potential as a whaling site. For decades the men of
Savoonga joined the people of Gambell in their pursuit of the bowhead.
However, in the early 1970s, with the introduction of the snowmachine,

the people of Savoonga, who had long been disappointed with their share of the catch, began their own tradition.

Sixty-five miles from Savoonga, located on the island's southwest cape, was an old village called Pugughileq. Pugughileq was a midden of whale bones, bleached a chalk white by the sun, on which the villagers once hung and dried their seal nets. Here the men of Savoonga built rough plywood shacks, heated with oil stoves during the April bowhead hunt.

"Whaling is a lot of waiting," Heimo recalls. "I sat next to Nathan—he was the captain—on a hill that looked south. Nathan glassed the open water and watched the wind. He was hoping for a north wind to clear out the ice, so we could chase the whales. He saw a few whales blow, but the wind was out of the southwest and we were locked in by ice. While we waited, Nathan told me that Eskimos were the world's greatest travelers. He said that an Eskimo discovered the moon by building a ladder of driftwood to it. The only thing he couldn't figure out was why he didn't leave behind a sealskin flag to show the world that an Eskimo was there first."

Heimo was astounded by Nathan's ability to stay awake. With fifteen hours of light, the old man glassed tirelessly. Before he finally surrendered to sleep, he joked with Heimo that he slept, always, "with one eye open."

The men waited three-quarters dressed, hoping for a favorable wind and Nathan's cry. They waited for three days, and then finally it came. He had sighted a whale—"*Aghvook!*" Forty men were ready to go in a matter of minutes. Nathan climbed into the stern of the *angyaq*. "*Oooo-hooo-kkk!*" he yelled. "One, two, three!" Heimo and six other men ran alongside the thirty-foot *angyaq*, pushing it like bobsledders across the ice on its ivory runners. Then, as if they'd been training for this moment for years, the hunters simultaneously leaped into the boat when Nathan barked out the *k* of "*Ohook!*" Their timing was perfect, literally flawless. It was as if the men were joined together by some invisible thread. But Heimo jumped late, preoccupied with the spectacle, determined not to miss a detail. The men had already grabbed their paddles and were lunging at the water like racers when Heimo cleared the gunwales. Heimo took his paddle, stroked twice, and then noticed Nathan motion to one of the men to raise the sail. It was less an order than a gesture, a slight nod of the head, like a buyer bidding on a steer at a cattle auction. The sail caught the wind, and the men fell silent.

Nathan negotiated a narrow lead, and then the ocean opened up. When the whale blew again—"Puhhh!"—half a mile out, it was electrifying. Heimo heard the man next to him, Nathan's sixteen-year-old nephew, draw in a long breath, as if to suppress a desire to yell out loud. Heimo's whole body trembled, his muscles tensed. The *angyaq* covered the half mile quickly, and then Heimo saw the whale, swimming languidly, unaware that it was being pursued. No one moved now except for the striker, who drew his arm back. The thirty-ton bowhead was only twenty feet from the boat.

"Shit," Heimo says, "it was the scariest thing I ever felt. *Aghvook*—the word kept speeding through my head. *Aghvook, Aghvook.* I tasted blood or something in the back of my mouth. That metallic taste."

Then the striker struck. Seconds later the bomb exploded, and Heimo felt the whale shudder. It was furious now, flailing in the water. Heimo was ready to throw the float until he saw that the harpoon had not stuck.

Only seconds after Heimo realized this, another *angyaq* was over the whale. He saw the striker throw the harpoon and felt the bomb go off and saw the whale shudder again. The whale tried to dive, racing for the ice, but it was too badly hurt. The harpoon had stuck this time, and the throwers tossed out their floats. The whale drifted toward the surface of the water and made a halfhearted attempt to escape, but its blow had turned to blood. When the Yankee whalers saw blood spitting out of the whale's blowhole, they'd exclaim, "The chimney's on fire!" knowing that the whale was as good as dead.

Nathan's radio crackled at full volume now. The other boats, *angyaqs* and aluminum skiffs, which would haul the whale to shore, had been alerted, and they were speeding to the site. When the last boat arrived, the whale turned belly up, and everyone cheered. They'd gotten their whale and they still had one strike left.

Ropes were fastened to the whale and the boats worked together to tow it in. When they arrived back at camp, Heimo couldn't believe his eyes. Half of Savoonga, it seemed, had been radioed and turned out to see the hunters and their catch. Anyone with a working snowmachine had made the sixty-five-mile trip. Heimo watched as two men from the boat that had delivered the final, deadly strike climbed on top of the whale and began to cut off huge slabs of *mungtuk* (whale skin with a layer of blubber) with long, twelve-foot, ulu-shaped knives. The juicy, black-and-white *mungtuk* was then divided among the people.

In mid-January of 1981, en route to his cabin on the Coleen River after spending the holidays in Fort Yukon, Heimo considered telling the bush pilot that he would not be going to St. Lawrence Island in the spring. At the last moment, just before the pilot returned to Fort Yukon, he reconsidered. What the heck, he thought, I'll go for one last adventure.

At the end of May 1981, near the end of the walrus's summer migration north, Heimo joined a group of hunters from Savoonga. Their destination was a prime walrus hunting spot among the spring's last, large ice floes just northwest of the village of Gambell on the island's far western shore. They traveled by what was locally known as a "speedboat," a wooden V hull with an eighty-horse Evinrude engine. The fog was thick when they left Savoonga, so they took a compass bearing—60 miles west-northwest. Five hours later, confused by the absence of any ice floes, they emerged from a fogbank. Heimo knew something was wrong as soon as he saw the mountains. They were the mountains of Siberia along the Chukchi Peninsula, not far from the Siberian coastal town of Provideniia. The coast was close, which meant that they were in Russian waters. They hadn't compensated enough for the strong southerly currents. Though Heimo had been living largely without news from the ouside world for over four years, he knew enough to realize that this was bad. It was the height of the Cold War, and he and his friends were in Russian waters.

The severity of the situation dawned on Heimo when a Russian patrol boat gave chase. There were men in the bow of the boat with guns and another man with a bullhorn. Heimo and his friends could either give themselves up or duck back into the fogbank and make a run for it. They chose to run.

Looking back, Heimo thinks that his friends fled to protect him. Eskimo hunters occasionally entered Russian waters. Russian patrol boats would sometimes investigate, but that was usually the end of it. However, when the patrol caught sight of Heimo, a white man, it was suddenly more interested.

"Spy," Heimo says now. "They must have thought I was a spy, hoping to slip into the country through Siberia." To this day, he is convinced that if he had been caught he would have had a tough time explaining to them that he was a simple walrus hunter.

Shortly after losing the patrol boat, Heimo's boat collided with an ice floe, ripping a hole in the boat's side just below the gunwales. His friends hadn't seen the floe in the fog, which covered the water like a thick wool blanket. He and his friends bailed frantically until it was obvious to them that they could not bail fast enough. Quickly, one of the men tore out one of the boat's seats, which was nothing more than a plywood board. Then he tore out another. He held one of the boards over the hole on the outside of the boat while another man held a plywood seat over the hole on the inside. From a toolbox, which they always carried with them, another man grabbed a hammer, gathered a small handful of nails, and nailed the two boards together. The boards didn't completely stanch the flow of water, but by bailing, too, they were able to keep the boat afloat. Five hours later they arrived in Savoonga, cold, wet, and tired, but alive.

It is late July 2002, and we are sitting outside the Korths' cabin on the upper Coleen River near their summer kitchen, which is nothing more than a small fire pit with an iron grate over it surrounded by lawn chairs and rough-hewn spruce benches. We have just finished our supper—boiled porcupine, or "quill pig." This morning, not far from the cabin, Heimo killed it with an ax. He singed it over the fire to remove the quills, and then gutted and skinned it. Edna boiled it for two hours and then browned it on the grill. Knowing I've never eaten porcupine, everybody watches me take my first bite. "Delicious," I inform them, which it is, though I think they were all hoping I'd retch with disgust.

"Up here you got to eat what you can get your hands on," Heimo says.

"No," I say, protesting. "I'm not kidding. I'll never again look at a porcupine in the same way. When I see one I'll think supper. It tastes like pot roast."

"Oh, yeah," says Heimo. "Soon everybody will be serving it for Sunday supper down there. Ah, excuse me, would you please pass the porcupine."

Supper is over and Krin is doing the dishes. The night air has cooled, and after a week of utter rabidity, the mosquitoes have finally decided to give us a break. Heimo has just finished telling us the story of almost losing the boat, and their lives, to the ice floe. Edna holds his hand, fingers interlocked, a silent admission of how different her life would be had the walrus hunting trip turned out differently, had Heimo's Eskimo friends not acted quickly to patch the hole in the boat.

Heimo pulls Edna close and kisses her on top of the head. "You know those Eskimos," he says. "They're resourceful. They can fix almost anything." Heimo's comment is an informed observation, not a blanket generalization. During my winter visit, one of the snowmachines was running poorly, and Heimo cursed his inability to figure out what was wrong with it. "An Eskimo could fix it," he said. "I've seen them take apart entire engines, figure out the problem, fix it, and put the engine back together in an afternoon."

"Mom can do that, too," Rhonda yells from the hammock. "Mom's the mechanic in the family." Rhonda and Krin and Krin's new husky puppy, Firth, which Krin named after one of the rivers in northeast Alaska, are all lying in the hammock together. The hammock was a gift from Fred Thomas to Krin for her thirteenth birthday. It sags under their weight. They swing back and forth only inches above the ground.

"It's true," Heimo says, hanging his head in mock shame. "Edna fixes everything around here."

"Yeah, right," Edna replies, as she often does to Heimo's verbal taunts, jerking her hand from his.

"That's right," Krin yells. "Mom's better at fixing things than Dad."

"I'll fix you," Heimo shouts, and jumps up out of his chair. The girls see him coming and scatter. Firth scampers after Krin, yapping and bit-ing at her heels; Krin runs for the woods. Rhonda makes a break for the cabin, but reconsiders and dashes for the tent, which Heimo and Edna have been sleeping in since returning to the river because it's cooler than the cabin. Heimo chases Rhonda around the tent until she sprints for the cabin, ducking under the volleyball net, which is tied tightly be-tween two black spruce trees. Heimo follows, but forgets to duck. He is on his back now, having lost the battle with the net. Nobody inquires to see if he is hurt—instead we all laugh hysterically.

After his brush with death while walrus hunting, Heimo might not have been allowed to return to his cabin on the Coleen had he and other rural Alaskan trappers not been accommodated by a large and contro-versial piece of legislation called the Alaska National Interest Lands Conservation Act.

"What is to be the fate of all this land?" John McPhee inquired in 1976 in his book *Coming into the Country*. McPhee was referring to the vast lands that had been held in public trust from the time the United States acquired Alaska in October 1867, and more recently, those super-vised loosely by the Bureau of Land Management. With statehood in 1959, Alaska was guaranteed 105 million acres. With the Alaska Native Claims Settlement Act of 1971, Alaska Natives received 44 million acres. Besides 2 million acres of private property, what remained was 224 million acres, a chunk of federal land larger than any other state in the union, though almost a quarter of that federal land had already been protected as national forests, parks, and refuges.

Nearly five years after *Coming into the Country* was published, and prior to his final trip to Savoonga, Heimo was asking the same question: What would happen to the land? More important, what would come of the land along the Coleen River? Would his way of life be tolerated or would it be expunged with the stroke of a pen? Dare he dream of one day raising a family in the place he loved? One thing was for certain: Because of a promise included in the Native claims legislation, conservationists would get their due.

When ANCSA was passed, an Alaska planning group was formed to examine a variety of management possibilities on "d-2" lands, which had been withdrawn from state selection. All of the agencies involved—Fish & Wildlife, the National Park Service, the Forest Service, and the Bureau of Land Management—scrambled to make their selections and meet a congressional deadline of December 18, 1978.

It all looked as if the issue would be settled by the summer of 1978, but in October the Ninety-fifth Congress adjourned without enacting the appropriate legislation. When it became evident that the December 18, 1978, "d-2" lands deadline mandated by Congress would not be met, Secretary of the Interior Cecil Andrus exercised his authority under the Federal Land Policy and Management Act (FLPMA) and withdrew 110 million acres from state and mineral selection. Two weeks later, President Jimmy Carter used the authority granted to him by the obscure Antiquities Act of 1906 to give national monument status to fifty-six million of those acres, incensing countless Alaskans. Alaska, many claimed, was being "locked up." Some citizens of Fairbanks burned Carter in effigy, and a secessionist movement was born.

Nowhere was this land withdrawal greeted with greater antagonism than in the bush. Every suspicion, every resentment harbored about government and the outside world was comfirmed. Rumors had been swirling for years, passed on by word of mouth or crackling over the radio, fueling a general sense of paranoia, a feeling among trappers, miners, and residents of bush communities that, whatever happened, their interests were not going to be considered.

I asked Lynette Roberts, who homesteaded on the Yukon with her husband, Steve Ulvi, how the land debate was greeted along the river, and she replied without hesitation, "With great hostility. There was this general sinking feeling that life as we knew it was over, which had everything to do with the fact that almost everybody was squatting, trespassing." Because of the proposed Yukon-Charley Rivers National Preserve, the section of the Yukon River between Circle, Alaska, and the Canadian border, including Eagle, was ground zero for the protest movement. The joke was that the Park Service knew how to manage only scenery and not people. It would come in and, if need be, forcibly remove homesteaders from the land. (A few years later, it would pay them as seasonal employees to dress up as trappers, don the garb of homesteaders, build fish wheels, and hang fish for the tourists who'd flock to the area to catch a glimpse of what life along the river was once like.) Trappers all over the state were alarmed. Some heard that their presence, which had always been tolerated, was said to conflict with the "necessary and appropriate" use of the land and that subsistence living was incompatible with wilderness preservation, albeit nominally. Others heard that they were being belittled as nothing more than neopioneers, engaged in a social experiment or playing a game of wilderness survival as a lifestyle choice. Then there were the horror stories, some based firmly in fact, of pompous, briefcase-toting Bureau of Land Management agents, the first symbols of the new order, jumping out of helicopters to assert the government's sovereignty over the land, delivering threats and eviction notices.

Randy Brown, who spent fourteen of his sixteen years in the bush along the Kandik River, where he and his wife, Karen Kallen, eventually raised two boys, remembers the time well—the consternation and the confusion. "Reapportionment was inevitable," he says. "But this was a land grab of dramatic proportions. There was surveying going on everywhere, I mean everywhere—federal officials drawing up park boundaries, mineral surveys, timber surveys. They came in by helicopter to the upper Kandik, not too far from our cabin, to do timber surveys. Everybody was making claims—Native Corporations, the state, the BLM, the Forest Service. It was a crazy time, and we were caught in the middle of it, unsure of what was going to happen to us and the way of life we'd chosen."

Roger Kaye, then a biological technician and land use planner with the U.S. Fish & Wildlife Service, was one of those federal officials with the unenviable task of traveling throughout the bush and arranging meetings to explain, as best he could, the coming regulations to bewildered trappers and villagers. He and his boss, Lou Swenson, barnstormed across the countryside, visiting seven villages in twenty days. "We did a conscientious job of trying to help them understand what was going to happen. There was a lot of misinformation out there." Lou Swenson, who later served as manager for the Yukon Flats

National Wildlife Refuge, adds, "The new regulations tried to maintain the status quo, and we tried to help people understand that. It was a completely new idea of refuge management. We didn't act like big bad government guys. Everything was authorized unless prohibited rather than the other way around. Refuge managers in the Lower Forty-eight would have heart attacks. But Alaska was a very different situation. People in the bush were relieved to find out that little had changed—they could still use snowmachines and dog teams, hunt, fish, cut wood, you name it."

Finally, years of rumor, innuendo, and provisional meetings came to an end, and the trappers, at long last, had a general idea of where they stood. In the waning days of the Ninety-sixth Congress, the "d-2" land reform was consummated with the Alaska National Interest Lands Conservation Act (ANILCA), and on December 2, 1980, President Carter signed it into law.

ANILCA placed 104 million acres, 28 percent of Alaska, under some form of federal protection, replacing the monuments with wildlife refuges, forests, wild and scenic rivers, and wilderness preservation systems. With a stroke of the pen, the nationwide preservation movement that was launched on behalf of the Alaskan wilderness was validated and rewarded. ANILCA more than doubled the size of the country's national parks and wildlife refuge lands and tripled its wilderness preserve acreage. *Living Wilderness* called it "the strongest, most daring conservation action . . . in American history." The Sierra Club called it "the last great first chance." *Time* magazine labeled it "a masterpiece of compromise."

This is not to say that conservationists were entirely satisfied. Many lamented the lack of restrictions in the 23.5 million-acre National Petroleum Reserve, adjacent to the Prudhoe Bay complex, which occupies more than one-half of Alaska's North Slope and was established in 1923 during the Harding administration, when the Navy switched from coal to oil. It was a strategy that seemed sound in 1923—set aside oil reserves to ensure national security—but conservationists argued that it was no longer practical in light of the country's enormous energy needs, which only Persian Gulf sources could satisfy. The decision to set aside Section 1002 (referred to as ten-oh-two)—a 1.5 million-acre chunk of Arctic coastal plain and the last section of Alaska's 1,000-plus miles of Arctic coast not reserved for development—for assessment of its oil and gas reserves was particularly galling to conservationists.

Conversely, many Alaskans—particularly politicians, businesspeople, and the Alaska congressional delegates—denounced ANILCA and the conveyance of de facto wilderness into the protective and restrictive hands of the federal government. It was a land grab, they contended, without precedent in U.S. history, a conspiracy hatched and orchestrated by Lower Forty-eight politicians, most of whom had never even been to the state.

From the moment he set foot in Alaska, Heimo had been living with an uncertainty about what would become of the land. Being a newcomer, and feeling powerless in the face of inevitable and cataclysmic changes set in motion by the discovery of oil and, subsequently, the building of the pipeline, he did the only thing available to him: He went about his life and hoped for the best.

What Heimo and other Alaska trappers eventually got was a 186-page document that articulated a less restrictive approach to wilderness management that was in keeping with Alaska's unique circumstances and that enabled Heimo and some of the trappers to remain on the land. ANILCA explicitly allowed for the continuation of subsistence practices by Alaska's rural residents in most of the national interest lands, including the expanded Arctic National Wildlife Refuge, where Heimo lived, acknowledging that those living in the Alaskan bush "may be the last remnant of the subsistence culture alive today in North America." It also granted rural residents the right to use snow machines, motorboats, and other methods of transportation that had "traditionally been employed . . . by local residents." Significantly, in a section titled "Use of cabins and other sites of occupancy on conservation system units," it articulated a limited tolerance for backwoods cabins. ANILCA clearly spelled out the National Park Service's policy: Those who built cabins on federal land after 1978 were out of luck; ANILCA made no accommodations for them; they would lose their cabins. Trappers who built before 1978, but after 1973, could apply each year for one-year permits; those who came before 1973 were ordered to renew their permits every five years. National Wildlife Refuge regulations were slightly more liberal. They granted renewable five-year permits to anyone who built his cabin before 1978, which meant that Heimo, had he deliberated longer about coming to the Coleen River, would have missed qualifying for permission to live in the Arctic National Wildlife Refuge. ANILCA further stipulated that permits could be tranferred only to the immediate family and were rendered null and void with the death of the "last immediate family member of the claimant residing in the cabin." Finally, applicants were required to acknowledge that they had no interest in the property on which the cabin stood.

When Heimo decided to go to Savoonga in the spring of 1981 and wrote it off to adventure only, he was not being entirely truthful with himself. He also went to celebrate. While in Fort Yukon for the holidays, he had heard the news about ANILCA. The details were vague, but for the first time since he came to the Coleen in June 1978, he was certain that he could come back and lead a life that was no longer imperiled by prohibitive legislation. He could keep his cabin and continue trapping as long as he abided by the permitting process. He didn't like the new regulations, but he was willing to do whatever was required of him for the chance to live out his dream. But more than anything else, he came to Savoonga because of the presence of a pretty girl by the name of Edna Rose.

Heimo met Edna Rose, or Miti Dowin (her Yupik name), for the first time in the winter of 1975. He saw her often after that. He was friends with her father, Emerson, and frequently stopped by the house to visit. He was also a friend of her uncle's, Jackson Mokiyuk. Jackson trapped fox, and it was he who taught Heimo how to prepare furs, how to make the proper cuts so as not to damage the fur, how to care for the fur once the animal had been skinned.

Edna was a year older than Heimo. She was attractive, there was no doubt about that, and available, too. But Heimo had promised himself that he would not get involved in a village romance. Savoonga was just too small. In such a small village, gossip was a kind of pastime, and

Heimo was determined not to fuel its fires. Although he hadn't come to Savoonga in search of a wife, Heimo had to admit—on the trapline, he was often lonely. And he hadn't had a girlfriend since high school. There'd been other women, but they were brief flirtations, not relationships. Wouldn't it be nice, he thought, to share the beauty of the river with someone he loved?

One of Heimo's favorite stories concerns an evening in the spring of 1978 when he was sitting with Emerson in the living room of Emerson's house. Heimo hadn't seen Edna since the previous spring, and when he arrived she was there. He tried to conceal his excitement, chatting with her as casually as he could. But he couldn't fool Emerson. When Edna left, Emerson went to the kitchen and returned. "Heimo," he said, "would you like something? Coffee maybe?" Heimo answered "No." "Tea?" Heimo answered "No" again. "Juice? Water?" Heimo shook his head. "A wife?" For a moment Heimo was taken aback. Then he chuckled. "Sure, how about Edna Rose?" "Edna Rose?" Emerson replied, "Not for ten million dollars."

Heimo didn't have more than a few hundred dollars to his name, much less $10 million, but he was interested. There were complications, however. There were children involved: Melinda and Merlin. For Heimo, who had been on his own since he came to Alaska, the thought of being with a woman he loved was exciting. But an instant family? He didn't know if he was ready for that. And then there was Emerson. Though Emerson was his friend, Emerson had witnessed Edna's difficult recovery after the death of her fiancé, only to see her treated poorly by a man who was incapable of fidelity. Heimo was his friend, but Emerson was determined not to let Edna be hurt again.

Heimo's first real chance to be alone with Edna didn't happen until the summer of 1981. Heimo needed a break from Fort Yukon, so he accepted an invitation from a friend to stay in Nome for the summer and do carpentry work.

These were still Heimo's drinking days, and Nome had more taverns per capita than any town in Alaska. One night Heimo was drinking at a bar called the Board of Trade, or the BOT. Many of its patrons affectionately translated BOT as "Bottom of the Toilet." The BOT was a rough, hard-drinking bar. Surely the last person Heimo expected to meet in there was the woman who would one day become his wife. But in June 1981 Edna strolled in, or rather hurried in. She saw Heimo sitting at the bar and ran to him. She told Heimo that a drunk had taken an interest in her at another bar and that she had slipped out, hoping he wouldn't notice.

Edna and Heimo talked that night at the bar. Heimo made her laugh and he was a good listener and Edna confided in him. She told him things that she had not talked with anyone else about. Walking her home that night, Heimo summoned the courage to finally—after all these years—ask her out, and Edna, with little deliberation, accepted.

There is already a distinct chill in the air though it is only late July. Last night the temperature dropped below freezing, and this morning we woke to discover an inch of snow on the ground, clinging to the fireweed and the kinnikinnick. Winter is preeminent here. Combined, spring, summer, and fall—when bush families like the Korths cut wood, lay in their winter meat, make repairs to the cabin, dig an extra outhouse hole, enjoy the sun, and mentally prepare themselves for the snow and cold to come—amount to nothing more than a four-month prelude to the long season of winter.

This day, I am walking to the high cache with Edna. She and Krin just flew in yesterday, a full week after Heimo, Rhonda, and I arrived. Edna takes a deep breath, filling her lungs with the scent of spruce and the air's cold bite. "Smells like home," she says. "It's good to be home." Edna tells me that she is always happy to leave the cabin in spring and go to Fort Yukon for the summer. But two months is enough for her. "By mid-July," she says, "I can't wait to get back out."

We are going to the high cache to get the generator because today is wash day, and Edna has piled five huge cloth bags filled with clothes around an ancient-looking Hoover washing machine, which sits in the middle of the cabin yard. The machine is a relatively new addition. For years Edna did all her wash with a washboard, and even though she must now haul two five-gallon buckets of water from the river for each load—she estimates that she has at least twelve loads—using the Hoover is easier than scrubbing clothes all day.

On the way to the cache, we walk by my little two-man Moss tent, which is set back in the woods about forty feet from the cabin yard, outside the perimeter of the solar-powered bear fence, which was given to Heimo by a friend. The friend is an ardent environmentalist, and Heimo jokes that he was less concerned for their safety than he was for the bears, since an all-purpose law allows the Korths to shoot a bear in defense of "life or property."

"Bear bait," Edna says, looking at the tent and my fly rod leaning against a tree. There has been a grizzly prowling around the cabin yard, and Edna jokes that she regards my tent as the first line of defense. Each afternoon, after the day's work, I've set off for the river, calling myself, much to Heimo's amusement, a "subsistence fisherman," in order to supply fresh, tasty Arctic grayling for our supper. Edna knows that there's nothing that attracts a grizzly like the smell of fish. Though I wash up in an ice-cold pool downriver every evening, it is a pro forma precaution. Soap or no, I'm bear bait when I crawl into my bag at night.

"If a griz comes, I'll be up a tree quick as Krin," I say, "and then I'll send him to the cabin."

"Yeah, right," Edna says, looking at the trees, knowing full well that I'm not agile enough to get up one before a grizzly makes a meal of me.

Walking back to the cache, Edna and I stop to fill a small plastic container with blueberries. It is kind of a halfhearted effort. Soon Edna, Krin, and Rhonda will head out to the tundra for a full day of berry picking for canning.

Hunched over a blueberry bush, I ask Edna, somewhat tentatively, about her first date with Heimo. Edna is a steadfastly private person, still mistrustful of my motives, and she usually recedes in response to my questions. But she seems glad to talk about their first date in Nome.

They went fishing for Dolly Varden, and when it became clear that the fish weren't going to bite, they spent the rest of the day wandering the trails outside of Nome on a friend's motorcycle. That evening they went out for pizza. "Milano's Pizza," she says, as if pleased that she still remembers the name. She also remembers the story she told Heimo that night about her father.

When Edna was a young girl, she had been sick and feverish for a week. One day, a woman came to the house to tell Edna's father, Emerson, of a dream she'd had the night before. In the woman's dream, Edna was lying on the ground with her chest open and her beating heart exposed. Three shamans circled Edna. When the woman asked the shamans what they were doing, they replied, "Take her. We cannot get to her soul." Shamans were still a very important part of Eskimo society, and when the woman finished telling Emerson of her dream, Emerson marched over to the shaman's house and threw a large rock onto his roof, as a warning to him not to be casting any spells on his daughter. The next day, Edna's fever dropped, and two days later she had fully recovered. Edna knew that Heimo would appreciate the story, because he knew her father as normally a kind, mild-mannered man. The image of Emerson tossing a rock onto the shaman's roof in a fit of anger, risking the shaman's retaliation, too, gave both Edna and Heimo a good laugh.

"What did you think of Heimo?" I ask, emboldened by Edna's lack of reserve. I ask the question casually, giving her the opportunity to ignore it if she chooses. Perhaps it is the calming effect of the soft morning sun and the snow dripping gently from the leaves of the cottonwoods, but she doesn't hesitate. "I liked him," she says, "but I always thought he was just a weird trapper who lived alone."

Edna stops then, checking herself, as if she is uncertain how much to reveal. I wait, and minutes go by, and neither of us says a word. "A weird trapper?" I say, breaking the silence at last. "But what did you think of him after your first date?"

Edna doesn't respond. She stands and walks in the direction of the cache. I follow her. She stops at the ladder to the cache and puts down her container of blueberries and ties her shoe. Without looking up, she says, "I thought he was the nicest guy I ever met."

CHAPTER 9

A Family of His Own

Heimo and I are sitting on a rock ledge overlooking the Coleen River valley after a half day of hiking. It is early afternoon and only now is the fog, which has hung over the valley since yesterday evening, beginning to rise. Heimo is glassing east, hoping to spot a bull moose wandering in the dense white and black spruce thickets along the river. He glasses continuously, carrying on a narrative in a whisper. Although a moose's big ears make it look like a Maurice Sendak creation in *Where the Wild Things Are*, the oversized ears are what allows it to escape the stew pot. So we whisper.

"Not for ten million dollars," Heimo imitates Emerson, Edna's father, and chuckles softly. "No amount of money could pay for what Edna means to me. But every time I think of that—ten million dollars—it makes me laugh, because eventually all it took was twenty-five grayling, some moose meat, half a moose stomach, and a wolverine skin." That's what Heimo brought with him from the river and presented to Emerson when he and Edna returned to Savoonga in January 1982 for their wedding.

Heimo explains that by the summer of 1981, when he and Edna were dating in Nome, word made it to Savoonga that he had asked Edna to marry him, and Emerson, fortunately, had already had a change of heart. While Heimo was working up the courage to ask Emerson for Edna's hand, Emerson took the initiative and called him.

Heimo puts down his binoculars for a moment and laughs out loud. "'That's good, Heimo,'" he says, impersonating Emerson on that day. "'I like you. My boys like you. That's good. My wife like you.'" It was Emerson's way of saying that he knew Heimo would take good care of his daughter.

After spending the summer of 1981 with Edna in Nome, Heimo returned to Fort Yukon. But this time he was not alone. He had Edna on his arm, and her daughter Millie, too. Merlin, Edna's son, stayed with Edna's parents in Savoonga. After a week of visiting with friends, Heimo, Edna, and Millie left Fort Yukon for the cabin. For much of the flight, they were over the expansive, flat, pond-pocked wilderness of the Yukon Flats. But as they neared the Stranglewoman Mountains, Edna saw the land change. To the north was mountain country, and for the first time she understood why the Natives of Fort Yukon said that Heimo lived "above the clouds."

An hour after taking off from Fort Yukon, the pilot landed on a gravel bar not far from the river. Heimo held Millie's hand and stayed by their gear while Edna walked along the bank of the river. Admiring the Stranglewoman Mountains to the southeast and the rugged peaks of the Brooks Range to the north, Edna felt an exhilaration she had not experienced in many years. The Coleen River—it would be a new beginning for her, and for Millie, too. Millie pulled away from Heimo, but she didn't run down the gravel bar to be with Edna; she ran twenty feet into the woods. Millie laughed and giggled and danced around the trunks of two large white spruce trees. When Millie left Nome that summer, she had never even seen a tree before. Now, along the river, she was surrounded by them. There were trees so high she had to lie on her back to see the tops.

Heimo kept his eye on Millie, but he watched the river, too. Though it was already late August, it had been a wet summer in the Interior, and the river was high, uncrossable. Three years before, with his brother Tom, he had made the mistake of trying to cross the river at high water. It was not a risk he was willing to take again. In those three years, he had learned one cardinal rule—never take unnecessary chances. In the Arctic, good judgment is often the dividing line between life and death. So instead of trying to make it to the cabin, he, Edna, and Millie bided their time and camped along the river's east bank, within shouting distance of the cabin. For five days they hunted, gathered berries, explored, and chopped wood.

Despite having grown up around guns, Edna was new to hunting. She was the second oldest of five children, and as a youngster her father had taught her how to shoot—first a pellet gun and then a .22—and she had caught on quickly. By her midteens she was eager to hunt with her dad, but she knew that was impossible. She was as good a shot as any boy in Savoonga, but on St. Lawrence Island women were not allowed to hunt. It was considered bad luck and strictly forbidden.

With Heimo, there were no such restrictions, however. Edna was free to hunt; in fact, Heimo encouraged her. There were three mouths to feed now, and if he could depend on her to shoot a caribou or a moose, that was all the better.

By their second night on the river, Edna got her chance to show Heimo that she was a capable shot. Millie was already asleep in the tent, and Heimo and Edna had just finished washing up in the river. They were sitting around the fire, talking about what their lives would be like together, when Heimo heard a branch crack. Grizzly, he thought, and grabbed his gun. A minute later six caribou stepped out of the woods—four cows and two bulls. Heimo handed the .22 to Edna. "Take the back one," he said. "The big bull." It was still light out, so Edna took aim. She shot twice at eighty yards and the bull fell on the second shot. The caribou scattered. Three cows ran back into the woods, while the remaining bull and the fourth cow ran upriver. After thirty yards, they stopped, and that's when Heimo pulled the trigger on his 300 Winchester rifle and dropped the bull where he stood.

Edna ran upriver and stood over the animal she had shot. She had killed a caribou! Hardly a man on St. Lawrence Island, let alone a woman, had ever shot a caribou. It was nearly midnight when Heimo and Edna finshed gutting and cutting up the bulls. Edna was covered in blood up to her elbows. She had grown up cleaning fish and the birds her father hunted, and one thing Heimo never had to show her was how to use a knife.

The following day, Heimo began Edna's bush education. The first thing he was going to do was to teach her how to use an ax. Because there were no trees on St. Lawrence Island, it had never been something she needed to know, but on the Coleen the ability to use an ax was an absolutely essential skill.

Heimo showed Edna the correct stance and how to grip the ax and slide her hand down the handle when she swung. Then he lay a thick log in the moss for her to practice on. At first, Edna swung the ax wildly. But she was determined. Heimo could see it—her aggressive posture, the ferocious expression, the horrible grunting. "Whoa, Edna, calm down. You don't have to kill it," he cautioned her, holding six-year-old Millie and standing back at a safe distance, trying to suppress his laughter for fear of making Edna self-conscious. "Take it easy, Edna. You're going to wear yourself out, if you don't kill yourself first." Edna just rolled up her sleeves, wiped her forehead, glared at him, and swung the ax even more fiercely.

It wasn't long before Edna was using the ax with a precison that impressed Heimo, so they moved on to the next step—splitting wood. Edna had good hand–eye coordination, and learned quickly. After a morning of instruction, she was splitting wood like a regular woodswoman. She loved the feeling of the ax in her hand, but mostly she loved the smell of the wood. At first, each time she'd split a log, she'd pick it up and hold it to her nose. Only then would she let Millie, who proved to be an eager helper, add the log to their growing pile.

Nearly a week after arriving on the Coleen, they walked a few hundred yards upriver and found a spot where the current had slowed and the river bottom was shallow and knitted with gravel bars, and they crossed. Heimo led, holding Millie on his shoulders, and Edna followed him. When they reached the opposite bank, Heimo pointed to a tall stand of white spruce trees a quarter of a mile off the river. "That's home," he said. Edna and Millie led now, following the trail into the woods. Millie spotted the cabin first, one hundred yards down the trail. There it was. She pulled Edna by the hand.

Before either of them went inside the cabin, Edna, still holding Millie's hand, walked around the cabin yard. The yard was dark, shadowed by high trees. Where is the sky? Edna thought, and mentally she marked the dead trees that she was going to take down. When Edna saw the woodpile though, she was disappointed. Heimo had already laid in most of the winter's wood the previous spring. No matter. Edna announced that she and Millie would take down the trees, cut and stack the wood themselves, whether they needed it or not. "I want to be able to see the sky," she said, homesick for the treeless spaciousness of St. Lawrence Island.

It is early August, and it has been five days since Edna and Krin arrived back on the river, and Edna and I are sitting by the fire among the circle of chairs and benches they call their summer kitchen. There is a slight chill in the air, but the fire is not for our warmth—Edna keeps it going to drive away the opportunistic mosquitoes. Rhonda and Krin have gone to fetch water, and Heimo is a quarter mile downriver, using his spotting scope to see if the caribou are coming. For days, he has talked of little else. He watches Mummuck Mountain almost compulsively now, like a farmer studying the sky and waiting for rain, as if perhaps he can will the caribou to come.

Edna is dressed up. She wears a colorful flannel shirt and long feathery, Navaho-like earrings. Her hair is pulled tight against her head like a ballet dancer's and plaited into a long, silky braid, which brushes against her lower back when she pokes at the coals of the fire. The Korths are expecting company, three friends from Connecticut, who are supposed to come in this evening by bush plane. Years ago Heimo and Edna had helped them and their friends out of a tough spot, when a bush pilot infamous for taking poor care of his clients dropped them off on a lake two miles from the river. It wouldn't have been so bad, except for the fact that the three friends and the rest of their group were hoping to paddle the river. They had several tons of gear, canoes, food, and other provisions, and had anticipated being dropped off much closer. Heimo had gone to investigate when he heard the plane and discovered them out on the tundra wondering what their next move would be. He showed them a shortcut to the river and helped them haul their gear. Edna prepared grayling for the group of twelve.

Edna is particularly excited about their arrival because one of the three guests is a woman. It's rare that a woman comes out. Edna plans to take her berry picking on the tundra. She puts another log on the fire, holding it far away from her body so she doesn't get dirty. "You should have seen it," she says, leaning back in her chair.

"What?" I ask her.

"His cabin," she says, looking at me as if I haven't been following the conversation. "When I first saw it, I thought, What in the world are Millie and me getting ourselves into? I won't live like this. It wasn't exactly a woman's dream, you know." Edna laughs about it now, an easy, cheerful laugh.

The cabin was twelve by ten, with a tiny peephole window and a ceiling so low that Edna could hardly stand up straight without bumping her head. If the trees made her claustrophobic, the cabin was far worse. It made her feel like she was trapped under the ice, like all the air had been sucked from her lungs.

When Edna and Millie went inside the cabin, Heimo remained outside, pretending to sharpen his knife. This was the part he had been dreading. When Edna and Millie came out of the cabin, he saw their faces and knew immediately. "Raise the roof," Edna said. Heimo was so embarrassed by the cabin, he didn't argue. He would not only raise the roof, he'd put in a sleeping loft, too. He had to work fast though—they were sleeping in the tent temporarily, and it was already early September. It would get cold soon, and Edna and Millie had never experienced temperatures like those they would see on the Coleen.

If ever there were a woman cut out for the bush, it was Edna. Edna had spent much of her childhood in harsh conditions; the weather on St. Lawrence Island is gray and wet for much of the year, enough to defeat even the hardiest of souls. And Edna was used to cramped, spartan conditions. Every November, her father would load up his sled and ready his fifteen-dog team, and the family would make the thirty-mile trip to their fox camp. They'd spend much of the winter and spring there, returning to Savoonga in May.

But life on the Coleen would test her. Normally, for an Eskimo, whose world revolves around the extended family, living in such isolation—the Korths' nearest neighbor lived fifty-five miles down-river—would be out of the question. In Eskimo society, family bonds are valued above all else. Solitude is a sign of unhappiness, estrangement. After Edna made the leap of faith, though, and agreed to join Heimo on the river, she was determined to adjust and to learn to love the Coleen as much as she loved her "weird trapper."

Beginning in late September, a week after the first snow of the season, Edna and Millie tended a snowshoe hare snare line, which Heimo had laid out in a small loop leading from and back to the cabin. With her father Edna had learned to trap white fox, using longspring traps with a pan held by a dog, which released the trap's jaws, but on the Coleen wire snares were more effective, and Heimo showed Edna and Millie how to make and set them.

It was good for Edna and Millie to have time alone on the snare line. At six, Millie had already suffered enough. She had grown up without a father, and now she missed the only home she had ever known—Savoonga. On the snare line, Edna and Millie talked of Savoonga and how they missed eating seal meat and *mungtuk*. They also practiced identifying the tracks they found in the snow—the pointed pods of a cow moose, the four-toed pad of a wolf, the large, round tracks of a lynx, the elongated pad of a porcupine. They made a game of it, seeing which one of them could see and name a track the quickest. Sometimes Heimo would join them and quiz them, pointing out the distinguishing characteristics of each print. Only when Edna and Millie discovered the huge, pigeon-toed tracks of a roaming grizzly with its pronounced claws did Heimo's warning always to be on guard against grizzlies seem real—too real.

By early October, nearly six weeks after her arrival, Edna had also made another discovery—she was pregnant. She had intuited it weeks before, but now she was certain. One day in early October, after walking her line, while Heimo and Millie stayed at the cabin boiling new snares in spruce boughs to rid them of their scent, she returned to the cabin and told them both. Heimo whooped with joy. They were going to have a baby! He picked Edna up and swung her around, then realized what he was doing, and set her back down as carefully as he could. Millie didn't react. Later that night Edna promised Millie that she'd be happier when she had a sister or brother to play with.

In addition to adapting to their new surroundings, Edna and Millie also had to adjust to the Interior's cold, and to autumn's advancing darkness. One day in early November, Heimo noticed a pronounced ring around the sun, a luminously colored sun dog, and he knew then that even colder weather was coming soon. Sure enough, on the following day, a north wind off the Arctic sent temperatures to minus 35 degrees. Edna and Millie had never experienced 35 below before. Edna developed headaches, brought on by the intensely cold, dry air. Heimo checked his traps—he was used to 35 below—but other than tending to their snare line, Edna and Millie didn't wander far from the cabin. At night, to alleviate her headaches, Edna set pots filled with ice on the woodstove and breathed in the steam.

That December, their first together as a family, Edna and Millie were ready for a break. But they had no plans to go to town. Heimo had been hoping for a good fur year, but after an outstanding 1980-1981 season, his fur take by Christmas amounted to only thirty-five marten, and much of that money was needed for supplies. What money he had left over from the previous season they'd already set aside to pay for plane tickets to Savoonga for their January wedding and for wedding expenses.

One night, while Millie was asleep and Heimo was washing up after skinning out a marten, Heimo suggested turning on KJNP. "We can sit in bed and listen to *Trapline Chatter*," he said.

"Always KJNP," Edna grumbled. They hadn't gotten a message in over a month. Didn't anyone care that they were out there?

Heimo and Edna listened to twenty-five messages. "No more," Edna said, and reached to turn off the radio. She flicked the switch, and Heimo flipped it right back on. Edna turned over, her back to Heimo.

Then she heard it: "This message goes out to the Korths on the Coleen River. We're sending out a plane to bring you into town for Christmas." The announcer read the rest of the message, and when she finished, Edna was bouncing up and down at the edge of the bed. "We're going to town! I can't believe it! We're going to town!"

When their friend and bush pilot John Peterson showed up three days later, he handed Edna an envelope. Edna studied it.

"C'mon, open it up," Peterson said.

Edna tore the envelope and pulled out the letter. It was a petition signed by their friends in Fort Yukon, demanding they come into town for Christmas.

Heimo looked at the letter. "We got no money."

No big deal Peterson told him. The flight had been paid for, and their friends had already bought presents for Millie, too.

It is late July and Heimo and I are cleaning Arctic grayling on a gravel bar just downriver from the cabin. Only seconds, it seems, after I slit open the belly of the first fish, the gulls appear. "I guess they know me by now," I say to Heimo, half convinced the gulls have learned to recognize me. For the past week, I have fished daily, trying my luck in nearly every pool within two miles of the cabin. The river hasn't disappointed me. For each fish I keep I throw one or two back. For an entire afternoon, I won't see a single gull. Yet as soon I leave the water and grab my willow stick through which I've threaded the graylings' gills, they suddenly appear, like a dog that crawls out from under the back porch when it hears the rattle of its food dish. When I crouch down and cut into the first fish, they cruise overhead—mew gulls and herring gulls—115 miles from the Arctic Ocean, screeching and squacking impatiently for their next meal.

I finish cleaning the fish and grab the largest of the bunch. "Look at this one," I say, holding up a twenty-two-inch lunker, feeling inordinately proud of myself. I hold it by the belly and pull the dorsal fin, which fans out like that of a minitaure sailfish. Up close, the fish is goggle-eyed but pretty, its gunmetal gray splashed with variations of green and blue. Heimo doesn't even look up. He knows that catching ravenous grayling, even with a fly, is hardly an angler's feat. Besides, after a summer of gill-netting twenty-pound king salmon, he is unimpressed with my haul.

"It's gonna taste good tonight," I say.

"Yuck," Heimo replies. After almost three decades of eating grayling, he no longer is fond of them and will eat them only in a pinch. His favorite fish is the salmon, whose pink meat he thinks is far superior to the white meat of grayling.

Rain falls as Heimo puts the finishing touches on the final grayling. Until yesterday it has been a dry month marked by sun and brilliantly blue skies, though August is usually the rainy season up here. "This is what Savoonga's like every day," Heimo says. "Cloudy and rainy. But the Arctic's a desert. You know that, don't you? We get fifteen inches of precipitation a year up here, less than Arizona. But in Savoonga, this is what you get day in, day out. The Interior is to Savoonga what San Diego is to Seattle." Heimo stops for a moment, considering the analogy he's just made, and then he makes a small correction. "That's true," he laughs. "Unless you're talking about December and January, when the sun never clears the horizon around here."

Except for its weather, Heimo has fond memories of Savoonga. It is, after all, where he met Edna. It is also where he was married—January 25, 1982. It was Edna's birthday, her twenty-seventh. The wedding was at the Presbyterian Church. Since Edna is related to almost everyone in Savoonga, much of the village was there for the ceremony. The Reverend Alice Green performed the wedding. Green had come to the island in the late 1930s. The saying in Savoonga was that she "baptized, married, and buried." After over forty years of service to the church and the village, she planned to retire. Edna and Heimo's wedding would be her last.

Edna wore her hair loose down to her waist, and she wore a light blue wedding gown that she and Heimo had chosen together at J.C. Penney in Fairbanks. Heimo sported a fresh haircut and a light blue suit to match Edna's gown; he hadn't worn a suit since he was sixteen. The pants and the dress shirt made him itch, though, and his face itched, too. Edna wouldn't allow him to get married in a beard, so he'd shaved that morning. All that remained of his foot-deep field of a beard was bushy sideburns that—wedding or not—he refused to part with.

After six years alone in the bush, all the attention on his wedding day made Heimo feel like escaping to the ice pack and hiding behind a pressure ridge. He was in love with Edna—there was no doubt about that—but if it had been up to him, they would have simply exchanged their vows privately and quickly, and that would have been the end of it. After the ceremony, he would have thrown his suit in a pile on the floor and gone out walrus hunting with Herman on the ice floes. Instead he was standing in front of a crowd of people, dreaming, to calm his nerves, of setting fox traps. He was so anxious he needed to be prompted by Reverend Green to say, "I will," and then when it came time for the kiss, still flustered, he forgot to lift Edna's veil. The guests erupted into gales of laughter, and Heimo blushed like a bashful young boy. After the kiss Edna held her hand over her mouth to keep from laughing, too.

Just over four months after their wedding, Coleen Ann Korth, whom Edna and Heimo named after the Coleen River, was born in Fairbanks—May 29, 1982. By mid-July, they were back on the river, and Heimo immediately began to work on a new cabin. The four of them—Heimo, Edna, Millie, and now Coleen, too—would need more space than what the little cabin could provide. First, Heimo laid out the cabin's dimensions—sixteen feet by sixteen feet. Then he cut the trees. It was hard building alone. Edna helped when she could. While Edna was working with Heimo, Millie held Coleen in her arms when the baby slept and rocked her when she cried.

During the first few weeks, Edna often took the girls to the river to a nearby gravel bar to avoid the mosquitoes. It had been a dry summer, and the river was low, so they were able to wade comfortably to an expansive bar twenty feet from the riverbank. On the gravel bar, Edna lay down a blanket, and together she and the girls enjoyed the breeze and the gurgling of the river. Sometimes while Coleen and Millie slept, Edna daydreamed. The last six years of her life had been difficult—first the death of her fiancé and later the discovery that her boyfriend and the father of her son, Merlin, was an incorrigible womanizer. Edna had hit a dead end. But on the Coleen, she dared to dream again. She was in love with a generous, responsible man. They would raise a family together. They would live simply. It would be a hard life, but the girls would grow up happy. Millie and Coleen would learn to be comfortable in the woods, to fish and hunt, to identify birds and gather berries, to paddle a canoe, snowshoe, ski, and perhaps trap, too. Though Edna had only stayed in school until the tenth grade, she and Heimo were determined to give Millie and Coleen a good education. The girls would get even more attention than children in Fairbanks did. Edna would oversee their studies. She knew she was smart; she picked up things quickly, and what she lacked in formal education, she would make up for through sheer effort. If need be, she would learn herself, and she would teach the girls, as best she could. A good life.

One day, while sitting with the girls on the gravel bar, Edna felt a searing stab of pain. She had just finished demonstrating for Millie the coarse whistle of a gray jay when it hit her. The pain dug at her abdomen and left her gasping. She tried to ignore it, but when it returned, thirty minutes later, she couldn't. This time it lasted for nearly a minute. She had to lay Coleen down on the blanket because she didn't have the strength to hold her. When it subsided, she took the girls back to the tent and described the symptoms to Heimo. They both hoped it was a freak pain and that it would soon disappear, but instead the pain grew progressively worse over the next few days. The sharp stabs were accompanied now by a dull but nearly constant ache.

Two weeks later, John Peterson, the Korths' friend, who was now running a big game guiding and hunting operation along one of the rivers to the north in the Brooks Range, stopped in for a brief visit en route to his hunting camp. Heimo heard his plane and hiked out to meet him at the nearest gravel bar, where he'd landed, three miles downriver. "Thank God you stopped," Heimo said. "Edna's sick, and I'm worried about her." Peterson had to deliver supplies to his hunting camp, but he promised to stop in again in two days on his way back to Fort Yukon. In those two days, Edna's condition deteriorated. Her skin turned yellow with jaundice. Even the whites of her eyes were yellow. Worst of all, she couldn't eat and could hardly get out of bed.

Two days later, Peterson landed downriver. Edna told Heimo that she couldn't make it; there was no way she could walk that far. Heimo was frightened now and his response was more strident than he intended. "You got no choice," he told her.

It took Edna three hours to cover the three miles. Heimo carried Coleen and provided a shoulder for Edna to lean on, and Millie walked on her own. A mile from the gravel bar, Edna had to stop to feed Coleen, who was wailing with hunger. When they finally made it to the plane, Edna nearly collapsed. Heimo had to lift her into the seat. Then there was Coleen. What were they going to do about Coleen? There was no other way; Edna would have to take Coleen with her, and Millie would stay at the cabin with Heimo.

Peterson flew Edna and Coleen to Fort Yukon and then rushed her to the clinic, where they diagnosed her condition as cirrhosis of the liver. The nurses there had seen so many alcohol-related illnesses that they never considered it might be anything else. Edna insisted that she was not a drinker, and only then did the nurses call the Fairbanks hospital to consult with a physician. When the nurse described the symptoms, the doctor knew immediately—a gallbladder attack. Get her to Fairbanks on the next plane, he demanded, or she might die. Arrangements were made to leave Coleen with a friend in Fort Yukon. When Edna arrived at Fort Yukon's tiny airport, the daily commuter plane to Fairbanks was taxiing down the runway. They radioed the pilot and made him turn around. Edna arrived in Fairbanks at 7:00 P.M. that evening and was rushed to the operating room. Two hours later, she was recuperating from surgery. The doctors had performed an emergency gallbladder operation, an operation that saved her life.

By the time Edna and Coleen returned to the river two weeks later, Heimo had the new cabin finished. It was big but crudely and hurriedly built. With fall coming on, there was a real possibility of snow, and Heimo did not have time to lay in a floor. Edna lay spruce boughs over the dirt floor, for warmth and to contain the dust. But there was nothing she could do about the lack of light in the cabin. Inside it was dark and gloomy because Heimo had not had time to peel the logs.

For Coleen's first birthday, Heimo and Edna threw a big party. It was late May and they'd just left the river. They'd spent a few days in Fort

Yukon, but were now in Fairbanks, renting a cabin without indoor plumbing. Heimo was peeling logs for the summer for a builder, hoping to earn enough money to buy supplies for the upcoming trapping season. Many of their friends showed up for the birthday celebration, and Erich and Irene Korth came, too.

Heimo picked up his parents at the airport in an old broken-down car he'd bought for the summer. When Heimo saw his mother pushed off the plane in a wheelchair, he was struck by her appearance—how dramatically her health had declined. It had been just one year since Heimo and Edna were in Wisconsin. As a wedding present Irene Korth had bought them the plane tickets. Though she had already been diagnosed with cancer, she was full of life and energy, on her feet for much of the day, cooking big meals, doing household chores, and dispensing an abundance of affection. "She loved Edna and me up," Hemo remembers. Now, though, she was gaunt and frail. She and Erich had been to the Mayo Clinic in Rochester, Minnesota, but the cancer, which began in the pancreas, had metastasized to the liver. Irene's skin now had the shiny yellow hue of jaundice, as Edna's had when she'd had the gallbladder attack. Quietly, while they waited for their bags, Erich Korth told Heimo how sick Irene had been. Publicly she expressed hope that she'd recover, but privately Irene confessed to her husband that she knew it was only a matter of time. The pain was almost constant now, Erich said, and as a last resort Irene had been to see a faith healer.

Irene's final wish, before she died, was to see her granddaughter, Coleen. It was a happy visit, marred only by what happened two days before Erich and Irene were scheduled to return home.

Heimo, Edna, and Erich Korth were out hauling water; Irene wanted to spend as much time as she could with her granddaughters and insisted on staying behind to watch Coleen and Millie. It was a dry summer all over the Interior, and lightning had sparked a number of fires nearby. Fairbanks skies hung heavy with smoke. The Bureau of Land Management was using World War II bombers to spread retardant. When Irene saw the bombers fly overhead, she panicked. With Coleen in her arms, and holding Millie by the hand, she fled the cabin and ran down to the main road. She was wandering along the road, as cars sped by her, babbling incoherently, when Heimo, Edna, and Erich found her. They were being bombed, she howled, just like during the war, and they needed to find a place to hide.

The planes were all too reminiscent of the war. Irene was born in 1929 in Hausen, Germany, fifteen miles south of Frankfurt. While her brother was sent to the Russian front, where he later died, and her father was forced into military service, she and her mother and three sisters spent much of World War II in a bomb shelter, hiding from the savage one-two punch of the British and American air campaign. It was an experience she never forgot.

Edna took Coleen in her arms and pulled Millie against her leg, and Heimo comforted his mother, embracing her until her trembling stopped. "It's nothing, Mom," he repeated again and again. "We're okay. We're going to be okay."

A day later, when Heimo took them to the airport, Irene Korth admitted that she was embarrassed by the incident. She didn't know what had come over her. When Heimo hugged her good-bye, he knew that he would never see her again. She had always supported his decisions, even if they had puzzled her. He would miss his ally, but his greatest regret was that Coleen would grow up without having known her.

Before leaving Fairbanks for the trapline, Heimo traded his car to a friend in exchange for a seventeen-foot canoe. The canoe represented an important step in the Korths' lives. Just transporting their gear and supplies to the cabin had always been a two- or even a three-day chore. Now, if they landed upriver, they could load the canoe with supplies and float down. If they landed below the cabin, they could line up. It would also make transporting meat less of an ordeal. When Heimo shot a caribou or, worse, a moose, he had to carry all the meat back to the cabin before he could hang it. It was grueling, backbreaking work.

After a brief stopover in Fort Yukon, Heimo arrived at the cabin in late July in poor spirits. He had called his mother one last time before he left Fort Yukon, and she'd resisted, hanging up. "Bye, Mom," he said, "I gotta go. I really gotta go. I love you." Both of them knew they would never talk to each other again.

Five days later, Heimo waited for the Arctic Circle airplane that would bring in Edna and Coleen. Millie had already flown back to Savoonga with a family friend to be with Edna's parents. When Edna and Coleen didn't arrive, Heimo worried. Was it weather, mechanical problems? What he didn't know was that Edna and Coleen and the pilot had to make an emergency landing on a gravel bar one hundred miles downriver on the Porcupine.

An hour into the flight, the pilot broke the bad news to Edna. The plane's throttle was stuck, he said. We'll have to land. "What?" Edna asked, adjusting her headset. "What?" she raised her voice. "We have to land—now!" the pilot answered. "Hold on and don't let go." Edna held Coleen as tightly as she could, hugging her to her chest and locking her fingers. Then she looked out the window. The pilot was descending quickly. "Please, God, don't let us crash." She kissed Coleen. When she looked out the window again she spotted the gravel bar. She pulled Coleen close, and leaned back and braced her feet against the bottom of the pilot's seat. When the plane hit with a loud "thunk," the pilot instantly cut the engine. Edna looked out the window. Would the bar be long enough? Then she closed her eyes. "Huhhhhh," she heard over her headset, a long expulsion of air. Only then did she dare to look out the window. The pilot had brought the plane to a stop just before the river. Edna's leg muscles quivered.

The pilot didn't waste any time radioing for help. Ten minutes later, it started to rain. A bit colder, Edna knew, and the rain would swiftly turn to snow. She was determined not to wait in the plane and freeze, so she put Coleen in her backpack and pulled its drawstring so that only Coleen's head was showing and left the plane. Then she gathered wood and kindling for a fire. For three hours, she and Coleen and the pilot huddled around the fire to stay warm before they were rescued. That evening, back in Fort Yukon, Edna sent Heimo a *Trapline Chatter*, alerting him that she and Coleen were okay.

The following day, after an uneventful flight, Edna and Coleen made it to the cabin. They were there for only two days when Heimo decided to line the canoe upriver to check out a second cabin site, which he had already cleared with the U.S. Fish & Wildlife Service in Fairbanks. Over the summer, after examining the records of his fur take since arriving on the river, Heimo came to the conclusion that he was trapping out the local fur-bearing population. He was especially concerned about the marten and the beaver, which, unlike the wolf, wolverine, lynx, and fox, had small ranges, and were more susceptible to trapping pressure. His marten take revealed an undeniable trend: 66 marten for the winter of 1978-1979; 105 marten in 1979-1980; 121 marten in 1980-1981; 59 marten in 1981-1982; and 35 marten in 1982-1983. New country was the only solution, so he'd gone to the U.S. Fish & Wildlife office and proposed the idea and was given the go-ahead.

Heimo loaded the canoe with food, a lantern, sleeping bags, a tent, a shotgun with slugs for bears, and his 22.250 in case they came across caribou. Heimo lined the boat upriver, while Edna walked along the bank with Coleen on her shoulders. Coleen loved to be *umuck*ed, the Siberian Yupik word for toting someone on your shoulders. She loved the vantage point and waved to Heimo from the riverbank. Heimo waved back and occasionally shouted, "I love you, Guroy," their affectionate nickname for Coleen. After the way she'd devoured her cake at her birthday party, they started calling her "Guroy," a Yupik word that translated to something like "Little Piggy."

Four miles upriver, near the mouth of Marten Creek, Heimo shot a caribou, so they set up camp and hung and dried the meat. He shot two geese that evening and roasted them over an open fire. After three days, they continued their journey. When they reached the spot that he and the Fish & Wildlife official had plotted on the map, he was thrilled. The location was ideal—lots of good timber in which to hide his cabin, dead trees for firewood, high ground, and what looked to be a year-round spring. They overnighted at the future cabin site, and the following day they floated down to the lower cabin, where Heimo began working on the floor. He'd brought in some plywood, vowing that he would not allow his family to spend another year with a dirt floor. Covered by spruce branches, the dirt floor was cold in winter and muddy in spring. There were needles and dust everywhere. Heimo had signed on with Keith Koontz again that August to guide hunters, so he had to work fast. He did not like the idea of leaving Edna and Coleen alone, but he had no choice; 1982-1983 had been a poor fur year and guiding was good money.

Three weeks later, Heimo returned from hunting camp. Coleen was fifteen and a half months old now, and she had inherited her father's love of walking. Edna told Heimo how she and Coleen had hiked up and down the river, and Heimo could see how proud Edna was. When Coleen came to hug him, Heimo noticed that Edna had tied bells to her coat. "What's that for?" he asked her, and Edna explained that Coleen was a born explorer like her father. "She loves to get away from me and go off on her own," she told him. "Once I thought I lost her. I found her by the banks of the river. It really scared me. She could have fell in so easily. After that I tied bells to her coat so I always knew where she was."

That evening the moon was nearly full and Edna, Heimo, and Coleen went for a walk along the river. Heimo *umuck*ed Coleen, and from his shoulders, she cried out and pointed to the moon, "Moo, moo."

The winter of 1983–1984 began mildly with very little snow and temperatures that rarely dropped lower than 10 below. By January, however, the warm spell abruptly ended. On January 7, Heimo loaded wood into the woodstove and then went outside to check the weather. His breath crackled in the dry air; the tops of the trees hardly moved at all. No wind, Heimo thought—a sure sign that it was bitterly cold. The thermometer, attached to the black spruce tree just outside the cabin door, read 55 below. Heimo returned to the cabin, deciding that it was too cold to check his lines; 55 below—it wouldn't last. But he was wrong. The weather didn't break until January 23, when warm southerly winds whispered in, ending the cold's frigid grip over the southern foothills of the Brooks Range. Then, in early February, the weather changed again. Temperatures locked in at minus 35 and didn't budge for more than three weeks.

To make matters worse, a bush pilot had stopped in to deliver word that Heimo's mother had died in December. Though he had known that previous summer that her death was imminent, Heimo was hit hard by the news.

That winter Heimo had his worst trapping season since the early days on the middle fork of the Chandalar River. By spring, he had only managed to catch fifteen marten. Because the snowshoe hare population was down, lynx were scarce, too. Even wolves, which were normally plentiful along the Coleen, were hard to find; Heimo caught only two. Only wolverines, of which Heimo got six, saved his year from being a disaster. Nevertheless, after two poor seasons in a row, Heimo knew that he and Edna would have to make a change. He did the math and figured out that they would have barely enough for supplies for the following season, particularly after the plane tickets. In April, before breakup, Edna and Coleen were flying out to bring Millie back from Savoonga. Heimo asked Edna to leave Coleen with him, but Edna knew that Coleen would just be in Heimo's way. Besides, Edna said, Coleen needed to get out. None of them had seen another human being since the previous July.

Before she and Coleen left the river, Heimo and Edna finalized their plans to spend the next season upriver.

On April 8, just before Edna and Coleen flew out, Heimo wrote his friend Jim Kryzmarcik from Wisconsin.

> Jimmer,
>
> It is now April 8th and we are at the trapline cabin. We will be moving upriver about 20 miles to build a new cabin, more fur up there. I brought the boat up there dragging it behind the snowmachine a couple weeks ago. I set up the tent and stove at the same time. Edna and the kids will be up there in about a week. . . . Well this winter has been the poorest trapping season I had on the river.

Heimo included a ptarmigan feather with the letter.

While Edna and Coleen were gone, Heimo hauled up the canoe and supplies by snowmachine and began cutting trees for a new cabin. On April 21, a day later than Heimo expected them, Edna, Millie, and Coleen made it in. Spring was late and the snow was still a foot deep, so the pilot had an easy time finding a gravel bar to land on. Heimo picked up Edna and the girls with the snowmachine and ferried them back to the tent camp.

Far from being a hardship, living in their temporary tent camp was idyllic. At night they spread a sleeping bag over a bed of spruce boughs and slept under caribou skins. Coleen lay between Heimo and Edna, and Millie snuggled against Edna's back for comfort and warmth. Edna was glad to be back home.

Edna and I have gone to the river to haul the last two buckets of water. After a full day of washing clothes, Edna has only one more load to do. The sky is a faded, almost fragile blue, and we stop to watch two birds soar among the wisps of clouds. One has a tremendous wingspan. The other is smaller, with narrow, bent, streamlined wings. "Golden eagle," Edna says, "and an osprey."

I have been accompanying Edna for a portion of the afternoon. She has been unusually talkative—lighthearted, even—perhaps because the burden of doing laundry has finally been lifted from her shoulders. The cabin yard is a web of impromptu clotheslines, rigged for the occasion, but that doesn't matter; Edna is nearly done. The relief is evident in the way she moves. She jumps a small channel of water between the gravel bars. For a moment she reminds me of Krin.

Edna plunges her bucket into the river and sets it down on the gravel bar. Earlier she'd been telling me about Savoonga, about her father's fox camp, and she picks up now as if the narrative thread had never been interrupted. "When I was young," Edna remembers, "there were stories, always stories. My little friends and me used to go to an old woman's house to hear them. She'd tell us stories and she'd fall asleep—she was very old—and we'd nudge her awake. Now they have TV, and things have changed."

"Gotta rest my legs," she explains, sitting down next to me. She picks up a rock and tries to skip it from a sitting position. It skips twice and sinks. "They're lost," she says. "The people in Savoonga. They're trying to hold on to their language and their dance—that's good—but the hunting is disappearing. They don't need to hunt. They can collect their welfare checks. I hunt and trap. Why can't they? We own the island." Edna is referring to the fact that the residents of the island refused to participate in the Alaska Native Claims Settlement Act, choosing instead to retain the fee simple title to 1.136 million acres of land on the island. "We thought that owning our own land would make things different, but it didn't change." Her people, she thinks, are wandering in a world in which they have no firm footing, caught between the traditions of the past and the uncertainties of the future. Only whaling still has the power to bring the people of St. Lawrence Island together. On the other hand, the island's two Native Corporations are trying to initiate business ventures. One new effort allows islanders to sell ivory, artifacts, and whalebones discovered during spring "subsistence digging" forays among the ancient and abandoned villages of the island and then sell them to auction houses across the world.

Suddenly Edna falls silent. It is a habit I am now familiar with, so I say nothing. "Do you understand?" she asks, after scratching at the gravel with a stick. I assure her that I understand her feelings about her former home. "Do you understand?" she asks again, looking at me for the first time since she started talking about Savoonga. "I love Savoonga, but it is hard for me to see what's goin' on there."

When Edna and Coleen returned from Savoonga with Millie, Heimo was glad to have his girls back. Though the adjustment of having people around after six years of living alone was difficult for Heimo, he had come to love, and depend on, Edna and Coleen's presence so much that he no longer enjoyed being alone. Even Millie, it seemed, was happy to be on the river again, reunited with her mother and Coleen and, Heimo hoped, perhaps him, too.

For a month they peeled logs in the morning and hunted in the afternoon for ptarmigan and spruce grouse. The pace was relaxed, casual. They would build a cabin in a new place, and their fortunes would turn—or else. They'd talked about it—this ominous "or else"— obliquely at first, the prospect of having to leave the trapline. And they always arrived at the same spot: Another bad trapping year, and they'd have to consider leaving; they'd have no other choice.

But for a month, at least, they were able to forget. While Heimo and Edna peeled logs in the snow along the river, Millie and Coleen played tag and hide-and-seek on the bank above, and most of the time, Heimo and Edna knew where Coleen was by the sound of the bells. When the sound faded, Heimo bounded up the bank and called for her. More often than not, she refused to answer, and Heimo followed her trail, sometimes deep into the woods. He'd find her hiding behind a tree with her hands covering her eyes, believing as all children do that if they can't see you, well, then, surely you can't see them.

Heimo scooped her up in his arms and ran through the woods. "I got you, I got you," he yelled. And then the two of them searched for Millie. Sometimes, in the late morning, Coleen tired and then she fell asleep on the caribou skin, which Edna laid on top of the snow like a picnic blanket. Millie would sit next to her and read.

Breakup didn't come that year until May 22. When it did, the Korths' spring idyl ended. It was as if the reality of their situation suddenly struck them. They had no intentions of going to Fairbanks or Fort Yukon that summer, and the mosquitoes were already ravenous; they would only get worse. By the time mid-June arrived, Heimo knew that they would have to spend the majority of their days on the gravel bars, far away from the trees and the underbrush. It was the only way to escape the swarming mosquitoes. Though he wanted to go to town as much as Edna, it was just too expensive. They could not afford to buy even the most basic supplies. Better to stay at the cabin and live off the land, subsisting on geese and what they could gather—willow leaves, Indian potato, and wild onion. But soon enough the geese migrated through, and then they ate whatever they could get their hands on—porcupine, late-season ducks, ground squirrels, grayling. It was too soon after breakup for grayling to be in the river, but they were lucky enough to find some in the creek.

On June 2, Heimo remembered that they'd left a twenty-five-pound sack of cornmeal in a fifty-five-gallon drum at the lower cabin. He told Edna that he was going to go and get it and bring it back the same day. But then he reconsidered. The water was still too high to line the canoe back up the river. He could float down alone and hike back, but that would mean leaving the canoe at the lower cabin for at least another week, and they'd probably need it before that. Heimo suggested that they all float down. Because there were more lakes, there would be more ducks and geese at the lower cabin. And surely, they wouldn't have a problem finding Indian potato, willow leaves, and wild onion. Besides, they both knew it wasn't a hard float; they'd discovered that the previous spring. Edna agreed; they'd float down together. That was the best plan.

On the morning of June 3, Heimo read the temperature—a crisp 30 degrees—but the sky was clear in every direction. At least they would not have to contend with rain. Heimo loaded the canoe, and then he positioned Millie in the middle and set Coleen in Millie's lap. Edna took the bow, and Heimo sat in the stern to do the steering.

Two miles downriver, Heimo saw a sweeper, a large tree hanging low over the river, and he knew then that they were in trouble. It had not been there the previous spring, he was sure of that; it must have toppled during breakup. He paddled furiously to try to maneuver around it, but the current pulled at the canoe. They hit the sweeper full force and the canoe flipped. The next thing Heimo knew, they were in the water, a deep hole. God, was it cold. Heimo surfaced and saw Edna hanging on to the canoe. Instinctively, he grabbed for Millie. It was then that he realized that she no longer had hold of Coleen.

What happened then Heimo will never forget. He had hold of Millie and he saw Coleen float by. He saw his daughter float by, but there was nothing he could do. He couldn't let go of Millie. So Heimo dragged Millie to shallow water. He swam out and pulled Edna and the canoe out of the deep water, too. Then he ran to the bank and raced downriver. "Coleen!" He was screaming it now. "Coleen!" He would see her and then he would dive in and rescue her, and everything would be okay.

Heimo ran a quarter of a mile downriver and then he ran back. Maybe Coleen was stranded on a gravel bar. If so, there was still time to save her. When he reached Edna and Millie, he realized he needed to help them. He was shivering from the cold, and he knew that if they didn't get warm, they'd both be severely hypothermic. Now he went into autopilot. He helped them both up the bank and then he gathered kindling and an armful of deadwood. He arranged it and then he tried to strike a waterproof match. Only he couldn't; his hands were shaking. "Goddamnit." He tried again and again. When the match finally lit, the fire went up in a blaze, and Heimo ran back downriver, looking for a trace, Coleen's pink boot, anything that might help him find her. Then he ran upriver again. As he neared the fire, he began to grasp the truth. Coleen was gone.

At the fire, Edna was hugging herself, rocking back and forth, and crying hysterically, "mama, mama. I want my mama." Heimo knew they would have to make it to the other side of the river, that it was important to get Edna and Millie under caribou skins. The fire had not been enough; Edna and Millie were shaking uncontrollably. Heimo carried Edna to the canoe and set her in it and then he got Millie. He searched for a large log to use as a paddle and pole. Then he sat down in back of the canoe and pushed it off into the current, but the river immediately tugged at them. Heimo battled against it, and when they reached a spot where the water was shallow enough, he jumped out. He held on to the canoe and slowly shuffled his feet along the river's rocky bottom until he was at the bow. Then he grabbed the bow rope, pulled the canoe onto a small sandbar, and carried Edna and then Millie up the bank. It was then that he lost it. In his rage, he punched trees and heaved huge rocks into the river. Minutes later, spent, he yelled Coleen's name one last time.

Back at the tent camp, he covered Edna and Millie in caribou skins and then tripped the new emergency locator transmitter. Then he went to the gravel bar and scratched out SOS with his foot. That evening, the Civil Air Patrol out of Fort Yukon was looking for them. CAP had been notified by Alaska's Rescue Coordination Center (RCC), where all ELT messages are sent. Heimo, Edna, and Millie were all out on the gravel bar now. Heimo had built a fire to keep them warm and to enable the pilot to find them easily. The only problem was the ELT signal was coming from the tent camp where Heimo had set it off. When the plane came, the pilot searched among the trees and never bothered to look in the direction of the gravel bar. Heimo ran down the gravel bar. He waved his arms wildly and shouted at the top of his lungs. "We're down here, you stupid son of a bitch. We're down here. God, please let him see us." Then he saw the pilot pull up and circle around in the direction of Fort Yukon. Until the pilot gave up his search, Heimo believed that maybe—somehow—Coleen might still be alive. When the pilot turned for Fort Yukon, his last glimmer of hope faded. He had failed to save his daughter.

Later that evening, a friend of the Korths, a pilot for Arctic Circle Air, heard that the RCC was still getting hits from the Coleen River, hours after the pilot had given up his search. He took matters into his own hands and borrowed a company plane and flew out to the river. He found Heimo, Edna, and Millie still on the gravel bar and noticed that someone was missing, so he air-dropped a message—"If it's an emergency and you need a helicopter, wave your arms." When Heimo waved, he tipped his wings to acknowledge that he understood and air-dropped another message—"I'm going to get help." He knew there was a helicopter based out of Arctic Village, where the University of Alaska was doing archeological work, so he radioed them and had them send out the helicopter. Five hours after their friend discovered them on the gravel bar, Heimo, Edna, and Millie were in Arctic Village, where news of their tragedy quickly spread among the villagers. Late that night, with the sun just beginning to fade, they arrived in Fort Yukon, where they were met by a group of friends. The following day, Heimo went out in a helicopter with two Alaska State Troopers and flew up and down the river much of the afternoon, but never found a sign of Coleen.

Four days later, a service was held in Coleen's honor at the Assembly of God Church. Much of Fort Yukon was there. Heimo and Edna were numb. But when the service ended and Heimo turned to thank everyone for coming, he stared into the crowd of people and for the first time he cried.

CHAPTER 10

Summer

I arrive in Fort Yukon in mid-July 2002, and Krin is in the yard playing with her husky puppy, Firth. But I hardly recognize her. She has cut her hair as short as mine and spiked it with what appears to be an entire bottle of gel. "Pretty haircut, Krin," I say, startling her. "How's your summer been?" She glowers at me and manages a gruff "Thanks," but ignores my question. "Where's your mom?" I ask. She points to the cabin without saying a word.

I shuffle my feet, knock on the screen door, and walk in. Edna is working inside, surrounded by stray clothes and boxes. "A yard sale?" I say, joking. Edna wipes her forehead with her arm. "No," she laughs. "Just packing for the Coleen. I'm tired of doing this every year."

The cabin is a mess, but I get some sense of its layout—one large room, perhaps thirty feet by twenty feet, with a small kitchen, an eating area with a table, a living room with two chairs, a coffee table, a television, VCR, computer, stereo, and three sleeping areas, dilineated by sheets hanging from the ceiling to the floor.

Seated in one of the chairs is a leprachaun of a man with whitish gray hair and sparkling blue eyes. Despite the heat—at the airport they'd told me the temperature was in the low 80s—he wears a flannel shirt and a jeans jacket, which he's buttoned to the top.

"This is Fred Thomas," Edna says.

Fred smiles, but doesn't get up, so I walk over and extend my hand.

223

Travel anywhere in Alaska's Interior and people know the name Fred Thomas. He's one of the last of the old-time trappers. Fred was born in Fort Yukon in 1919, the son of a white man from Wisconsin and a Gwich'in woman. He started running a trapline at the age of six and doesn't plan on stopping anytime soon.

I offer to help Edna pack. "Sit," she says, shaking her head. Then she goes to the refrigerator and pours both Fred and me a glass of orange juice.

Heimo has warned me that Fred, like many Natives, could be shy around strangers, so I sit down across from him and don't say a word. Unexpectedly, he speaks first. "So you're the *cheechako* from Wisconsin?" he says, his eyes gleaming.

"I suppose so," I answer. "Probably greener than the guys who came up in the seventies."

This inspires him, and he forgets his shyness. "They were a funny bunch," he says. "And ugly, too, especially Heimo." He belly-laughs and looks in the direction of Edna, who is smiling at him.

"Fred and Heimo are always joking," Edna says, since Heimo isn't here to defend himself. He left for the river early yesterday to prepare the cabin for Rhonda and me, arriving first, then for Edna and Krin, who are scheduled to fly in a few days later. He has to set up the outdoor kitchen and the tent, in which he and Edna sleep during the summer because it's cooler than the cabin. He also has to cut the grass in the cabin yard to discourage the mosquitoes, and remove all eighty-four of the roof poles that we peeled in spring and stored in the cabin over summer.

"Those guys had to learn fast, and they had to forget everything they knew when they got here," Fred says, as if he's still amazed that most of them survived. "Two or three of the fellas prit-near starved. One of them ate voles to stay alive. A couple of 'em shot themselves. It's a hard life."

I venture a question. "Why do you do it, then?"

"Well," he answers, "it wasn't a choice. You gotta remember; it's the only life people like me ever knew. There was no other way. But that was then. There's general assistance now, enough money for the people here not to have to trap anymore. But me, I'll keep trapping. You might say I'm just used to it."

Krin charges in and the screen door creaks and then slams shut with a sharp crack. She grabs a mirror and holds it in front of her face, oblivious to us, or perhaps in spite of us. She puts on eyeliner, lipstick, and then rubs another gob of gel in her hair. She is a thirteen-year-old girl who, once fond of snowball fights and climbing trees, now has become transformed into a young woman. When her hair is sufficiently spiky, she bounds out the door.

Fred continues. "There was a cycle back then, not anymore really. People used to come into town in June with their entire winter catch and go back out in fall time." In the fall of 1919, when Fred was only ten months old, his father and mother lined up to their cabin on the Black River, a trip that took them thirty days.

"Fall time?" I ask, knowing that traveling the rivers so close to freeze-up was risky.

"Yeah," Fred says. "Fall time—late July, early August," and then I realize that in the Interior, Mother Nature determines the seasons. By the time the autumnal equinox rolls around, people are sometimes a week or two into winter.

"That's the way it worked," Fred explains, slurring now because of a toothache that's started to bother him again. "Goddamn tooth," he fumes, gritting his teeth. "I'd better be heading home."

Fred gets up, and I stand to say good-bye. I tower over him by almost a foot. Looking at him, it is hard for me to imagine him carrying an eighty-pound moose quarter out of the woods, but legend has it that he and his brother Albert were two of the toughest guys in the bush, strong despite their size and virtually impervious to cold. They'd cover their lines at 50 below, when one mistake meant the difference between life and death.

Fred says good-bye to Edna and me, walks out the door, and shuts it softly. A minute later the phone rings. Outside I hear someone shriek and then the sound of stampeding feet. I go to the door to see what all the commotion is about. Next thing I know, Krin and Rhonda are wrestling to see who will answer the phone. Rhonda grabs Krin around

the waist and pulls her back and dashes in. She flops down in a chair—
the epitome of a teenager—and talks with a friend on the phone. I try
not to listen. "Soda" and "AC" are the only two words I hear.

When Rhonda hangs up, she jumps to her feet. "Hey, welcome to
Fort Yukon," she says. "Wanna walk to AC?" Krin is waiting at the door.

"If he goes, I'm staying," she blurts out.

"Guess Krin's out of luck," I say. "Maybe I'll bring a Mountain Dew
back for her."

"I'll get my own," she says, snubbing me.

Outside the Alaska Commercial Company store—AC, for short—
where Rhonda has worked as a checkout girl for the last seven weeks, a
bunch of kids are hanging around on their bikes. One of them, a thin
boy, wears a Michael Jordan jersey that hangs just above his knees. A
young girl sits on the handlebars of his bike. His boom box is turned up
to full volume.

"White America," Rhonda says. "Eminem."

Though I'm not sure what I'd expected, I'm surprised when we walk
inside the AC. It's a thoroughly modern store with two levels. On the
first floor, the store sells an assortment of items: tools, household clean-
ers, meat, frozen food, even fruits and vegetables, which come with astounding price tags. Grapes are $10.99 per pound. Downstairs, the AC
sells clothes, rugs, toys, sewing supplies, furniture, and, Rhonda says excitedly, "Sunglasses!" We each buy a pop and then we go downstairs,
where Rhonda tries on a variety of glasses, modeling them for me. The
money she made over the summer is burning a hole in her pocket. For
$12, she buys the funkiest pair on the rack. Satisfied with her purchase,
she asks, "Hey, you want a tour of Fort Yukon?"

Our first stop is the large new Gwich'in Tribal Office building where
Rhonda introduces me to a number of people. "When are you going out
to the cabin?" one of the women asks Rhonda. "Oh, tomorrow, I guess,"
Rhonda replies gloomily. "I'll stop in again to say good-bye."

Every year, Rhonda tells me, it gets harder and harder to leave Fort
Yukon and return to the cabin. "It's fun here," Rhonda says. "We have
friends. We can shoot pool at night, buy Slurpees, go to the AC, watch
movies on the VCR. There's just more to do." Leaving the building,

Rhonda says, "Even though I'm half Eskimo, I feel more Gwich'in than Eskimo because we've been coming here all my life."

We double back along the gravel road in the direction of the town's radio station. Though Fort Yukon is a twenty-first-century town, in some ways, it still has the look and feel of a Hudson's Bay fur outpost—log houses, privies out back, dirt and gravel roads.

At the post office, Rhonda tells me to wait while she checks for their mail. Four-wheelers fly by spitting up so much dust that I grab my bandana and hold it over my mouth and nose. "Nothing," Rhonda says, running out the door. "But don't tell Krin I just did that. She'll get mad. She loves to check the mail. She rides up here every day on her bike."

Farther down the road, we reach the Fort Yukon radio station, Gwaandak Radio, KZPA, 900 AM. During the summers of 1994 and 1995, Heimo worked as a disc jockey here, subjecting the town of Fort Yukon and much of the bush to a music flashback: Fleetwood Mac, Moody Blues, Jimi Hendrix, Steve Miller, Sly and the Family Stone, Led Zeppelin, and anomalously, Enya. Although dead air was forbidden, Heimo never quite mastered the silence-filling DJ banter. Nor was he willing to serve up the diet of country tunes that so many people expected from KZPA. Nevertheless, inside there's a plaque that bears his name.

At the Fort Yukon High School, a multimillion-dollar building with state-of-the-art facilities—new computers, Internet access, video hookups—Rhonda shows me where vandals recently smashed twenty-seven windows. "That happens a lot," she says.

Next on the tour is the town drug dealer's house, the local moonshiner's place, and the Arctic Circle Baptist Church, where all the women are ordered to wear dresses, and the University of Alaska Fairbanks Interior Campus—Yukon Flats.

"Do you want to see the Episcopal Church?" Rhonda asks. "It's pretty cool."

Rhonda is right. The Episcopal Church is a quaint red log building with white trim, Fort Yukon's oldest church. After Alaska was purchased from Russia, it was divided among the various denominations of missionaries. The Episcopalians got much of the Interior.

Inside, many of the pews have plaques dedicated to the memory of former Fort Yukon residents: Florida Yasuda, Old Alexander, Charlotte Englishshoe. Some of them date back to the early 1900s. The baptismal font honors the memory of Hudson Stuck, otherwise known as the dogsledding bishop, the first archdeacon of Alaska, and author of *Ten Thousand Miles With a Dog Sled*. In the back room, we discover Gwich'in hymnals, collecting dust, because few people in town still speak the language.

After visiting the church, we make our way over to the Hudson's Bay Cemetery, where a large monument reads:

> In memory of the People of the Hudson's Bay Company who died at or near Fort Yukon between the years 1840 and 1870, many of them being pioneers and discoverers and explorers of various portions of the Yukon and Alaska. Erected by the Hudson's Bay Company 1923.

I walk around the cemetery, glancing at the headstones, trying to imagine how it must have been to live in Alaska's Interior in the 1800s. A poem I discovered in a collection at the university library in Fairbanks, by Belle Herbert of Chalkyitsik, Alaska, describes what it was like for the Native families, many of whom were living lifestyles that had changed little in thousands of years:

> Ah, grandchild, times were very hard and people
>   worked hard.
> Grandchild, we survived on the food they
>   hunted and shot.
> If we stayed in one place, there wouldn't
>   be any food.

"Come on," Rhonda shouts to me. "There're too many mosquitoes. We gotta keep moving. Let's go down to the river." For the first time I look at my legs—I am wearing "greenie" hiking shorts, perhaps the only man in Fort Yukon who's not dressed in jeans—and they're covered with mosquitoes, which are rising out of the uncut grass in small, dark clouds. I haven't seen so many mosquitoes since my wife, Elizabeth, my brother, Jeff, and I hiked through the jungles of Papua New Guinea. At least there's no malaria or dengue fever or Japanese encephalitis here, I console myself.

We return to the cabin, completing a large circle, passing a number of small log cabins along the way. On a shed I see a sign that reads "Native Power" in bold black letters. I know how Heimo would respond to the sign. "Guy's on a culture kick," he'd say, believing that those Natives who live the traditional life—trapping, hunting, fishing—have little need to proclaim it. A guy like Fred Thomas, for instance. A few houses down, six dogs snarl at us from a cabin yard.

"Thank God, they're all chained," I say to Rhonda.

"They better be if the guy wants to keep his dogs," she says. "If people see an unchained dog, they shoot it. The dump is full of dog carcasses."

Back at the cabin, Edna is transplanting some of her flowers and an apple and chokecherry tree to take out to the Coleen, and Krin is riding her bike while Firth chases her and yaps. Firth is still young and unsteady on her legs, so she spends more time tumbling and rolling than she does chasing.

The bush pilot makes two sweeps of the gravel bar, testing the wind and checking the bar for any obstructions before he decides to land. On another bar, large trees, torn from their roots and manhandled by the river during breakup, lay scattered among the stones and sand. Next spring, when the river is again transformed into a wild, rushing torrent, these trees will be gone, rolling and splashing their way to the Porcupine. Heimo creeps up the river in his canoe, hardly making any progress against the current with his three-horse engine.

We land and wait for Heimo to meet us at the gravel bar. After a quick "Hi," he loads our gear into the canoe. "It'll take me a while," he says. "I have to paddle. Motor's screwed up. Keeps cuttin' out on me." Then he eases the canoe into the river. "Meet you on the other side of the island," he yells back to us. "Watch out for bears. I've seen a lot of tracks farther upriver."

Rhonda and I slip on our hip boots and wade the river to reach the island. The river is down, only knee high and a limpid green. I can see the stones on its bottom as if there is no water separating us, as if the river itself doesn't exist.

When we reach the willows, they hum with the sound of so many mosquitoes I feel as if I'm at a NASCAR race. I walk quickly, swinging my arms to keep them at bay, aware that biologists have discovered rotting caribou, killed by marauding mosquitoes, that have been completely drained of blood. The sand is a calligraphy of tracks—moose, porcupine, the wide three-toed imprints of cranes, the webbing of goose prints, but no grizzly tracks. Heimo made better progress than he expected and is already waiting to take us across when we reach the far side of the island. "Water's muddy," he says. "Maybe caribou cross upriver or maybe bank collapse. I go upriver later and look."

I look at Rhonda and smile, and she understands my amusement.

"After a couple of months in Fort Yukon, we always come back talking like that."

"What?" Heimo asks. "What?"

" 'Maybe caribou cross upriver or maybe bank collapse,' " I imitate him. " 'I go upriver later and look.' "

"How's this?" Heimo asks, and affects a cultured English accent. "I daresay it was the caribou or perhaps a bank collapsed. Either way," he says, drawing out a long "I" in "either," "I intend to check after dinner."

"No," I say, "it doesn't suit you. Stick with 'I go upriver.' "

Heimo insists that Rhonda and I put on our life vests and then he paddles us across, aiming the bow of the canoe at a forty-five-degree angle to the current. A willow branch stranded in the middle of the river taps out a staccatto beat on the water's surface. Once across, Heimo jumps from the canoe into a slow, shallow pool. With three quick half hitches he secures the canoe to a branch dug into the river bottom. Then he grabs our bags and trudges up to the cabin, muttering about the "goddamn motor." I follow Rhonda. She stoops and grabs the leaf of a fireweed plant and eats it.

"God, I'm going to miss it here," she says, chewing the leaf.

It's a decision that Heimo and Edna and Rhonda, too, have been agonizing over for much of the last year—whether or not Rhonda should go "Outside" to attend high school. Over the summer, they made up their minds and arranged for Rhonda to live with Heimo's younger brother, Tom, in Appleton and attend the same high school Heimo did—Appleton East. In late June, Heimo and Edna called me from Fort Yukon and asked if I'd be willing to escort her, to let her fly out with me. "Of course," I said, realizing how difficult it would be for them to let go. They'd lose Rhonda for an entire school year and possibly for good. It would be hard on Heimo and Edna, and of course Rhonda, but I knew it would be equally hard on Krin.

Sitting around the fire after supper, while mosquitoes hover around our chairs, waiting for our bug spray to wear off, Heimo and I talk about what leaving home will mean for Rhonda.

Heimo is wearing only a T-shirt, and I can see that summer in Fort Yukon has taken its toll. Despite his running regimen—four miles a day—and spending every morning on the river with Fred Thomas tending gill nets, he looks as if he's put on at least ten pounds.

"Millie tried it," Heimo tells me. "She lived with my brother Erich and his family, but that didn't work out good at all. It's going to be different with Tom, I think. And I have confidence in Rhonda. She's got good head on her shoulders, too." I stare at Heimo when he says this, and he averts his eyes. Then, finally, he lifts his head and breaks into a laugh. "Just kidding," he says. "She's got *a* good head on her shoulders, and I have faith in her. She was brought up with good values. I think she's going to make the proper choices. Besides, she needs to get out and see things. It's going to be hard on Edna and Krin, but it's the right thing to do. Except for summers in Fort Yukon, she's lived out here her whole life. There's a big world out there, and she should have the opportunity to see it. When she's finished with high school, if she wants to come back, she can. I hope she does, but that's up to her. As far as ANILCA's concerned, she can do that. It says that the permit can be renewed every five years 'until the death of the last immediate family member of the original claimant.' But after her and Krin, it's over. They are the last people in America that will ever be able to live like this."

Rhonda has been doing the dishes and listening passively to our conversation, her head half turned in our direction. "How do you feel about it, Rhonda?" I ask her.

She shrugs her shoulders and dunks the cup she's just washed in the plastic rinsing tub. "I don't know."

"Come on, Rhonda," Heimo says.

Rhonda speaks up now. I've witnessed it before—how much she needs her father's respect, the lengths she'll go to to make sure he's proud of her. She doesn't have it in her to disappoint him. She's her father's girl, his "little woodsman," whom he can always rely on to do the right thing.

"I'll miss this place," Rhonda replies. "I'm sure it'll be hard, but personal style is in, and I think I have a lot of personal style, so I think I'll be able to make friends quickly."

"I think you will, too," I say, though I know that in a largely white city like Appleton Rhonda may meet with racism.

"And you'll wear fur in winter to show them that you're proud of how you were raised," Heimo insists.

Later, when Rhonda and I are fetching water, I tell her, "It may be tough on you. Remember who you are and be proud of it. Some people might say nasty things. Don't listen to them; they're just idiots."

"You mean racists?" Rhonda asks, rescuing me from my ambiguity. "I can handle them."

Rhonda fills her bucket and I offer to carry it. "Sure," she says. "Thanks."

Walking back upriver, she points to Mummuck Mountain, and for the first time I can see why they call it that. *Mummuck* is a Yupik word meaning "breast." The nipple on the mountain is pronounced, the breast ample and rounded. Edna was the first one to notice it, in May 1984, shortly before Coleen died. "*Mummuck*," Edna said, pointing it out to Heimo, and the name has stuck.

"When the light is just right and caribou are on top of the ridge, you can see them from here without a spotting scope," Rhonda says.

"Have you ever been up there?" I ask.

"Sure," she responds, annoyed at my question. "What do you think? Three years ago I got my third caribou ever up there."

"So you got it when you were thirteen? When did you kill your first one?"

"That was on the Sheenjek in 1998," she says, "when we were living in the tent camp. I was twelve."

In the spring of 1998, before they left the Coleen, Heimo and Edna decided that they wouldn't return to the river until the summer of 1999. They'd spend the following season on the Sheenjek River. Heimo felt the Coleen drainage needed to rebound from his trapping pressure. But there was more to it than that; they went for the wolves and for adventure, too. The Sheenjek has a high density of wolves, and Heimo was hoping to catch half a dozen by spring. He and Edna were also excited about the prospect of exploring new country. Sixty miles west of their cabin on the upper Coleen, the terrain at the headwaters of the milky, glacier-fed Sheenjek River is rugged and mountainous.

Today it is raining. It looks as if it might clear up, but Heimo has decided not to try putting on the new roof. Instead we fish our way downriver, hoping to catch enough grayling to feed the three of us for supper.

"Only six. We'll catch that in no time," Heimo assures me.

"Too bad," I say. "I was hoping to spend more time on the river."

"Go ahead," Heimo replies. "Spend the day, and catch all the fish you want."

When Heimo first came up, he enjoyed fishing, but he no longer has any patience for it. And he has no tolerance for my fly rod. "Never play a fish, just horse it in," he says. There's no room for the finer points; he fishes to eat. So we do what I call "guerrilla fishing." Heimo is amused by the name, which only serves to make him fish faster. We walk down the riverbank at a good clip, and when Heimo spots a hole, he drops his spinner in and jigs it. He'll jig the spinner for a minute or so—no more—and if a fish doesn't bite, he moves on.

"It's not like fishing for trout down there," he says, "where you have to work the stream. If there are grayling, they'll bite. Grayling 'pod up.' Where there's one, there's more. Where there's none, there's none," he says definitively.

Guerrilla fishing. We catch our six fish in a remarkably short time, horsing them in like bait-and-bobber fishermen, and now we are about a mile downriver, lying on a sandbar in a meadow of goose grass. I have no idea what time it is, late morning, afternoon. It hardly matters. In summer, the sun circles above the horizon almost continuously. Morning, afternoon, evening, night—they are Lower Forty-eight constructs that are no longer applicable.

"Just think how many millions of years it takes for rock to be ground down into sand. And people take it for granted," Heimo says, sitting and grabbing a handful of sand, which he lets run between his fingers. "You know," he says, pausing for a long time, "this is where Coleen died. This is where the canoe turned over. About a year after it happened, I found Coleen's pink boot not too far downriver. Edna has it back at the cabin. But don't tell her we were here. She doesn't like to come here. She doesn't even like to hear about it. She's still afraid of the river."

Heimo says this and confirms my hunch. In spring I had watched Edna on the ice. She was cautious, walking on it only when it was necessary, and then she walked stiffly, as if each step was a matter of willpower. When she could avoid the river, she did. When the ice began to run and leads opened in the ice, her tentativeness struck me as something more elemental. It was fear, a fear born of painful experience and a memory that won't leave her.

"After Coleen's death," Heimo adds, letting the rest of the sand fall from his hand, "Millie was with us some, but she spent most of her time with Edna's parents. Maybe she felt guilty. Edna tried to talk to her, but she wouldn't talk about it, so me and Edna never knew. I don't know what it was, but Millie and me never hit it off. She resented me, and maybe I resented her a bit, too. As she got older, she didn't like to be out here. No fun, bad memories, I don't know. Anyway, when she turned fifteen, she went to Mount Edgecomb—Millie was really smart with books—a state-funded boarding school in Sitka, Alaska. I think she just wanted outta here. There was no holding her back. She said, '*Sayonara*,' and left for good."

After Coleen's funeral in early June 1984, Heimo, Edna, and Millie were led outside to a gathering, a traditonal Gwich'in potlatch, with moose, salmon, fry bread, chicken, and potato salad. There they were presented with $500 in cash, which the town had collected for them. People as far away as Arctic Village donated money. It was a godsend. The Korths were down to their last $4. But money couldn't patch the hole in their hearts.

A week later, the three of them left Fort Yukon to return to the river. While Edna and Millie waited on the gravel bar where the plane had dropped them off, Heimo made the trip to the cabin site. He alone would ford the river and test the current. It was better that way.

Wearing hip boots, Heimo leaned against the current. Still churning with spring runoff, it slapped coldly at his thighs. Where the river slowed, he could see grayling holding in the deep holes. He crossed the river's main channel, searching for the shallow water where the sun illuminated the gravel underneath, and then a smaller channel. As he approached the far bank, near the cabin site, what he saw on the gravel bar that had once been Coleen's playground was almost more than he could take. He remembered how she had loved it here, playing tag, building sandcastles, throwing stones into the water. There among the knee-high willows were Coleen's footprints, indentations from the pink boots she loved. Heimo kneeled down and touched one of the prints, then he proceeded to do the only thing he could. He walked up and down the gravel bar and stamped them out. Edna, he knew, would never be able to bear it. Then he splashed water on his face and wiped his eyes with his shirt and lined the canoe upriver to where Edna and Coleen were waiting.

When Edna saw the canoe she balked. She wouldn't go downriver in it. "I'm gonna walk," she said. Heimo explained that the river was too high, the current too fast for her to keep her feet, for him to try to carry Millie. "You got no choice, Edna," he said. Edna eventually agreed, but she refused to paddle. Instead she sat in the middle of the canoe, gripping Millie with one hand, clasping the canoe's rail with the other.

For the next three weeks, Edna, Millie, and Heimo worked for eighteen hours a day, taking advantage of the sun, to build their new cabin. It was hard to summon the motivation, the energy to go on without Coleen, but by midday they were lost in their work and they could forget, if only temporarily. It was the work, Heimo says, that saved them.

We are lying in the sand, under the summer sun, which even at this latitude feels hot, and Heimo is telling me the story. "I have issues with Fort Yukon, but the people there really helped us," he says. "Even strangers. But that's the way Fort Yukon is. For all its problems, the community rallies when a tragedy occurs. People forget their differences. A guy flips his boat, and his enemy will save him."

"So Brantley"—Edna's brother—"helped you, too," I say. "When you left Fort Yukon, didn't he come out and help you build the cabin?"

"No," Heimo says, "we'd finished it long before that. Edna and Millie had to go to town in January because Edna was having bad problems with her teeth. That's when Brantley came out. I told him that I could use his help while they were gone. But that wasn't the real reason," Heimo confesses. "I could have managed on my own. There was just the trapline, cooking meals, and hauling water. The truth is, I couldn't stand the thought of being alone. I couldn't stomach the idea of being out here by myself after Coleen."

Heimo grabs a stone and throws it into the woods, struggling to find words. "You never get over it," Heimo says. "You just try to get used to it."

"Thinking back," Heimo concedes, "it was probably a stupid thing for all of us to go down to the lower cabin, bad judgment, I don't know. I had a dream the night before it happened. I dreamed that Coleen was going to die. Same with my mom, too. When I found out about my mom, I remembered the dream I had. They say my *oma*, my grandmother on my dad's side, had those kind of dreams, too. I didn't pay any attention to the dream. I thought it was nonsense."

When Edna returned from Fairbanks, she and Heimo had little to say to each other. They hardly spoke and almost never hugged. Heimo had fits of temper. He yelled and screamed when the snow covered his trapping trails, when the snowmachine stalled. There were days when he could not get out of bed, when he could not have cared less about trapping.

Edna could only sob. One morning, after Heimo and Millie left to check one of Heimo's short lines, Edna crawled into bed, pulled up the covers, and buried her head in a pillow. When Heimo and Millie returned in the early afternoon, Edna was still in bed. The small pile of wood that he had brought in that morning lay next to the stove. The fire had gone out and the cabin was cold.

Heimo got the fire going again and made a dinner of fried caribou steaks, noodles, and canned spinach. He set Edna's plate on a bucket next to the bed. After he and Millie had finished their meals, he went to her.

"Please eat, Edna," he said.

"No," she replied.

Then Heimo lay beside her, and wrapped his arm around her. Edna sat up and pushed him away. "I want Coleen back," she cried.

"We had some terrible fights," Heimo remembers. "It was our way of getting out the grief. When we talked, we talked about divorce. Millie had to see all that. It was tough on her. Things were bad between Edna and me for a long time, and then Rhonda was born. They say a child can't save a marriage, but Rhonda being born saved ours. If she wasn't born I don't think we could have stuck together."

I wake early today to the sound of sandhill cranes croaking happily from the tundra. Despite the late spring freeze, which was hard on the berries, the cranes have been here for days now. They must have found a hardy patch of blueberries. When Heimo and Edna and Krin shoot some of the cranes this fall, their gizzards will be dark blue.

Last night Heimo announced that today would be "roof day." He has chosen well. The sky is a sea of pristine blue. Clouds lurk far to the north, but they will not pose a problem for us. According to KJNP, rain is not in the forecast.

Heimo begins what will probably be a full-day project by draping large sections of cloth over the inside of the cabin. When he's done with that, he and Rhonda and I climb onto the cabin roof and remove the moss, some of which crumbles and falls into the cabin below.

"It's gonna be a mess," Heimo says, "but this roof's gotta go. I put on this roof two years before you were born," he tells Rhonda. Rhonda smiles wanly. She knows what Heimo means—he built the roof the month after Coleen died.

We save as much moss as we can, planning to use it later, throwing it down onto tarps spread around the base of the cabin. Then we take off the old Visqueen and the layer of moss underneath it. When we finish that, we remove the old poles, pulling out the nails carefully to avoid bending them beyond repair. Heimo has brought out nails, but we will need to use some of the old ones. While we pull nails, Rhonda goes to the woods and gathers blueberries for lunch. At noon with the roof off, we stop for a ten-minute break and enjoy a piece of fry bread dripping with honey and freshly picked blueberries.

"Let's get the new roof on." Heimo sounds like a football coach trying to rally his team at halftime.

Rhonda, who has been inspecting the mess inside the cabin, says, "Man, that's going to take a long time to clean. And guess who's going to end up doing it?"

We climb onto the roof, and Heimo starts handing me the poles. I lay them down between the roof beam and the exterior wall, and Rhonda arranges them on each side of the roof, making sure there are no large gaps. She is also conscientious about laying moss under the poles along the exterior wall. Wood on wood means premature rotting. When Rhonda declares that the poles are set, I nail them, toeing them together where they meet at the top or nailing the ends to the main roof beam. Then I slide down the pole and drive in another nail, fastening the poles to the outside wall. After all the poles have been set and nailed, Rhonda and I fill in the gaps with moss.

"Why not just lay down the Visqueen?" I ask Heimo, who is watching our every move from below. "Why the extra step?"

Heimo answers abruptly, "Moss discourages condensation."

After the gaps have been patched, Heimo hands us a large roll of Visqueen, which we spread out incrementally, two feet at a time, covering each section of plastic with moss, all the while treating the Visqueen with extreme care for fear of puncturing it. Puncture it, and the roof is going to leak. When we have spread out the plastic and mossed each side of the roof, Heimo is finally content.

"Good job," he says, sounding relieved. "One day, twenty years from now, when Edna and I are grandparents, we'll need another roof. You won't mind coming up and giving us a hand, will you?" he asks me.

I don't respond. After having jumped from the roof, lost my footing, and somersaulted in the direction of the solar fence, I'm busy trying to assess the damage to my elbows and knees. When I'm confident that nothing is broken or torn, I answer, "Not at all. As long as you never let me try that jump again."

I am covered in spruce needles and dirt, a pathetic sight. "Don't worry," Heimo says. "I don't want to have to see that again."

It is early afternoon, and everyone is gathered in the cabin yard, including Edna and Krin, who flew in three days ago. Heimo is using his bandsaw to cut up the old roof poles for firewood. Krin is lying in the hammock holding Firth, and Rhonda is sitting in a camp chair playing chess on the computer. The girls begged Heimo to let them run the Honda gas generator and play computer games. Initially, he flat-out refused—he didn't want to waste gas—but they kept at him.

The dog, too, is something of a sore spot for Heimo. For years, he's been adamant about not getting one. As far as he's concerned, they're more trouble than they're worth, although the Natives of Fort Yukon say that a man should never live in the bush without a dog—a dog will alert you if bears are around. Edna and Rhonda finally prevailed, however. They convinced Heimo that when Rhonda left for school, Krin would need a playmate.

The computer is a gift from a teacher in Fort Yukon. The high school was getting new laptops, so the teacher gave the girls one of the old ones. It is hard not to be struck by the appearance of the computer here—the paradox. But Heimo is no purist, maybe never was. With two teenage girls, adhering to some ascetic notion of simplicity is impractical, if not impossible. He is a wilderness man, but a modern one, reluctant to shun something that allows him to make life better over the long haul. He struggles to keep it simple, but he feels no compulsion to fulfill anyone's romantic notion of what he should be. Romantics never last long in the bush. Heimo knows this. You modify your canon as the situation dictates or you leave. Rhonda tells me that he agreed to let them have the computer for the same reason he let Krin have a dog. He thinks it'll be good for Krin when Rhonda goes to Wisconsin. If Krin is happy, he's happy. It turns out he might even be motivated by a bit of self-interest. Rhonda tells me he is something of a computer junkie himself. In Fort Yukon, during the summer, he sometimes plays computer games for hours a day.

Krin coos at Firth and hugs and kisses the dog as if it were a baby. All the while, white-wing crossbills feed on spruce cone seeds high in the surrounding trees and discard the leftover cones in the cabin yard. The cones fall through the branches and hit the ground like heavy raindrops.

"Shhh," Heimo says, interrupting his sawing. "Shhh." We all look at him. No one is quite sure whom he is shushing. No one is talking. The generator continues to rumble.

"Hear that, hear that," Heimo says. "It sounds like 'Quick three beers.' That's an olive-sided flycatcher."

Heimo is cross today. For the last two days, he's been suffering from the flu. There's nothing that galls him like being sick. Fortunately, he and the others are rarely ill. If they get sick, they have a well-stocked supply of antibiotics and other medicines from the Fort Yukon Clinic, which Edna and the girls get free because they are Native.

Heimo's concern about his health borders on obsession. He has no insurance, but more important than that, he's concerned about the slow deterioration of his body, as if each illness accentuates his growing vulnerability. And the weak don't last, at least not in the Arctic. He gets a case of the sniffles, and he worries. His heart skips a beat, and he thinks he's having a heart attack. So he does everything he can to protect himself. To avoid exposure to potential parasites, which cause many diseases—brucellosis, trichinosis, liver tapeworm cysts, tularemia, sarcocystosis—he insists that Edna cook all meat well done. Years ago, he renounced all domesticated meat and processed sugar, which he believes are the root of many physical ailments. Because he is often gutting animals or working with traps or fur, he is also concerned about germs. He soaps and scrubs his hands as well as any surgeon. He avoids sharing glasses or eating utensils with anyone, including Edna and the girls. And when working with wood—cutting it, splitting it, hauling it—he always wears goggles. "To lose my vision," he says, "would be a fate worse than death."

To forestall his inevitable physical decay, Heimo works to keep himself in tremendous shape. "I want to die out here, and to do that I need to be healthy," he once told me, sounding disconcertingly like Yogi Berra.

Fred Thomas is his inspiration. At eighty-three, Thomas is still as active as a man half his age. So that he is still in good enough health to be out here when he turns eighty-three, Heimo does push-ups and sit-ups four times a week. He doesn't enjoy skiing, and after years of covering his trapline on snowshoes, he refuses to snowshoe for exercise. What he does love is running, even in the dead of winter.

During my winter visit, after a day on the trapline, Heimo would often emerge from the cabin dressed in a fluffy powder blue sweatsuit, the pants too short, barely reaching his ankles, bound for a little oval track he'd cleared in the tundra. The incongruity of the two images—the rough trapper, his beard coated with small pieces of ice, his trusty sidearm strapped to his waist versus the health fanatic, wearing a sweatsuit that looked more like a cozy pair of pajamas—always struck me as part hilarious, part psycho. Who spends his day on a freezing trapline and then clears out a track in the tundra so he can stay in shape? Who in his right mind runs in the Arctic at 25 below?

Four times a week, Heimo walked out to the track, where he'd perform a few preliminary stretches. Then he'd put his head down and grit his teeth against the Arctic cold and the assassinlike winds that whipped the tundra. Having no interest in joining him, I'd watch him run. His vapor cloud, which hung in the air like thick smoke, followed him around the track. Set against the frosty peaks of the Brooks Range, with the alders and willows coated in hoarfrost, it was easy to imagine him as the last person on earth.

It is early evening and Edna has just finished making sourdough biscuits. She makes bread nearly every day, kneading the dough by hand, so her forearms are large and sinewy, like a woodworker's. Now she is cutting up the fish I caught and cleaned this morning. Tonight, for supper, we're having one of my favorites—fried grayling. Edna will fry them over an open fire, and the smell will permeate the nearby woods. When she sets them on our plates, the fish pieces will be brown and crispy, and the soft white meat will peel from the bone in perfect fillets.

She cuts up the biggest fish, talking as she works. "You know, Coleen would have been twenty years old. If she were still living, these girls wouldn't be here today. Heimo and I were only going to have one. Then Rhonda came. It was the best thing that ever happened to me and Heimo."

The truth is that two and a half years after Coleen's death, the Korths almost lost Rhonda, too. It was 1986, and Edna was three and a half months into her pregnancy when she started bleeding. Believing at first that it was a miscarriage, she and Heimo were disappointed. But then the bleeding persisted. What should they do, they wondered? Should they wait to see if the bleeding stopped? It was too risky, they decided, so Heimo went out to a gravel bar, the same gravel bar where they had waited after Coleen's death, and scratched SOS into the sand, filling in the furrows with sparkling sheets of tinfoil. They'd give it a day, and if no one responded to the SOS, they'd trip the ELT.

An hour later a plane flew by; however, the pilot didn't acknowledge the SOS. Perhaps, Heimo and Edna hoped, he'd return by the same route later in the day. Sure enough, the plane flew over again, and this time the pilot responded to the signal. He landed and unloaded cans of gas to make room for Edna, and then flew her to the clinic in Fort Yukon, where medical care workers diagnosed the bleeding as "placenta previa," the condition in which the placenta attaches low and partially covers the cervix. Edna had lost a lot of blood. Realizing that they weren't equipped to care for her, the clinic workers sent her to Fairbanks. The doctor in Fairbanks diagnosed it as a more serious condition—"placental abruption."

With placental abruption, the placenta separates from the uterine wall before birth. There is often hemorrhaging, but the greatest danger is to the unborn child, who is deprived of oxygen. The doctor told Edna bluntly that her child would probably be born with brain damage and prescribed extended bed rest. Against her doctor's wishes, Edna flew back to Fort Yukon. Three weeks later, Heimo and Millie flew to Fort

Yukon, where they waited out the rest of Edna's pregnancy. Millie went to school. To make ends meet and to keep from dwelling on the doctor's prediction, Heimo worked as a house parent at the Vocational Education Center. On February 19, 1986, Rhonda was born.

"The doctor was wrong," Edna says. "I held Rhonda and knew that she was okay. A mother knows."

In another setting, Edna never would have told me this story. It's the sort of intimate story that she only trusts her family with and, sometimes, her small circle of friends in Fort Yukon. But tonight, surrounded by Heimo, Rhonda, and Krin, feeling secure, perhaps, she's much less reserved than she normally would be.

"You can see," she says, nodding in Rhonda's direction, "Rhonda turned out okay. But Rhonda was tough from the beginning—really tough. The summer Krin was born, that was our first year on the Old Crow. Heimo flew out early to set up a tent camp. Rhonda, Krin, and me flew in near the end of July, and Heimo walked to the drop-off lake to pick us up. It was a seven-mile walk to the tent camp, through tundra, but Rhonda walked the whole seven miles alone, over niggerheads, and she was only three and half years old. Heimo carried our gear and I carried Krin. We didn't arrive at the tent camp until 6:00 A.M. the next morning. There was no wind that night and the mosquitoes ate us up, but Rhonda didn't cry. She didn't even complain."

Tonight Edna is surprisingly at ease in my presence, so I risk a personal question. "How do you think Rhonda will do in Wisconsin? Are you worried about her?"

Rhonda overhears me and comes over and teases the fire with a long stick, pretending to tend to it. "So what do you think, Poop?" Edna says, calling her by her nickname. "How do you think you're going to do?" Rhonda shrugs her shoulders, returning to Krin and the chess game, disappointed perhaps that her mother didn't answer the question.

Edna shrugs her shoulders, too, as if she were mimicking Rhonda. "I don't know how she's gonna do. Good, I hope."

Edna's seeming indifference catches me by surprise, though it shouldn't. For the last few days, I've been struck by just how little is being said about Rhonda's departure, though it is imminent. It is as if both

Heimo and Edna, but Edna in particular, having already lost one daughter, have neither the strength nor the will to discuss the possibility of losing another.

Supper is over and Rhonda and Krin are snacking on fish tails, which they let cook on the grill until they're a crispy brown. A log cracks, and an ember flies out and rests on my leg. I brush it off. "Must have thrown a spruce log in there by accident," Heimo says. "Sorry. That's why when the Gwich'in made fires in their caribou skin tents they used only cottonwood. Spruce likes to explode."

Edna is looking through my book of Alaskan wildflowers. "The minister didn't know anything about flowers until I met him," she says, nudging Heimo, who is sitting next to her with his arm around her. Edna catches herself. "I mean the reverend. I taught him about crowberries and cloudberries. You can eat this one raw or in a salad," she says, pointing to a photograph of brook saxifrage. "And you can eat the roots of these two—wild celery and what the book calls Parry's wallflower."

"Damn mosquito," I say, slapping my calf loudly, interrupting her.

"Kill one," she says, without looking up, still paging through the book, "and all the rest show up for the funeral." Then she finds the page she's been searching for. "This one is just wild spinach," she explains, showing me the photograph of Arctic dock. "And this one—roseroot— you let it ferment, and it's really good."

Suddenly Heimo jumps up.

"What's going on?" Edna asks, startled by Heimo. "A bear?"

"No," Heimo says, tired of hearing about flowers. "Let's do something else. Let's get the phone book and let Jim try to pronounce the Eskimo names in Savoonga."

"Good idea," the girls shout. "I'll go get it," Rhonda offers.

This was something we did a few weeks into my winter visit, and the Korths remember it well. The way Siberian Yupik words are spelled often has little bearing on how they sound, so despite my efforts, I made a mockery of the language. For Edna, Heimo, and the girls it was nothing short of hilarious.

Ask Edna to spell a Siberian Yupik word, and she shakes her head. "I don't know," she'll say. I thought this was unusual until I learned that Siberian Yupik is primarily a spoken language. It wasn't until 1910 that a white man, Edgar O. Campbell, a medical missionary and Presbyterian minister, developed the first Yupik writing system. When Edna was in school though, it was English or nothing. She was scolded for speaking Siberian Yupik. And she was never taught how to write it.

The Siberian Yupik language is ideally suited to the world of St. Lawrence Island, a landscape of ice and snow. Siberian Yupik has almost sixty separate words for ice: *siku*, ice; *duvaq*, shore-fast ice; *iighwilnguq*, drifting floes of ice; *genu*, slush ice; *saleq*, new ice; *laaq*, ice run; *meghaat*, open water on pack ice; *kagim leghwaaq*, crushed ice. Heimo told me how sometimes Edna will caution the girls: "Watch out, that's wet water!" or "Walk there, that's frozen ice." They find it endlessly amusing, but for Edna it is anything but redundant.

Rhonda turns to the Savoonga section of the phone book, which is only a page and a half, and hands it to me. "Edna is related to everyone in there except for the Bs, the Ds, and the Js," Heimo chortles.

So I start. "Annogiyuk, Kinegeekuk, Mokiyuk, Pungowiyi, Waghiyi." By the time I reach the final name, Edna and the girls are doubled up with laughter, holding their stomachs, as if the gesture is choreographed, and Heimo is pounding his knee. He sounds as if he is sobbing.

"Tell him," Heimo says, trying to catch his breath. "Show him how."

Edna opens her mouth to speak. "I can't," she pleads. "I can't." A minute or so goes by, and she is finally ready to try again. "AnA-gai-yuk," she emphasizes the second *a*. "Kinekuk," long *e*, guttral *k*. "PungaWI," she says, swallowing the *g* deep in her throat, then accenting the last syllable. When she reaches Waghiyi, she breaks up again. "That's enough. Please, no more."

"Here, try to say this," Heimo says to me. "Bee-nick-took nukloo."

I try to repeat it. Edna can no longer restrain herself. She is sprawled out in Heimo's lap.

"What does it mean?" I ask, hardly able to get the words out myself, but neither Heimo nor Edna can speak.

Finally, Heimo squeaks out an answer. "Nice ass," he says. Then he looks to make sure that Rhonda and Krin haven't heard. But they have. They roll out of the hammock and into the dirt. Firth hops between them, barking and licking their faces. Edna jumps out of Heimo's arms and runs toward the trees in the back of the cabin, still wracked with laughter. "I can't stand it," she yells. "I have to pee."

Two weeks later and a long way from the Coleen River, Rhonda and I are sitting in the airport in Seattle, when she shows me her BIA card. It reads: "Department of the Interior—Bureau of Indian Affairs—Certificate of Indian Blood—This is to certify that the person named on the reverse is listed as or is a descendent of a person on the ANCSA roll, an official record of this office."

Rhonda explains. "I'm glad I remembered it. It means the Bureau of Indian Affairs will pick up my medical expenses. Uncle Tom will have to drive me to a reservation, though. I guess there's one about an hour from Appleton. Sometimes I wish Daddy would move us to Fairbanks. I could go to school there. It would make things easier. If he had the money, we could live in Fairbanks, and he could buy a plane and fly out during the week and trap. But that would kill him, I think. He can't stand town for very long."

I give the card back to her, and she studies it. "Only," she says, "I'm Eskimo, not Indian." She sticks it in her purse and then sniffs the air. "Smell that?" she asks, scrunching up her nose. "Plastic. I really don't like the smell of plastic."

She gets up to go to the bathroom and returns with a Coke, flopping down in the seat next to me. "You should have been there when I left the cabin."

"Maybe it's better I wasn't," I say. I had left the river a day earlier than she, hitching a ride back to Fort Yukon with John Peterson. "I'm sure it was very emotional."

"Yeah," Rhonda says noncommittally, as if that is the end of it. I return my attention to my book, and she says, "The night before I left, I listened to Enya and cried. She's Daddy's favorite, you know. I was upset, but I think it was hardest on Mom and Krin. Krin climbed in bed with me in the morning and just hugged me. She seemed okay, but when I left, she really lost it. Daddy carried me in his arms down to the canoe. He wouldn't talk. I think he was trying not to cry. Mom just cried and cried."

"How do you feel now?" I ask her, shortly after they announce our flight to Minneapolis.

"Okay," she says sadly. "I have to just keep imagining Daddy getting on his snowmachine first thing in the morning. You know how we always come out to kiss him good-bye for the day? Him all bundled up against the cold, heading for the trapline? It makes me happy to think about that."

CHAPTER 11

Closing of the Frontier

"Keeping it simple is extremely hard work," says Steve Ulvi. He and I and Stu Pechek, who trapped for a decade out of a cabin on Grayling Lake, fifty-five miles west of the Korths, are sitting by a campfire on a sandbar along Salchaket Slough, a side creek that feeds the Tanana River about an hour by boat outside of Fairbanks. We have just finished our dinner and a six-pack, and Ulvi is leaning back against a large dead-fall, eyes closed, puffing on his pipe. The smell of tobacco is sweet and pleasant and seems to work as a deterrent to the mosquitoes. "Simplicity was the unwritten code on the river," Ulvi elaborates, a wisp of smoke rising.

It has been twenty-seven years since John McPhee wrote about him and the Yukon River experience that was such an important part of his life. At fifty, the good looks are still there, the shattered blue eyes, the dramatic droopy mustache, his hair no longer blond but dark and streaked with gray, his body still strong but no longer coiled tightly from toiling in the woods. Ulvi is genial and laughs easily, but there's no mis-taking the intensity.

"It was our religion. When we left the river, we had three power tools: a chain saw, a thirty-five-horse Evinrude on a homemade, welded thirty-foot riverboat, and a gas-powered ringer washer. To live in the bush for six or eight years, let alone ten or fifteen, let alone nearly thirty, as Heimo has, is damn difficult. On the Yukon, we had a sense of community. It came with its responsibilities and pressures, sure—the pressures to keep it simple were enormous—but, all in all, it was such a positive experience. There were people up and down the river who were willing to help out in a pinch. Heimo and his family are out there, way up there, by themselves. That adds another dimension to the experience. Their isolation is compounded by the fact that so few people are doing it anymore." Ulvi stops talking and pokes at the fire with a long stick.

"More wood?" Pechek asks in his bass voice still tinged with the long vowel sounds of Minnesota's Iron Range. "Why not," Ulvi answers, smoke wafting from his nose and mouth. "Let's settle in." Pechek rambles off into the brush to collect more wood. Though I've just met him, I like Stu already. He looks as if he's just come off the trapline with his split-rail-fence physique, all knotted muscle and bone, not a pound to spare.

"You literally can count them on one hand, maybe two" Steve continues, "the people that are still out there. And the numbers are shrinking. When we left there wasn't a fragment of a doubt that we were doing the right thing. We got bored; we needed more intellectual and social stimulation; the kids needed a better education; they needed friends; we got tired of the isolation and the never-ending work. I admire Heimo, but there is no way I could have stayed engaged in that lifestyle for as long as he has."

If anybody knows what it takes to make it in the bush, it's Steve Ulvi. He and his wife, Lynette Roberts, and their two children lived on the Yukon from 1974 until 1984, honing their version of the simple life, and then they began a slow transition into Fairbanks, where they moved in 1991. After living on the river for a decade, it took Steve years to acclimate to the idea of being in Fairbanks. Had it not been for Lynette and the kids, he probably would have dragged it out another few years. But he knew it was the right thing to do, and he had a job, which made things easier.

In 1981, Steve took a position as a seasonal employee with the National Park Service to make ends meet. Then in 1984, he joined the Park Service full-time, and that's when they made their move into Eagle. They lived in Eagle for two years and then bought seven and a half acres of a Native allotment outside of town and built a three-sided cabin with tarps for doors and plastic windows. They still lived off-the-grid, ran dogs, and raised rabbits.

Steve admits that it was a big deal when he went to work for the Park Service. Some regarded it as a kind of heresy. "Eagle," he says, "was one of the hotbeds of opposition, and the Park Service presence wasn't always greeted kindly. But I figured that I was a local hire. I felt like I could make a difference. Another guy from the river and I had a big impact on how the Park Service's policies were implemented locally. We tried to fit in. Our first staff boats were nineteen-foot Grumman canoes with six- to fifteen-horse kickers [outboard motors]. In the long term, for Alaska and America, ANILCA was a good thing. But there was a price to pay. The old Alaska was transformed, but the land was saved. I'd love to be able to turn the clock back to 1952, but that just isn't possible. I believe we've done the right thing. I thank my lucky stars, though, that I was able to experience life on the river. I can't imagine what I'd be dreaming about or what I'd be like today had I not done it. But the truth is, this land that we've protected will be here for generations. The state and BLM lands will be crisscrossed with roads."

His pipe wedged between his teeth, Ulvi pokes at the fire with a stick. "Our lives along the river in the 1970s and 1980s will one day be interpreted as history by the National Park Service, as it now interprets the gold rush and the era of the stern-wheeler. We'll never see anything like it again. Our society in general suffers in small ways from that. The Alaskan and American sense of self suffers, too. We're losing a sense of who we are as a people, and it's not only because the land has been partitioned. The greatest threat to the bush experience is not the National Park Service, but the intense regulation of trapping, cultural homogeneity, and changing societal values. Does a wilderness impetus even exist? There are thousands of young men living on the outskirts of Bozeman, Montana. Montana's beautiful; we'd all be there if it hadn't been overrun. How is the rebellion manifesting itself these days? Where are the dreamers who want to turn the clock back?"

"There's damn little land left," says Dean Wilson, a longtime fur buyer. Wilson and I are sitting in his office at the Klondike Hotel on Airport

Way in Fairbanks, out of which he and his wife operate their fur-buying business. The room smells like a butcher shop and is cluttered with lynx, otter, red fox, and marten furs, dark and light brown wolverine furs, wolf furs stretched nine feet long, ranging in color from gray to tan to pure white to a deep, inky black. Danny Grangaard of Tok, one of Alaska's old-time trappers, a former hippie who came up in 1965 with hair down to his waist, has just brought in a pile of luxuriant wolf skins. Grangaard is regarded as perhaps Alaska's most skillful wolf trapper. "I'll catch more wolves than marten this year," he laughs, sipping black coffee, making light of the cyclical, but still disappointing, shortage of marten, whose population has hit a low not seen in many years.

Wilson is inspecting Grangaard's wolf skins and talking at the same time. "The pipeline changed everything. But it's not just the land deal. For fifty-six years, I've made my living by trapping, fur buying, hunting, mining," he says, scribbling notes, as best he can, in a pocket-sized notebook. Wilson was diagnosed with Parkinson's not long ago, and those trappers who have known him for his honesty and fairness say he's gone downhill fast. "It's a way of life that's disappearing," he continues. "It's being phased out, choked out, by a culture that doesn't understand it or like it."

Federal export fees and regulations, including in-person inspections of furs, notwithstanding, trappers have a bigger battle to fight. The poor image of trapping is something that neither Wilson nor Alaska's trappers can ignore. Sixty percent of the land in Alaska is held in federal trust. In other words, outsiders have the power to mold Alaska into their idealized image of what a frontier should look like, and public opinion in the Lower Forty-eight does not favor trapping. A trapper on federal land, though he may live in extreme isolation, like Heimo, cannot escape the heartfelt stirrings of animal lovers in Illinois.

Danny Grangaard leaves, and ten minutes later, Alex Tarnai, a trapper, who was born in Hungary and came to Alaska in 1976, walks in with his six-year-old son, Little Alex. Alex's hair has gone almost entirely gray, but even at fifty-nine, he is heavily muscled. He has the build of a gymnast and the gentle voice of someone accustomed to reading bedtime stories to a child.

I am hardly surpised to see Alex here today. Dean Wilson's office is like a local bait-and-tackle shop or a small-town diner, where folks wander in and out for much of the day just to shoot the breeze and catch up on the gossip. We visit for a while and Little Alex falls asleep in his father's lap.

"What's the state of trapping today?" Wilson asks Alex.

"What a large question," Alex laughs. Then, like a man who is used to taking his time to get things right, Alex pauses before answering. "Well, you can't do it like I did, but there are still opportunities," he says, pointing to a sign hanging behind him that reads "Trapline for Sale." "A young guy could come up and make it known that he wants to trap. He could come here and talk with some of the guys. There are any number of trappers willing to give up their lines. I'd give him one of mine, forty miles or so to start with. But nobody's coming and nobody's asking.

"It isn't just the lands issue," he continues, "but that certainly plays a part." When Alex Tarnai speaks of the effects of ANILCA, he isn't just relating stories he's heard. He experienced ANILCA firsthand. The problem with the 186-page document is that portions of it are necessarily vague, subject to the interpretation of various agencies and agency managers with distinctly personal visions of how the act should be implemented. In Alex's case, he hadn't even heard of ANILCA until the assistant manager of the 1,560,000-acre Nowitna National Wildlife Refuge, in the central Yukon River Valley, showed up at his cabin door in brand-new Abercrombie & Fitch outdoor gear with a briefcase a full two years after the Lands Act was passed. There would be "changes, new regulations," he told Alex, and proceeded to read some of those new rules to him. As the refuge's only full-time resident, Alex was made to feel "like an outlaw whose presence in the woods was dependent on staying in the agency's good graces." He was told that it was a "privilege" to be there, one that could be revoked at any time. Despite feeling bitter about the experience, Alex maintained a good relationship with refuge officials until 1987. That year, a federal wildlife refuge planner, whom Alex had come to know, made plans to pay a friendly visit. The Nowitna's refuge manager got wind of the visit and informed Alex that he was not entitled to have visitors because his cabin was a "work cabin" and not a "recreational" one. That's ridiculous, Alex thought, and his friend visited anyway. The manager, however, feeling that his authority was threatened, harassed them, flying overhead with a camera and a ticket book to document their violations. Worse yet, while Alex was out on his trapline, the refuge manager entered his cabin, ostensibly to check on his stove. That was it; Alex had finally had enough. He sued the U.S. Fish & Wildlife Service—many Fish & Wildlife officials later told him that they were sympathetic to his cause—claiming he was denied his constitutional right to associate with anyone he pleased and accusing the agency of illegal trespass. In a landmark case, U.S. District Court Judge Andrew Kleinfeld ruled in his favor.

Wilson gets up when another trapper comes in with a bundle of marten fur. Alex remains seated, holding little Alex. "The U.S. Fish and Wildlife Service treated me shamefully," he says. "But I don't hold a grudge. That refuge manager is gone, and my relationship with the agency is now very friendly."

It is late morning when I meet Bill Schneider in his office at the University of Alaska Fairbanks's Elmer E. Rasmuson Library. Schneider has served as curator of oral history at the UAF since 1981. In that capacity, he has interviewed many Native trappers who are still living in the bush villages, as well as white trappers who once made the bush their home. I have just left Dean Wilson's, and Schneider and I pick up on the subject of the last of the white trappers still living off the land. Schneider elaborates. "White guys trapping in the bush," he says, speaking slowly and thoughtfully, "are an 'endangered species.' The Natives get a lot of support, but there is no organization besides the Alaska Trappers Association advocating for the rural white trapper." He pauses and studies a large pair of headphones he's holding in his hands. "Wilderness is both the source of, and a respository of, our national myths about who we really are as a people. Yet the people who are left out there, living the myth, are more out of touch with American life and values than ever before. Ironically, we have always held in higher esteem those who make forays into the wilderness than those who live in it. We're creating an environment for ecotourism, but we're eliminating a culture dedicated to living on, and working with, the land."

"The lands issue dramatically changed Alaska," Randy Brown says emphatically. He and I are having lunch at Soapy Smith's Pioneer Restaurant, a Fairbanks institution situated a few doors down from the intersection of Cushman Street and 2nd Avenue. Two Street, as 2nd Avenue is often called, has been cleaned up in recent years, but it still has something of a reputation for drunkenness and decadence.

Brown is friendly, intelligent, and intense. Though he would surely resist the comparison, he looks a bit like Robert Redford in *Jeremiah Johnson*. He is still taut and fit and wears his copper-colored beard and hair slightly long, as he once did on the trapline.

What Brown says is true. The reapportionment of Alaska's 375 million acres changed Alaska's physical and psychic landscape. John McPhee was there while it was happening, while the lines were being drawn, but he never reported on the fallout. In 1976 and 1977, ANILCA was still an idea, legislation in the making; today it's not. Every square foot of Alaska has been surveyed and conveyed to one group or another—the Park Service, the BLM, the state, Fish & Wildlife, regional corporations, Native villages, Native allotments, private holdings. The map of Alaska is now a color-coded mosaic, a patchwork of neatly delineated boundaries. On the ground, these boundaries are anything but neat; state land abuts National Park Service land, which adjoins Native land, and the division is often indistinguishable. Hunters and trappers can get confused trying to figure out what's what.

For centuries, anyone who could use the land was welcome to it. Through the Homestead and Homesite Acts the government even enabled people to acquire land, free of charge, provided they "prove up," making nominal improvements to it. In a place like Alaska, however, this stipulation was rarely enforced. The Homestead Act, which was enacted in 1862 and was terminated nationwide in 1976, provided that any person over the age of twenty-one could obtain free title to 160 acres of government land. Although the program had been marginally effective west of the Missouri River in the Lower Forty-eight, it was a bust in much of Alaska. The Homesite Act of 1927, which was established only for Alaska and provided free title to five acres of land under terms similar to the Homestead Act, wasn't repealed until October 1986. Though it was more successful than the Homestead Act, the large-scale settlement of Alaska never occurred.

Randy Brown and his family experienced the partitioning of Alaska firsthand. In 1985, the land on which they were living was conveyed to Doyon, the largest of the regional corporations, covering the whole Athabaskan Interior and thirty-four villages. Doyon issued a trespass notice in 1990. Brown says, "We could have sued for grandfather rights, but how big of a place could we have sued for? Five acres, ten, one hundred—no amount of land would have suited our needs.

"After ANILCA, and before Doyon issued the trespass notice, we were working through a permitting process with a variety of different agencies. Dealing with the BLM was relatively straightforward. It offered ten-year renewable permits. Same with the state. However, on Park Service land, where we had our fish camp, the regulations were more complex; we needed a fish camp permit, a permit to cut wood. The frustrating thing was that the rules changed from administrator to administrator. Some of the people living on Park Service land just refused to abide by the process. Of course, the agencies were under no obligation to accommodate guys like me, but they did. Nevertheless, the land regulations precipitated an exodus, and now they prevent recolonization. If they were to allow people back in, the question is where to draw the line? Do you just allow limited colonization? At first, I think they'd be flooded, but a lot of people wouldn't stay. It's always been that way though. Lots came and few stayed. There are a lot of half-built cabins out there. People came to live forever and they left after a year or two."

Randy takes a big bite of his hamburger but doesn't stop talking. "I still get letters [Randy and Heimo were part of a 1992 National Geographic documentary called *Braving Alaska*] from people who are looking to get out into the country. I've heard the argument about society not making young men like us anymore, and I don't buy it. There are adventurers out there. When they contact me, I tell them to go into a village and let it be known that they're interested in going out to the woods. But to come out and jump off the way I did, that's a thing of the past. Now the land can be accessed by airplane trappers and snow machine trappers who blaze out into the country for a week, even a day."

After visiting with Brown, I call Alonzo "Lon" Kelly, an outdoor recreation planner for the White Mountains National Recreation Area for the Bureau of Land Management in Fairbanks. "I don't buy it," Kelly says. "I was the former realty specialist and later an outdoor recreation planner for the Fortymile River country with the BLM. I don't know what the Park Service did. But I don't put any stock in the accusation that it put people out. If people had wanted to stay, they could have. Living that life today is not out of the question. I'm not familiar with the exact agency guidelines, but if someone wanted to build a cabin on the BLM's 72 million acres, or at least on much of that acreage, he'd be welcome to present a proposal to us. He'd have to have been trapping the land for a while though, and he'd have to document his use with fur sale receipts or something and prove that there is no existing conflict with ongoing subsistence or recreational users. Then we'd consider it, I think. It's complicated, but in assessing the request, we'd follow the legislative framework of ANILCA and the Federal Land Policy and Management Act." Though Kelly is sincere, what he doesn't say is that even if a person were to follow the prescribed steps, the chances of the BLM giving him the go-ahead are anything but guaranteed. Such a messy bureaucratic process would have been anathema to the Randy Browns and Heimo Korths of the world, and there is no reason to think that today's would-be adventurers would react differently.

But it's those modern-day adventurers that Kelly doesn't see. "It's a nonissue these days," he says, unequivocally. "No one is interested in going out into the country."

I am sitting in Roger Kaye's house in the hills outside of Fairbanks, where Kaye surrounds himself with examples of America's woodcraft wilderness tradition—Philip R. Goodwin sketches, old guns and traps, first-edition books of exploration and adventure. Outside, the temperature slips to 25 below. Inside, the handsome woodstove, which acts as the centerpiece of the living room, gives the home a generous, hospitable feel. Roger's Japanese wife, Masako, has just prepared a delicious dinner of sushi, salad, and roast chicken. A friend of Roger's, Tom Paragi, a wildlife biologist for the Alaska Department of Fish and Game and a part-time trapper, brings with him a surprisingly good beaver stew.

After dinner Roger shows us a photo album of his days on the trapline. He trapped for only a year on Beaver Creek, forty-five miles south of Fort Yukon, but that year was formative. Except for the Arctic National Wildlife Refuge, there seems to be nothing he enjoys talking about more. "I get great satisfaction knowing that there are still a few people in the bush toughing it out, keeping those wilderness skills alive," he says, slowly turning the pages of the album.

Roger sips his wine and flips to a photograph of a wolverine. "It was a big one," he says, obviously still proud of his catch. Then he closes the album and leans back in his chair. "You have to understand," he says. "These bush rats would not have had this right in any other country. They came to the woods, built illegal cabins, and now they have the legal right to be there because ANILCA made accommodations for their life way. But ANILCA does not allow for the expansion of the bush rat experience. It couldn't be done and still protect the values that the refuge and other places like it were set aside for. The refuge is a place for wildlife, particularly for species not tolerant of civilization; a place of scenic values and scientific values; a setting for recreation. The refuge has other meanings, too. It is a place of solitude, mystery, discovery, exploration, a place of restraint, even sacredness. Many Alaskans don't think about the need to protect wilderness because we're surrounded by it here. The scale is enormous, and people can't conceive of it ever being diminished. They don't understand that Alaska is the last refuge for wilderness.

"That's not to say that if someone wanted to come up and trap in the refuge, he couldn't. In fact, he could as long as he didn't put up a permanent structure. He could trap out of a wall tent. That's permitted. In other areas of Alaska, a person could go through a realtor and buy land if he had that kind of money. Granted, it's not the same experience as *Coming into the Country*, where you could go out and build a cabin and essentially do whatever the hell you want. Those days are gone."

I leave Roger's house near midnight, and it occurs to me that it would be interesting to get Roger Kaye and Bill Schneider, UAF's oral history coordinator, in the same room. I recall my conversation with Schneider the previous week. We'd been talking about ANILCA, and the role of the governmental agencies. Schneider spoke vehemently: "I don't think it's justifiable for the lead agencies of preservation, which includes historical and cultural preservation, to discourage recolonization. There have always been people out there, living off the land. I often wonder what the constructors of our current wilderness ethic would say. Take Bob Marshall or Margaret Murie—these conservation icons all had local guides on their adventures in Alaska.

"In many ways ANILCA is a dead end for subsistence users," Schneider continued. "As much as it supports subsistence activities for this generation, I think its framers had trouble fathoming that subsistence could be a lasting value. I don't think they could imagine a young person choosing that way of life. They [the federal agencies] could glorify it, put up with it for a while, but I don't think they could imagine future generations doing it. If we as Americans don't create places and opportunities in our vast and bountiful land for people like this, whether they be Native or white, then we have lost important historical and cultural values. The argument, of course, is the land can't accommodate it, but we're not talking about large numbers of people."

Kirk Sweetsir, who owns Yukon Air Service, flew me out to the Korths' upper Coleen cabin in spring. We were over the Yukon Flats, where the snowy surfaces of countless small lakes are accented by muskrat push-ups and the tracks of peripatetic caribou. Sweetsir was punching the cabin's coordinates into his GPS and talking at the same time. "The experience will be increasingly less available to guys without money," Sweetsir said, "and more available to guys from Anchorage and Fairbanks. It's unfortunate, but civilization continues to creep into the most remote parts of Alaska. Heimo has built his firebreak against it, and he's trying to hold it off as best he can, though I think even he is aware of the inevitability of it—things will change.

"What gets to me is the somewhat unremarkable incrementalism that creeps up on people who are stitting still. All around them things are moving along and one day they realize that just because they're not bothering anyone, it doesn't necessarily follow that no one's going to bother them. It all seems a bit of a tragedy. We have no reverence for a person like Heimo. He's likely to die defending a vague idea of what his world ought to look like. Not long ago, he was one of many similarly situated people and they generated their own gravity. Now it's down to him. He becomes more of an anchronism with each passing year."

In mid-July, before going out to the river, I visit Harry Bader, director of Alaska's Department of Natural Resources (DNR) Northern Region. Bader elaborates on Sweetsir's idea. "People are moving out to the woods with all the capital that makes it comfortable. Their relationship to the land is very different from the guy who's out there, barely scraping by, trying to make a go of it. I call 'em trust fund homesteaders, and their presence on the land is so much more consumptive. Those who are dependent on the land import far fewer resources—less fuel, fewer modern conveniences, less of everything. But the Alaska way of life, the age-old practice of living off the land, is bumping up against Lower Forty-eight values that say, 'Watch the wolf, don't trap it,' and that changes the character of the experience entirely."

Bader is familiar with life in the bush. "I did my time," he laughs, making light of his experience. "I did it, and I enjoyed it. However, I was one of those just playing at it. At no time was I dependent on the land. I wasn't forced to shoot a moose or a caribou to stay alive. And I wasn't dependent upon trapping for my income." Bader lived outside of Eagle for a year, though by looking at him, it is hard to imagine him running a trapline at 40 below. I know better than to doubt him, though. "Harry can do just about anything," Stu Pechek told me before I met with Harry at his office in Fairbanks. Nevertheless, Harry's looks are deceiving. He is a small man and has the fine hands of a pianist or a jewelry maker. He is also very much an intellectual. He used to teach wildlife management and environmental courses at the university in Fairbanks, has his J.D. from Harvard, and is finishing up his Ph.D. in Forestry at Yale, making the trip to New Haven, Connecticut, twice a year.

We turn our attention to a large map, where he shows me the land he administers, 45 million acres of the state's 105 million total, a swath of country covering the crest of the Alaska Range north to the Arctic Ocean and stretching from Canada's Yukon Territory border to the Bering Strait.

Having heard about the DNR's land dispersal programs, I get right to the point. "Among those 45 million acres is there anywhere a person could just jump off and build a cabin, replicating, say, the experience of the guys who came up in the 1970s?" Harry reflects on the question, turning a pencil in his fingers, and then answers. "The simple answer is no," he says. "And I feel kind of awkward about that because that thing you're talking about is the defining attribute of Alaska and Alaskan culture, and I don't necessarily believe it's a good thing it's over. So, let me restate my answer. It's not entirely impossible for us to see something similar again. But the current regulatory and statutory system forbids that sort of going out."

Harry points out that the DNR has two land-dispersal programs: a subdivision program of presurveyed parcels and one for remote residential parcels. Both are designed to get property in Alaska out of state hands and into the hands of individuals. Both also involve the purchase of land. Neither in any way resembles what the "back to nature" boys did in the 1970s. What's closest to that perhaps is the DNR's "Trapping Cabin Permit," which allows a trapper to build and use a cabin on state land for temporary shelter while trapping. However, compared to the experience of guys like Heimo and Alex Tarnai, who simply picked a spot on the map, it is complicated, dispiriting. A trapper has to prove he uses the trapline on a regular basis. The trapline must also be long enough to warrant the building of a cabin. Additionally, a trapper must be able to provide tax returns reporting income from furs, receipts from fur buyers, and additional proof, such as receipts for tanning, if requested. Recently, very few people have taken advantage of this option.

"Unofficially," Harry says, "we have some trespassers, people who are living off the land on state land. We are trying to figure out how to allow them to stay, how to legitimize them through some sort of permit system. To me, to tolerate that handful of people—and that's all we're talking about—who are seriously trying to keep that way of life alive is well worth it. Thank God most of us don't want to be on the land; it couldn't sustain us. I'm glad it's just a few, but I fear it's too few. In ten years, I believe, we won't have any more people out there."

Heimo and I are gathering summer blueberries for breakfast. Last night, Heimo promised us all pancakes. Edna does the dinners, but Heimo, he's the breakfast man. It's a role he's grown accustomed to over the years. When he first brought Edna to the Coleen, she made one thing clear to him. She liked to sleep in later than 6:00 A.M., and she didn't make breakfast.

Strangely, I have a craving for pancakes this morning. I say "strange" because when I'm home I rarely eat them. Heimo told me it would happen. "You need carbos up here," he said a week into my earlier winter visit. Now, as we pick berries, I realize that I've been looking forward to eating pancakes for days.

After breakfast, Heimo and I pack for our hunting expedition. Though Heimo has been glassing Mummuck Mountain for the past several days, he hasn't spotted a single caribou. "Maybe they're down in the valleys north of Mummuck Mountain," he says. "We'll see. It don't matter really. I'm just tired of doing nothing. Don't get me wrong—I like sitting around as much as the next guy—but now I gotta move."

In early August, before the caribou come, there's not much that needs doing, and life along the river takes on the characteristics of a summer vacation. The new roof is on, and Edna has finished the loads of laundry. So the Korths pick berries, fish, take short hikes, glass for caribou, sharpen tools, play volleyball, and sit around the fire at night and exchange stories. The pace is relaxed, leisurely.

But today, Heimo is tired of relaxing. He needs to walk.

At the river, we throw our gear into the canoe, strap on our life vests, and are about to shove off, when Edna comes running toward us.

"What is it?" Heimo says, slightly annoyed.

"I forgot to kiss you," Edna answers. Heimo smiles now and they kiss. "Please be careful," Edna entreats us when Heimo starts the motor.

The idea of motoring upriver, though, is a fantasy; the water level is too low. A half mile up, we lay our paddles in the canoe and walk. We trade off lining. I begin, and while I line, Heimo studies the gravel bars, looking for tracks.

I'm trying to navigate a long stretch of riffles, when Heimo yells. I can't make out what he's saying, and then he yells again, "Wolf tracks!"

I clear the choppy water. "What's all the excitement about?"

"This time of year the wolves are following the caribou," Heimo explains. "I don't see any caribou tracks, but I bet we run into them up ahead." Sure enough, on the next gravel bar, while Heimo is lining, I spot some and call out to him. Heimo pulls the canoe onto the sand.

"A gob of tracks." He smiles. "They must have passed through here yesterday. When the caribou are migrating, wolves eat like fiends. The wolverines eat well, too. They gobble up what's left."

It is noon by the time we reach the base of Mummuck Mountain. We tie off the canoe and change from our hip boots into hiking boots.

Before beginning our climb, we traverse a boggy area. In Alaska there are three types of tundra: wet, moist and alpine. Wet tundra is a morass of tussocks and stagnant pools. Moist tundra is a maze of tufts and tussocks minus the pools and the sloppy sogginess of wet tundra. The tussocks in this stretch of moist tundra get the best of me, and Heimo easily outdistances me. He is waiting on the other side of a bog when I finally make my way out.

"Black-tipped groundsel," he says, pointing to a pretty yellow flower at the bog's edge. Panting, I consult my book.

"Yup, black-tipped groundsel." Yesterday Heimo and I identified the flower for the first time. I'm surprised that he's already committed its name to memory.

Now we begin our ascent through another long stretch of moist tundra. The walking is easier, though I still struggle to keep pace with Heimo. The moist tundra gives way to alpine, patchy areas of mosses, herbs, lichens, and shrubs, and then we ascend a series of benches. The underbrush turns to scree and large rocks are speckled with white, yellow, and black lichens. Heimo stops for a moment and kicks at the ground, scattering pellets. "Moose crap," I say, though I can't believe that a moose would be up this high.

"No, musk-ox," he answers. "I've never seen it up here."

The Inupiat call the musk-oxen *umingmak*, "the bearded ones." In 1969 and 1970, sixty-three musk-oxen were shipped in wooden crates from Nunivak Island in the Bering Sea to the North Slope of Alaska in an effort to reestablish the population. The total herd now numbers close to 400 animals. Twenty thousand years ago, musk-oxen roamed the Old World as far as southern France; cave paintings testify to their presence there.

Glad for the rest, I look back in the direction of the cabin and notice for the first time that the leaves of the balsam poplar have already begun to turn yellow. Out of the north, where the trees that creep up the Coleen River valley give way to an ocean of russet-colored tundra, a dry wind blows. Heimo zips up his jacket. "Almost fall time," he says. "Let's keep moving."

What Heimo loves to do more than anything else in the world is walk. He calls it "coverin' country." He moves effortlessly, hardly winded, all the while naming rocks and birds as he goes. "That's schist," he says, naming a metamorphic rock. "See that? American golden plover. There's a horned lark. And that one's a harrier. You can tell by the white rump." Skipping around a rock outcropping, he stops. "If I could come back as any animal, it'd be a Dall sheep. God, I love to hike in the mountains."

Fifteen minutes later, we reach the top of Mummuck Mountain, and Heimo takes off his pack and sits down near a benchmark erected by the U.S. Geological Survey in 1972. "We'll stay here for a while and glass." I sit down next to him. "Frigid arnica," I say, pointing to a hardy yellow flower that hangs on for dear life between two large rocks, springing up out of a cupful of soil. But Heimo is no longer interested in flowers. He is glassing now, studying the mountains to the north and west, which look remarkably like the rugged moors of Scotland. "Sometimes," he says, "there are caribou everywhere. I wish you could see that."

French explorers in Canada called the endless herds of caribou, the world's most efficient walkers, *La Foule*—"The Throng." To see *La*

Foule, as I had the previous summer, while camped on the Kongakut River in the Arctic National Wildlife Refuge with my friend Burns, is to be awestruck—there are so many caribou that an entire slope looks as if it is undulating. As they near, a chorus of grunting and clicking hooves accompanies the dramatic choreography of their movements. The Gwich'in used to intercept these migrating herds, trapping the caribou inside fences, which were often miles long. Snares were set inside the fences, and when the caribou were corralled, they became entangled. Gwich'in hunters then finished them off with spears or bows and arrows.

Much like the old Gwich'in hunters, who depended on the caribou for many of their needs, when the Korths shoot one almost nothing is wasted. They eat the meat and the organs. The tongue and cheeks, the meat on the face, the fat behind the eyes, the brain—these are delicacies. They also keep the head, which they will roast or use for headcheese. To make headcheese, Edna boils the head down to a thick broth, adds spices, onions, red peppers, and vinegar, and sets the broth outside to harden. By the following morning the soup has the consistency of soft, gelatinous cheese and will taste like, as Heimo describes it, "peppered jello." Although the Korths primarily use high-tech sleeping bags now, they'll make the hide, depending on its condition, into a blanket, for added warmth in winter. Edna uses the leg skins for *kamiks*, the sealskin-lined boots that she, Heimo, and the girls wear throughout winter; she boils the hoofs and bones for soup, and uses the leg bones and attached meat for stew. This leaves only the horns, which Heimo often sells to a Fairbanks horn buyer for $200 to $250.

Mummuck Mountain has always been one of Heimo's favorite caribou-hunting areas. During the summer, the animals take refuge in the high elevations to avoid the constant menace of botflies, warble flies, and mosquitoes. Today Heimo hopes to kill only one caribou, but how many he takes for the year will be determined by whether or not he gets a moose. Legally, his family, including Krin and Rhonda, is allowed to take forty caribou a year, ten each. If Heimo gets a moose, they'll take four or five caribou at the most. If he fails to shoot a moose, which is unlikely, they will take ten or twelve. This year, he plans to shoot only a bull caribou. While he was in Fort Yukon, Fran Mauer, a former Arctic National Wildlife Refuge biologist, came through town. In the course of their conversation, Mauer reported that there'd been a significant calf die-off, and Heimo is determined not to risk taking a cow of breeding age, which might drop a calf again next year.

Though Heimo used to hunt with a large-bore rifle, a Marlin .444, which he brought up from Wisconsin, believing that it took a big gun to bring down a big animal, after his experience on St. Lawrence Island, he learned the art of bullet placement. He now uses a 22.250, a small rifle with excellent ballistics. He calls it the flattest shooting gun made. The added bonus is that it doesn't blow a big hole in the animal, therefore little of the meat is ruined.

After ten minutes or so, Heimo sets down his binoculars. "Old Crow Flats," he says, directing my attention east. "It's full of lakes and swarming with mosquitoes. The Indians who lived in that area used to be called the Rat Indians because they took so many muskrats off the lakes every spring. Over there," he continues, motioning to the northeast, to a small creek that feeds the Coleen River, "that's where I want my ashes scattered. Edna and the girls know that. It might sound corny, but this land has given so much to me, when I die, I'd like to give something back."

Heimo leans back and closes his eyes. I close my eyes, too, and doze off. I wake up to the sound of his voice. "I'd be disheartened—would that be the word?—not to see caribou here because of oil. They can't tell me that oil development in ANWR [Arctic National Wildlife Refuge] won't affect the herd. That's a bunch of lies. I'd be sad to see that disrupted. I know what it can look like. This whole valley can fill up with caribou. Take away the caribou and you lose something. I don't want ANWR to be like the North Slope."

What Heimo is talking about are the drill pads, drilling rigs ten stories high, hundreds of miles of service roads, flow stations, pipelines, reserve pits holding millions of tons of drilling waste, with high concentrations of heavy metals, hydrocarbons, and other toxic chemicals, smokestacks, parking lots, and workers' barracks that characterize the North Slope oil development area.

Proponents of development (including the state of Alaska, oil's biggest promoter) argue that the disputed 1002 area (referred to as "ten-oh-two"), a 1.5 million-acre chunk of Arctic coastal plain, was exempted from refuge status for precisely this reason—to allow for the possibility that oil could one day be extracted.

In the early spring of 1989, it almost was. President George Bush the elder was prepared to sign the bill giving the go-ahead. Then, on March 24, 1989, the *Exxon Valdez* ran aground in Prince William Sound, spilling 11 million gallons of crude oil, leaving an oil slick that deluged 1,200 miles of beaches, effectively smothering the hopes of those who wanted to get at the coastal plain's oil deposits.

While the 1002 area was indeed placed in a special category by ANILCA, the legislation specified that the area's oil and gas potential would have to be weighed against the impact of development on the environment. The U.S. Fish & Wildlife Service has determined that oil drilling would be incompatible with the purposes of the refuge. Big oil's boosters, however, hope to waive provisions in the National Wildlife Refuge Administration Act and National Enviromental Policy Act in order to circumvent this clause and allow drilling.

The rallying cry of the energy policy of the current Bush is that the U.S. needs to tap coastal plain oil reserves in order to relieve our dependency on foreign oil and to solve the accompanying national security issues. What's often neglected in this argument is that the oil contained in the coastal plain amounts to a mere drop in the bucket when measured against the United States's monumental needs, which are now at 19 million barrels a day, or 6.9 billion barrels a year. Christopher Flavin of the Worldwatch Institute likens trying to stem our reliance on Middle East oil with coastal plain production to "trying to stop a major fire with a teacup."

U.S. Geological Survey estimates of the coastal plain's oil production potential were first spelled out in a report submitted to Congress by the Department of Interior in 1987 called *ANWR: Alaska, Coastal Plain Resource Assessment.* Based on a $33 per barrel standard, this document established a mean estimate of 3.2 billion barrels of economically recoverable oil. In other words, the coastal plain would meet the United

States's energy needs for less than six months. Over a 25-year field life, it would produce an average of 351,000 barrels of oil per day, amounting to less than 2 percent of our 19 million barrel-per-day domestic consumption requirements. USGS updates of those estimates in 1998 and 2001 did not materially change the mean estimate. According to the U.S. Environmental Protection Agency, improving automobile fuel efficiency by just three miles per gallon would save one million barrels per day. At that rate, in less than ten years, we would save more oil than would likely be pumped from the Arctic Refuge. And the oil savings would continue long after that.

What's also overlooked in the argument to develop coastal plain oil resources is the time involved in getting that oil to market. Terry Koonce president of exploration and production for ExxonMobil, estimates that, based on the usual three-to-four-year permitting process, it will take ten years to get the oil into the existing Trans-Alaska Pipeline.

Opponents of drilling maintain that because the coastal plain of the Arctic National Wildlife Refuge is only one-tenth the size of the coastal plain in the central Arctic (the site of Prudhoe Bay), there would not be sufficient space to accommodate the foraging and calving of the 126,000 Porcupine caribou herd. Unable to seek relief in the coastal waters from the insects that plague them, the caribou would be driven into the Brooks Range, where they would encounter high predation risks. In addition, after surviving the winter on "caribou moss"—little more than lichens—they would be deprived of the protein-rich cotton grass of the coastal plain, an environment that Fran Mauer, former refuge biologist, calls "the best place in the world for raising calves." Although the caribou have become the environmental symbol, the cause célèbre, in the battle to save the refuge, the lives of many more animals are at stake: polar bears, hundreds of thousands of migratory birds, musk-oxen, wolves, moose, wolverine, Arctic fox, and Dall sheep.

Despite the claims of the oil industry and many of Alaska's politicians that its impact would be localized, a mere "footprint" on the land, the U.S. Geological Survey says that oil on the coastal plain is scattered into many separate pools. In other words, the effects of development realistically could not be contained even with revolutionary technology such as directional drilling. Drilling rigs would be spread across the land.

The National Petroleum Reserve Area (NPRA), an environmentally sensitive area lying just west of the current North Slope oil fields, is the industry's newest target. "They're making a real run at getting all of it," says Allen Smith, Alaska senior policy analyst at the Wilderness Society. "Not only are they pressing for oil and gas development in the Arctic National Wildlife Refuge, they plan to lease more land in the NPRA in the next couple of years than they've leased in all of Alaska in the last fifty years. It is a scandalous giveaway of America's Arctic that will needlessly sacrifice millions of acres of our natural heritage."

Bear Mountain lies directly north of Mummuck Mountain, where Heimo and I have been sitting, glassing, and talking for the last hour. The original 8.9-million-acre Arctic National Wildlife Range was established in 1960, under the Eisenhower administration, to preserve the unique wildlife, wilderness, and recreation values of this area, and Bear Mountain was its southern border. "Thank heavens, this is a refuge," Heimo says, standing up, his arms outstretched as if he is greeting God. "If the BLM or the state owned this, there'd be roads and mines, you name it. Look at the Red Dog Mine," he says, referring to the world's largest supplier of zinc and its most northerly mine, which lies just west-northwest of here, outside the Noatak National Preserve, one of the earth's largest watersheds. "Look at all the problems they're having. Rick [a friend from Fairbanks] accuses me of being a NIMBY—not in my backyard. It's not true, but even if it was, you gotta remember—my backyard is the Arctic National Wildlife Refuge, nineteen and a half million acres."

Heimo grabs his backpack and his gun and bounds away. Though earlier he was discouraged that we hadn't seen any caribou, he is in good spirits now, even if there are no caribou. We're walking, covering country again. "They're going to come," he says. "That's almost for sure. I just hope you get to see it before you go back home."

We dip down into a creek bed, and Heimo lies on his stomach and slurps the water right out of the stream. Then he cups his hands and splashes it onto his face. "God, that feels great," he says. "Go ahead," he says, seeing me hesitate at the lip of the creek. "Dunk it. It ain't that . . ." Before he can finish his sentence, I plunge my head into the water. Two seconds later, I come up screaming bloody murder. It feels like someone has taken a chisel to my temples.

"Damn cold, huh?" Heimo laughs.

We ascend another hill and Heimo is glassing west now in the direction of the Sheenjek River valley. Minutes later, he lowers his binoculars as a trans-Arctic jet rumbles high overhead. "Are you bothered by that?" I ask.

"Heck," Heimo answers, skipping down a steep slope like the Dall sheep he loves. "Those I can take. Besides, sometimes it's just good to know that the world is still going."

CHAPTER 12

Fall

"Tell us everything," Edna says. It is mid-September, and she, Heimo, and Krin are sitting outdoors around the fire at the Korths' cabin on the upper Coleen River. They have been waiting for me. Because the pilot encountered headwinds on the way up, I am quite late. Edna says she should go in and prepare dinner—moose tongue, onions, and potatoes—but all she wants to do now is hear about Rhonda. "Dinner can wait. How is Poop?" she asks.

Only then does it dawn on me that Rhonda is not here. In August I'd escorted her to Wisconsin and she stayed with my family and me for five days, but when I arrived on the river I expected to see her. In fact I almost asked where she was. There was Krin, lying in the hammock, reading a John Grisham novel and cuddling Firth. But where was Rhonda? Hauling water?

I haven't seen Rhonda for six weeks, but we talk regularly by phone, so I fill them in.

"So she's doing well?" Heimo asks when I finish.

"She seems to be," I say. "Oh, she's homesick, but I think she's enjoying herself. She can't stand all the noise, though. Even in our little town, she complained about it. She's made some good friends at school, and she likes her classes. She's even joined the choir and is talking about trying out for a play."

I look at Krin, and she is beaming. Heimo notices it, too. "Krinny," he says, "if Rhonda does well, and Tom can take it, then you get to go when Rhonda's all done."

Edna gets up smiling, pleased with my report, and walks to the cabin. Heimo goes to the cabin to get the satellite phone so he can check to see if they've received any e-mail messages, and rather than sit with me, Krin dashes off into the woods like a child of nature, followed by Firth.

Heimo joins me at the fire and punches a series of numbers on the phone. Two minutes later, he yells out, "Got a message." Edna runs from the cabin and Krin bursts out of the woods, and they both crowd around him. It's a short message from Rhonda. Heimo reads it out loud. Rhonda tells them that she has a cold, but other than that, she says, she's happy, doing well, singing her heart out.

Heimo turns off the phone and returns it to its protective case. "Why were you so eager to hear about Rhonda from me if she sends e-mails all the time?" I ask.

"E-mails aren't the same," Heimo says. "They only allow you a hundred twenty characters per message, though sometimes Rhonda will send two or three of them back-to-back. Besides, I think it was a comfort to Edna."

The satellite phone is a relatively new addition. However, calls are so expensive—$1.50 a minute for the Korths to call out, $6.00 a minute for Rhonda to call them—that Heimo and Edna plan to use it only as a last resort or in the case of an emergency, and every once in a while to call Rhonda, so that they can hear her voice. The most immediate benefit is that the phone allows the Korths to get e-mail messages from Rhonda, more personal messages than she'd be willing to leave on *Trapline Chatter*, and certainly a lot faster than regular mail, which one friend or another will fly out once every three months or so.

"Breakfast," Krin calls from outside the Arctic oven. I unzip the tent and then the rain fly and poke my head out. Krin doesn't dash off for the cabin. She stands there smiling, with Firth nuzzling her legs.

"Krin," I say, "you sound so pleasant this morning."

"Quit sleeping," she says stridently, "and come out here."

I have been reading and am already dressed, so I slip on my hiking boots and am out in less than a minute.

"You sure are slow," she says. "Bet I could climb that tree faster than you." She points to a large white spruce without any low hanging branches. Though I've always been proud of my climbing skills, I assess the tree and realize that it would be a difficult shinny, so I decline her challenge. Besides, I know better than to try to compete with Krin. She's a veritable Jane. In spring, I saw her work her way up a tree that I'd declared unclimbable.

"Chicken," she says, taunting me.

"No," I reply. "Just old."

"You're not so old," she says. "When I'm your age, I bet I'll be able to climb it. And by the way, while you were sleeping or reading or whatever, I was out hunting." Krin points to the meat rack from which two spruce grouse are hanging. "I shot them so you won't starve." At that she sprints for the cabin and ducks in through the door. Seconds later, I hear her yell, "Breakfast!"

Inside, Heimo is sharpening his knife and Edna is spooning the oatmeal that Heimo has made into four large bowls. KZPA, 900 AM out of Fort Yukon, is playing country music again. "God," Heimo says, looking up from his knife. "I get sick of country all the time."

I sit down on a bucket. "The honey is down there," Edna says, handing me a bowl and gesturing toward the table. "And the cinnamon is right here. I know you like cinnamon."

Edna gives Krin her bowl, and Krin sets it on her sleeping cot while she sorts through her box from the Gateway Correspondence School, which the bush pilot brought in when he dropped me off. The books in the box catch my eye. I set my oatmeal at my feet and ask her if I can look at them. Krin's required reading for the year is Mark Twain's *The Prince and the Pauper*, Charles Dickens's *David Copperfield*, Esther Forbes's *Johnny Tremaine*, and Sir Arthur Conan Doyle's *The Hound of the Baskervilles*.

"Of course, you already know this one by heart," I say, paging through Doyle's classic. Returning it to her, I repeat Holmes's line in my most ominous voice: "In those hours of darkness when the powers of evil are exalted . . ."

"I wish Poop was here," Edna says, taking a bite of her oatmeal.

"So do I," Krin agrees.

It occurs to me again—Rhonda is gone—and for a moment the cabin seems empty. Looking around, I spot a photograph I took of Rhonda and Krin in the spring. It hangs above Heimo and Edna's bed, push-pinned to one of the wall logs.

How dramatically Rhonda's world has changed in three short months. She is living in Appleton, Wisconsin, a city of 70,000, and attending the same high school Heimo went to, though the city and the school have grown considerably since Heimo was a young man. The transition, I know, has been hard for her, but she's been optimistic about it, excited about the possibilities. For Edna, left up here to imagine her daughter's life in a place she's only visited once, it is occasionally heart-breaking. Sometimes she checks for e-mail messages from Rhonda two and three times a day, depleting the phone's battery. Of course, she worries about Rhonda. Is she happy? Is she making friends? Is she doing well in school? It hurts to have Rhonda so far away, but Edna knows the alternative is worse. If she had not gone to Wisconsin, who would have supervised her homeschooling? At sixteen, Rhonda is now doing advanced algebra, writing difficult essays, and neither Heimo nor Edna can help her anymore.

Heimo finishes his third bowl of oatmeal. "Let's go look for moose," he says, getting up from his bucket. A friend of his from Fairbanks is coming out to hunt, and Heimo wants to make sure there's a moose around for him. Heimo shot his own a few days ago.

Fortunately for Heimo, the moose has extended its range all the way north into the treeless, wind-whipped mountains of the upper Coleen River country, and he can reliably count on getting one each year. In fact, moose can now be found as far north as the Arctic Ocean. Prior to the 1960s, their territory didn't reach much beyond the marshes and woodlands of the Yukon Flats. Fred Thomas remembers that it was rare to see a moose when he was growing up.

Moose are survivors, capable of subsisting on frozen willows, bark, and twigs during the winter, while they wander the deep snowdrifts of the creek beds to keep out of reach of the wolves. While a grizzly can kill a full-grown moose with one swat to its head, wolves rely on stealth and sheer numbers. When the wind is right, they are on a moose before the animal has a chance to react. They wear it down, cripple it if they can, by attacking its hocks. Then they go for the nose. Eventually, when the moose has little strength left, they rush in for the kill, biting and severing the jugular vein. Before the animal has even bled to death, the wolves begin their feast.

Thirty minutes after breakfast, Heimo and I are fording the river. I stumble and step into a hole, and the cold river water laps over my hip boots. "Youch," I yelp, bounding toward him.

"Better keep your eyes open. It's not summer anymore," he warns me, making reference to my propensity in July for wading into the river until I was waist deep. The joke was that I wore hip boots only for show, since I regularly disregarded the river's depths when stalking a rising grayling. In summer the water was cold, but not so cold that I was unable to endure it for the time it would take me to make a few casts.

Only four days short of the autumnal equinox, I'll have to break this habit of mine, since the first day of fall usually signifies the beginning of winter on the upper Coleen. Perhaps Mother Nature has other plans though. It has been warmer than usual, Heimo tells me. The robins are still here, a full two weeks after they should have hightailed it south. Fall-like weather was slow to come, and now winter's cold appears equally reluctant. However, this could change in a day. Tomorrow I could wake up, walk out of the Arctic oven, and be ankle deep in snow. If the sun is any indication, winter is on its way. It is tired, listless-looking, and casts only a dim yellow light over the land. It's hard to imagine that only two months ago it was working nearly a twenty-four-hour shift.

"Look at that," Heimo says, pointing to a riverbank where a grizzly has excavated gaping holes and piled up mounds of dirt in search of Indian potatoes. It hardly seems worth it—so much energy expended just to get at a few tasty tubers. But this time of year the bears are getting ready to den up, and they're ravenous.

"The wolves didn't howl last night, but they were howling almost every night before you came," Heimo tells me, as he examines a bear print. "You'll like hearing that, won't you?" He gets up and slaps the dirt from his pants. "I like it, too, but come winter"—he winks at me now—"I'll be trying to trap them."

In Alaska, where opinions are fierce and often as intemperate as the weather, few issues elicit more rancor than the trapping of wolves. In 1998, Alaskans were given a chance to voice their opinions. Ballot issue #9 proposed to eliminate the snaring of wolves. It was defeated by a 64 percent majority and left a lot of bitterness on both sides. There are those who regard the wolf as a killing machine, a wasteful predator. Mention Farley Mowatt's book *Never Cry Wolf,* and most trappers will simply scoff and say that Mowatt, whom they refer to as "Hardly Knows It," knows "nothing" about wolves. For others, including many people in the Lower Forty-eight, the wolf is a charismatic symbol of the outdoors, an animal to be revered and protected.

The day that Danny Grangaard brought his wolf skins into Dean Wilson's office, Wilson and I had a talk about wolves. "The environmentalists," he explained, "would swear that wolves eat only the old, sick, lame, diseased, and carrion. Other than that, maybe a few rabbits and mice. Wolf haters think they're wanton killers. They think the only good wolf is a dead wolf. I find both views a little extreme. Natives used to dig out wolf dens in spring and kill the pups to keep the population in check so there was enough wild game for their families. Sometimes wolves will kill indiscriminately—the sick or the healthy, it doesn't matter to them—and just let the kill lay. Maybe they'll come back to it, maybe they won't. I've never really understood that. Other times they will come in and consume diseased, sick, and winter-killed animals."

Now Heimo and I leave the bear diggings behind. We're walking along the bank when he stops. He glasses east, across the river, in the direction of the heavy timber. "Nothing," he says, letting the binoculars fall to his chest. "I thought I saw some movement." Then he looks at me. "You don't understand how I can talk about wolves like that, do you? How one night I can enjoy the sound of them howling and the next morning I can talk about trapping them." He continues: "I'm very sincere when I say that I try to trap humanely. I use the right-sized traps for the right animal. The animal's always going to feel pain, but if the trap is too big or too small, they'll feel much more of it. Public opinion about trapping is already so bad. I don't need to make it worse."

I tell him that I've always loved wolves, that seeing one in a trap might be hard for me, but that I respect his right to make a living off the land, and if that means trapping the occasional wolf, well, then, so be it. Trapping, and hunting, too, is what Heimo does; it's part of what binds him to the land. If he is more callous about the death of an animal than many of us, it is because death is woven into the fabric of his life. He kills to live.

Heimo sits down on the bank and dangles his feet over the river like a little boy sitting at the end of a dock. "People have always worn fur up here. Heck, in Fairbanks even the greenies do. It's practical. And you'd be hard-pressed to find a perfume that doesn't contain beaver castor. Now, to me, that's the most wasteful thing in the world, killing an animal just so people can smell good." Heimo grabs a smooth round stone and chucks it into the river. "I'm getting worked up, ain't I?" Then he jumps to his feet. He's agitated, and he needs to walk, and it's clear that he has no intention of waiting for me.

"Did I tick you off?" I shout to him as he cuts into the forest, leaving me at the river.

"No," he yells. "But I'm going to walk you till you drop."

Fifteen minutes later, we cross a creek. The thin film of ice that has formed on the creek's surface cracks under our weight, sounding like vegetable oil being poured into a hot skillet. We scale the creek bank and pick up one of Heimo's trails. One hundred yards down the path, Heimo stops. "Ax cutting," he says, stooping and running his hand over a tree stump. "It was probably made by a Gwich'in or an Eskimo hunter around the mid-1800s. They were still using stone axes then. You can tell by the cut. It's rough." Heimo runs his hand over the stump again and then points to a small clearing in the forest. "Over there is where I sometimes cut wood."

We're at least three miles upriver, and I can't understand why Heimo travels so far upriver for wood, when there are countless dead trees not more than a quarter of a mile from the cabin.

"I'm saving those for our old age," he says, "when Edna and I will be glad to have firewood close by. While I can still do the work, I use the trees way up here."

Today is the autumnal equinox, and Heimo, his friend Rick from Fairbanks, who hopes to bag a moose with his bow, and I are walking and scouting. Heimo stops occasionally to cow-call, cupping his hands around his mouth to amplify his interpretation of the bawling of a lusty female searching for a suitor. He calls and we wait, hidden among the willows along a dry creek bed. He calls again, and we listen for grunting and the thrashing of horns. Satisfied that there's no bull around, Heimo says, "Let's go," a big grin lighting up his face. We are off again. We cut through a dense copse of willows and then begin a steep climb. Heimo powers up the incline, nearly bounding, losing himself in the utter joy of the hike.

Earlier we were discussing the incremental advance of civilization. The mines, the oil fields, changing values, antitrapping sentiment, and tourism continue their inexorable advance on Alaska's remote wilderness, threatening to undo Heimo's way of life. I'd brought up the subject before, and he had evaded it. But now I press him. This being my last visit, there are some things I have to know. "Would you ever consider leaving?"

"The simple answer is no," Heimo says. "I can't imagine myself doing anything else. How could I ever leave the place I love?"

Still, love it or not, the option of leaving the bush, at least temporarily, and relocating to Fairbanks or a smaller Alaskan town is one he cannot completely exclude. It would be difficult for Heimo, very difficult, but it is a sacrifice he has entertained. Oil development probably wouldn't drive him away, nor would a mine, nor would a sudden influx of tourists. But he might consider leaving for Rhonda and Krin.

For Edna the adjustment to town would probably be less complicated. To some extent, she is living Heimo's dream. She's learned to love the life, and she'd miss the cabin and the quiet, no doubt, but being in town would sure be a lot easier than being in the bush. She could cook on a range rather than a woodstove, use a real washing machine, have a bathroom with a flush toilet, a mirror and a medicine cabinet, hot and cold running water, and most especially, she could enjoy the company of other women.

How Krin would react is hard to say. Part of her yearns to be surrounded by boys and girls her own age. The other part is young enough and innocent enough to enjoy the serenity and isolation of the river—a dash through the woods with her dog, climbing a tall tree, gathering blueberries, digging for Indian potatoes in spring.

"There's not much money in it, but I never want to do anything else," Heimo said this morning, while slipping on his hip boots for the day's hunt, sounding much like his friend Fred Thomas. I'd asked Thomas what trapping meant to him. "Well," he said, his eyes shining, "if you're asking me would I do it all over again if I had the chance, you bet." Ernie Johnson, a trapper whom Bob Marshall, founder of the Wilderness Society, once asked something similar, said, "I can make better money as a carpenter, but I am staying out here because I like it among these ruggedy mountains better than anywhere else in the world."

It's not to say that Heimo is without financial concerns. His catch for the winter of 2001-2002 was seventy marten, eight wolverine, four beaver, and two wolves. With marten bringing only $38 apiece, it was a so-so year. He'll have to do better this winter. With Rhonda away at school, there are books to buy, clothes, and an occasional ticket to Fairbanks. Once she gets to Fairbanks, Heimo can rely on the generosity of pilot friends to fly Rhonda out to the cabin. His friends won't ask for anything in return, except perhaps some of Edna's delicious moose pockets smothered in gravy.

Heimo and I are sitting on a ridge overlooking the Coleen River valley and enjoying the cheese sandwiches and homemade bread Edna sent us off with. Rick found a comfortable spot underneath a tree and promptly fell asleep. Because of their big ears moose have an extraordinary sense of hearing, so Heimo and I are whispering. But it doesn't matter. Rick is snoring loudly, doing his best impersonation of Fred Flintstone. If there's a moose in the area he's heard us and is long gone.

I tell Heimo what Ron Bennett said about him. Bennett is a friend of

Heimo's from when they were both single trappers. "Heimo said from the very beginning that he was going to be a lifer," Bennett told me. "He's the last of the mountain men. You gotta envy him doing what he wants, but he's not really planning for the future. Trapping's a dead end. Besides, there are too many other things to do in life. How much country can you see? How many different ways can you trap a marten?"

Heimo laughs at this. "Ah, that's just Bennett. He soured on the country, and he's just sore that I haven't soured on it yet. If he's waiting for that, he'll have to wait until the day I die. I like this country more all the time. Fortunately, I got Edna. She loves it out here as much as me. Without her, I never would have stayed."

Heimo plops the last bite of sandwich into his mouth. "See that small mountain over there? That's what we call Guroy Mountain."

"Yeah, I know," I say. "You and I were up there last summer."

"What I didn't show you was Coleen's grave," Heimo adds. "We never recovered her body, but after she died, I built a cross for her and chiseled out an inscription using a screwdriver and a hammer. Edna filled in the letters with a Magic Marker. It says, 'Coleen Ann Korth 5/29/82. Died 6/3/84.' We put up the cross at the top of the mountain. When we're at the upper cabin, we climb Guroy and spend the afternoon and talk about Coleen. We bring fresh flowers. It's hard on Edna, but it's something we like to do."

Heimo pauses. "Did I ever tell you that we petitioned the Board on Geographic Names to get them to name that peak over there Coleen Ann Mountain? We submitted a proposal for state approval. What the state wrote back really chafed me. The letter said that she was of no 'historical significance.' So I wrote the governor, Steve Cooper, and Congressman Don Young. They both fought for it. But the board still said no. They said we needed a petition. I did that, too. I started a petition and got hundreds of names. They still said no. Finally, I just got tired of trying."

Tomorrow I leave the river, but for today there is work to be done. Late yesterday afternoon, Rick shot a moose. When the arrow hit, the moose thundered off, crashing through the forest. We followed the blood trail and eventually found it a quarter mile from where Rick stuck his arrow. He had punctured the moose's kidney, so it didn't go far.

Rick was excited. The moose was huge with an immense symmetrical rack, nearly 74 inches across, Rick figured, admiring it as a possible Pope & Young bow-hunting record. For Heimo a moose means only one thing—meat. He doesn't give a hoot about records, so he went to work on it, and was soon buried up to his elbows in flesh and blood. Rick took pictures—I couldn't blame him; it was an impressive animal— and then he pitched in, too. With the two of them working on the moose, there was little I could do but watch. After nearly two hours of cutting, they were almost finished, and Heimo instructed me to build a fire. We had given up on the idea of getting the meat back to the cabin that night. We were downriver and it was too dark to line a canoe loaded with moose upriver. The hope was that the fire would smolder for much of the night and keep away the bears.

The plan then was to go back to the cabin and get a good night's rest. The following morning Rick would get his plane, which he had parked on a gravel bar above the cabin, and try to locate a gravel bar near the kill site where it was safe to land. While he was doing that, Heimo and I would float down in the canoe, load the meat, and paddle downriver to whatever bar Rick found. It was going to be a lot easier than the way Heimo usually does it.

Heimo has to pack out his moose alone, for one thing. That's why he always takes a small one. And he likes to get his early in the rut when the meat and the organs are at their tastiest. Later in the rut, after the lusty bulls have been lapping up cow urine, the liver, in particular, is no good. He also makes sure to shoot his moose near the river and always upriver so he can float it down. Years ago, when he was younger and stronger, he wasn't so picky. But it didn't take him long to figure out that he was making a lot of extra work for himself.

It is early, and Rick has already gone off to get his plane and search for a gravel bar downriver. Heimo and I are polishing off the last of the oatmeal, which he will replenish when he goes to Fort Yukon and then to Fairbanks to buy food supplies for the winter. Edna is sitting at the edge of her sleeping platform, using part of a caribou horn to scratch her back. The caribou horn back scratcher was a birthday present from Rhonda and Krin. Using a hand-powered drill, they bored a hole in the end of the horn and slipped a piece of leather through the hole. To the leather, they attached fur from a white fox. It is not only functional, it is a work of art, too.

Krin is huddled in the corner of her sleeping cot, writing in her journal, and protecting it as if she thinks I am going to steal a look. I have no doubt that that would be a losing battle for anyone who tried.

"Don't worry, Krin," I say. "I'd sooner tangle with a grizzly than try to see what you're writing in that journal of yours." Heimo laughs. Krin just puts on her headphones and turns up the volume on her portable CD player.

We hear Rick's plane overhead, and Heimo says we'd better get going. Just in case a bear is feeding on the kill, he brings his shotgun and slugs, and we go to the river to get the canoe. When we reach the bank, Heimo whispers, "Look." I follow his gaze upriver. Not more than fifty yards away is a large bull moose browsing among the willows along the riverbank. "Too bad Rick didn't wait to shoot this one," he laughs. "It'd sure be a lot less work." We climb into the canoe, and the moose hears us and high-steps deep into the willows.

Twenty minutes later, we're near the kill site. I tie off the canoe and Heimo pumps five slugs into the shotgun. Watching him, I realize something's up. When he calls me over, I know he means business.

"There could be a grizzly feeding on that moose, and he'll defend it till death," he says. "You take the shotgun, and I'll take my forty-four. Be ready to shoot. If you hear a 'woof, woof' and the crashing of brush, you know he's coming. You won't have much time. Whatever happens, don't freeze. Freeze and we're fucked."

The moose meat is about 150 yards in. We walk side-by-side, five feet apart, with our guns ready. My heart is beating like a stock car engine. "Don't freeze," I say to myself. "Whatever you do, don't freeze."

Thirty yards away, I can see the moose. I look at Heimo and he holds up his hand—wait here. He takes another five steps, stands up on his tiptoes. "It's okay," he says, turning. "No bear in sight." For the first time I understand how a man could wet himself from utter relief.

Now we have to lug out the moose, load it in the canoe, paddle to whatever gravel bar Rick has found, and then carry it to the plane. I jump right in. "I'll take a quarter," I tell Heimo. Each quarter is a hundred pounds of deadweight, and once I wrestle one to my shoulders, I realize that a lifetime of weightlifting has done little to prepare me for this experience. I stumble through the brush and tussocks and am winded by the time I reach the canoe. Heimo's right behind me. "This ain't nothin'," he says. "Before I got the canoe, I had to carry them all the way back to the cabin. Sometimes it took me two days to get the whole moose out."

By the time we've loaded Rick's plane, it's 2:00 P.M. Rick leaves Heimo with the nose, the brisket, the tongue, the head, and the horns, and we still have to line the canoe back up to the cabin. Rick will fly to Fairbanks, hang the meat, and fly back out the following morning to pick up Heimo and take him to Fort Yukon. Then he'll fly back to get me.

When we reach the cabin, it is late afternoon. Edna and Krin are outside, sitting around a fire. They are both glued to the flower book that I gave Edna as a present. When Heimo and I walk into the cabin yard, struggling under the weight of the meat, they don't even acknowledge us. We hang it next to the meat from Heimo's moose and cover it all with large blue and green plastic tarps. Clouds have moved in, and Heimo is worried about rain. If rain gets to the meat, it'll spoil faster.

Heimo goes to the cabin and comes out with a hand-crank meat grinder. "Edna's promised to make moose tacos tonight," he says. Edna finally looks up from her book. "Maybe I will, maybe I won't," she taunts him.

"Come on," Heimo pleads with her. "Rick brought out some vegetables. We better use them before they go bad. We'll have tacos tonight and moose nose and tongue."

"We'll see," Edna replies, and returns her attention to the flower book. She flips through a few pages and then gets up and walks to the cabin. "Okay," she says. "I guess we're having moose nose and tongue and tacos, too."

"Yippee," Heimo hollers.

Two hours later, Edna steps outside the cabin door. "Dinnertime."

I load up my plate with tacos and a piece of the twenty-inch moose tongue, which Edna has cut into five large slabs. I slice off a small bite of the tongue and plop it into my mouth.

"What do you think?" Edna asks.

"Tastes like a fine cut of steak," I answer.

"Hold on," Heimo says. "That's a low blow, comparing moose tongue to beef. Keep that up and all you'll get is nose."

Edna and Krin laugh at the joke. I had moose nose as an appetizer. Made up largely of fat and cartilage, moose nose is definitely an acquired taste, and when Heimo asked if I wanted a second helping, I promptly declined.

Tonight is my final night in the Arctic, and Heimo and I are at the river, fetching water. The afternoon's clouds have disappeared, replaced by shimmering plumes of green smoke and throbbing bright red bands— the northern lights—which tease the sky with intimations of the coming winter.

"This is going to be my twenty-eighth year in the bush," Heimo says, watching the sky. Then he bends, dips the bucket in the river, and pulls it out. "I can't tell you how many times I've hauled water since I came to Alaska." Realizing he's forgotten to put on the lid, he sets the bucket down in the gravel. "Hauling water," he says. "It's not a concept a lot of people would understand anymore, is it? The other day Krin asked me why we had to live way out here, why we couldn't live like other people, if she'd ever have friends. That nearly broke my heart. Sometimes I wonder if Edna and me have done the right thing. Not that long ago, many lived like this. Now it's down to Rhonda and Krin. Maybe when they're thirty, they'll look back and realize that they lived a way of life that doesn't exist anymore, and they'll be thankful. I sure hope so. I've set up separate bank accounts for them in Fairbanks, college funds. There's not a lot of money in there, but I'd like them to be able to go to college and make their own decisions about life. Even if they wanted to live like this, though, I don't think it would be possible. As far as I can see it, this way of life is done. The Democrats want to outlaw guns and trapping and the Republicans want the minerals and the oil and want to build roads even to the most remote parts of the state. Don Young is now the chairman of the House Transportation Committee, and Ted Stevens is back in charge of the Senate Appropriations Committee, so you know they're going to make sure that Alaska gets a good share of the federal funds." Heimo kicks at the gravel.

"Did you ever think of leaving after Coleen died?" I ask him.

"Why would we ever do that?" is his answer.

"Some of your friends thought you might leave and never come back because, well, because it was too hard to live with the memories."

Heimo stares at the ground and shuffles his feet and then he raises his head and gazes off into the distance. He doesn't speak. Instead he brushes his teeth with his tongue. Then he exhales deeply, and I can see his breath rise from his mouth and dissipate in the air.

"We could never leave this place," he says, finally, looking off in the direction of the Stranglewoman Mountains. "Coleen is everywhere."

Back at the cabin, Edna is paging through her flower book, and Krin is finishing up the dishes. She has her headphones on and is dancing, swinging her arms, kicking her feet, and twirling in circles. I sit down on a bucket, and Heimo sits next to Edna and wraps his arms around her. "I sure am glad I have this woman," he says, and nuzzles her neck. Krin was not aware that I was in the cabin. She catches a glimpse of me and stops her dancing, though I can still hear the song's melody leaking from her headphones.

Edna digs into her pocket and hands me some #2 picture wire. "In case your plane goes down tomorrow," she says. "With this you can snare bunnies and stay alive, so you can get home to your wife and girls." Then she reaches behind her and brings out a pair of tiny Eskimo slippers that she's made for the youngest of my two girls, who will be six weeks old when I return home.

"Fox fur," she says, running her fingers over the auburn and gray fur at the top of the slippers. "For Rachel."

"Thank you," I say simply, knowing that Edna will be embarrassed if I make too much of a fuss over them.

Then I excuse myself for the evening. I bend to get out the door and replace the blanket over the opening. The northern lights have disappeared, but stars flood the land in a soft gray light.

I walk back to the Arctic oven, eager to put some wood in the stove and crawl into my sleeping bag. In the distance, though, I hear what I think is the howling of wolves. I stop, hold my breath, listen again, and the sound is gone.

CHAPTER 13

A Way of Life

Driving down Appleton's College Avenue, it is as I remember the street best—lit up for the Christmas season, tinsel laced across the avenue, and lights climbing the street lamps. Between Walnut and State Streets, I pass what used to be Sarge's Bar and is now an upscale martini lounge. I think of Heimo there, before he left for Alaska, when the crowd was of a very different sort, and he was trying to drown boredom in booze, all the while dreaming of a life that would one day transport him far from the five-day-a-week drunks and the dead-end existence that were laid out before him as straight as a section line road.

In an odd twist of fate, Rhonda has called Appleton home for the last four months. The place where Heimo felt that he was squandering his life is the same place where Rhonda dreams of making something of hers. Tonight her sophomore choir group from Appleton East High School is performing at the Lawrence University Chapel. Rhonda has been excited about the concert since September, calling me every other week to remind me to put down the date on my calendar. I've promised not to miss it.

My four-year-old daughter, Aidan, and I arrive at the chapel late. The concert is already in progress. Most of the seats are taken, so we sit in the back. Aidan immediately scans the stage for Rhonda. I spot her sitting in one of the front rows, off to the right. Her group is not singing yet. As if sensing us, she turns. I wave to her and pull Aidan onto my lap so that she, too, can see. Rhonda waves for nearly half a minute before Aidan finally notices her. Then Aidan waves excitedly, as if she's spotted a celebrity. The truth is that in her eyes Rhonda *is* something of a celebrity. She regards Rhonda with the awe that a young girl might feel for an older sister. Rhonda indulges her, calling her at least once a week. The phone conversations make Aidan feel important, grown up, but they are not entirely one-sided. For Rhonda, they serve a purpose, too. Their weekly talks make up for a lack of connection with her own family, helping to dispel the loneliness. Both of them say "I love you" before hanging up.

We listen to four choirs before Rhonda's group finally takes the stage. Thinner than when I saw her last, she looks quite beautiful in her white and black gown with her hair pulled back. She smiles at one of her friends—that amiable, sideways grin of hers—as they align themselves on the risers. Then the choir director nods, lifts her baton, and the song begins.

Rhonda's group performs several songs and then the other choirs ascend the stage to join hers for a farewell medley. When the concert is over, Rhonda comes to the back of the chapel. Aidan runs to her, and Rhonda sweeps her up into her arms and introduces Aidan to two of her girlfriends. Then she walks over to me.

"You look lovely," I tell her. She shrugs like a typical high-school student. "Thanks for the invitation," I continue. "We really enjoyed the singing."

Rhonda pulls the corner of her choir gown up to her waist and checks a lime-green beeper attached to her belt. Then she returns her attention to me. "My uncle doesn't want me anymore," she says. "I blew it. He says he can't trust me." Rhonda tells me the story, holding Aidan as she talks. She had skipped school, calling in sick. Though she was already grounded, she was caught by her uncle later that day riding in her boyfriend's car. Her boyfriend is nineteen and that was already a sore spot between them. For her uncle, it was the last straw. There'd been too many deceptions, too many broken promises.

Though I knew that there were problems, this sudden revelation catches me by surprise.

"What's going to happen?" I ask her. "What are you going to do?" Again, she shrugs her shoulders. By now, her friends want to go. Cake and refreshments are being served, and one of the girls mentions that she is hungry. Rhonda puts Aidan down. "I love you," she says, ignoring my question. "I love you, too," Aidan replies.

Then Rhonda pulls back the sleeve of her gown and shows me her gold bracelet. "It's gonna kill him," she says.

"Who's that?" I ask.

"My boyfriend," she replies. "He gave me this bracelet, and he doesn't know yet that anything is wrong. If I have to leave, it's going to be hard on him. We're close. He really cares about me, you know. He's been a complete gentleman. He opens and closes my car door for me. Isn't it pretty?" she says, pulling the bracelet from her wrist and placing it in the palm of her hand delicately, as if it were a robin's egg that had fallen from its nest.

"It is," I say, admiring it. "He must think a lot of you."

"I guess," she says, returning it to her wrist. "Anyway, I gotta go." She gives me a hug and then hugs Aidan again. Aidan waves to her as she walks away. "Daddy, am I going to get to see Rhonda again?" she asks.

As Rhonda walks down the aisle, chatting with her friends, with one hand still wrapped around the thick gold bracelet, I remember Roger Kaye's story. Rhonda was three, and she couldn't take her eyes off him. To this day he remains struck by that image—a child who hadn't seen another person outside of her father and mother in six months.

I have my own indelible image of Rhonda—30.30 in hand, trudging across the tundra toward Rundown Mountain and her trapline, braving the cold ache of the north wind, which had whipped the tundra into small, giddy whirlwinds of powder-dry snow. We were walking in the direction of the setting moon, which was large and lopsided, and the hardened snow popped under our snowshoes. To the southeast, the sun had barely clambered above the horizon, washing the land in a lean and faded light. Rhonda stopped to adjust her backpack. "Okay?" she asked, turning toward me. I nodded. Her face had been windburned a bright red, but she turned and continued on, leaning into the wind.

Only when Rhonda has disappeared with her friends does Aidan agree that it is time for us to go. Later that evening I stop in at my parents' house before driving home. "Should we take her?" my dad asks me. "She needs to stay and get an education," my mother chimes in.

"I'd love for her to be able to stay, too," I say, "but it's too much of a responsibility for you."

"We could do it," my mother says. "We're not that old."

"That may be," I say. "But it wouldn't be easy."

Ultimately the decision is made for us. On the afternoon of Thursday, December 26, Heimo calls me from Fairbanks. He makes small talk at first. It has been warm and the rivers froze up late, but the trapping season has been good. He's caught nine wolverine, seventy-eight marten, one lynx, one otter, three mink, and five wolves. Then he pauses, and I can hear him breathe in deeply. "Rhonda's coming home," he says quietly. "She doesn't know it yet, but I'm flying down to get her on Saturday. Edna and I made the decision that she should come back and that I should go and get her." Heimo's voice trembles. "She's really let us down."

The plans have been made. Rhonda is leaving Appleton just two weeks short of completing her fall semester. The comparisons to Heimo are inevitable. Heimo left high school prematurely, only two months before graduating. But this is where the comparisons end. Heimo left Wisconsin to pursue a dream. Rhonda, on the other hand, will return to Alaska reluctantly, regretfully maybe, having failed to realize hers. Failure, though, is perhaps too strong a word.

Rhonda's situation was an almost untenable one. Not only was she cut off from her parents and Krin—connected by satellite phone for five minutes once or twice a month—and the emotional balance that a family can provide, she was also trying to adjust to a new place and a very different culture. She was so intent on fitting in that she forgot her personal style; she forgot who she was. She wanted to act and dress like the kids and the stars—Lauryn Hill, Lil' Kim—she admired. At school, the students were split into cliques. There were the preps, the punks, the geeks, and the hip-hop crowd. It was the hip-hop crowd where Rhonda found her niche. Half Eskimo in a largely white high school, Rhonda felt more

comfortable with this multicultural group of African-Americans, His-
panics, Puerto Ricans, Native Americans, and white kids, too. She wore
baggy pants, tight shirts, braids in her hair. The hip-hop crowd was more
inclusive than the other groups, but the lines were well drawn.

People liked Rhonda. She was friendly, but tough, too, no-nonsense,
and kids were drawn to her. Teachers were, too. "The teachers loved
her," Joe Lamers, a guidance counselor at Appleton East says. "They
weren't surprised to see her go—she confided in some of them about
the problems she was having—but they were saddened by it. One
teacher told me that if she didn't have four of her own kids at home, she
would have opened her house to Rhonda. It was a real tribute to
Rhonda, I think. I can't imagine the changes she had to go through
coming from where she did."

Joe Lamers was one of the few who knew much about how Rhonda
had grown up. When others asked her where she was from, she simply
said "Alaska," never bothering to mention the bush or the Coleen River
or the Old Crow. You could dress street, but the key was always to look
like you came from money, and you couldn't be the daughter of a
hunter-trapper and live in a one-room cabin and claim that you came
from money.

Rhonda was trying on a new identity, and the details of her former
life didn't fit the picture. Besides, how could she have made them understand? These were suburban kids. Most of them had never hauled water
or ice, split wood, studied by kerosene latern, checked a trapline,
skinned a marten and tacked the pelt to a stretching board, gutted and
butchered a caribou, much less bathed in a tin washbasin, using water
heated on a woodstove.

Rhonda was also carrying a huge psychological burden. All of Heimo's
hopes for the future, hers, and the family's, too, depended on whether or
not she suceeded. She had the power to legitimize the choices he'd made
in life. If it worked out with Rhonda, he could remain in the bush and
still see to it that his girls got a proper education. He could straddle two
worlds. No one could accuse him of not doing right by his children. If
she succeeded, Krin would probably come out, too. If Rhonda failed, the
deal was off.

It was all too much for her: the freedom—it was the first time in her life that she was away from home for more than a few days, and she couldn't help herself. Sometimes, after talking with her on the phone, when she would confess her indiscretions, it struck me that she was trying to sabotage her experience, trying to force her father's hand, test his love. Daddy says he wants to die in the bush, but would he leave the place and life he loves for me?

A day after informing me that he was coming down to get Rhonda, Heimo calls me again. "It's all been very emotional," he says, whispering, his voice barely audible. "I called Rhonda last night to tell her that I was coming to get her. She's at Lisa's [Heimo's sister] now. She was really bawling, and I could hear Lisa in the background crying, too. Lisa's going to have a good-bye party for her, so she can see her friends one last time." Heimo pauses. I wait, thinking that he's dropped the phone. Then he blurts it out. "We're leaving the . . . bush." He tries to say it as matter-of-factly as possible, but he can barely get out the last word.

I catch my breath. "Leaving?" I ask.

"Yeah," he says. "Edna and I talked it over. There's no other way. We're going to rent a cabin in Central or Fairbanks. We're leaning toward Central. There's a school there. But nothing's for sure now. We may end up in Fairbanks. I don't know how we'll do it moneywise; it's going to be hard. We'll keep the cabin in Fort Yukon, but I don't want the kids going to school there—too many problems. I'll be flying back and forth between the cabin and town, if I can swing it. I'll spend three or four weeks on the river and two weeks in town. Then, after Krin graduates and goes to college, Edna and I will move back out. That's the plan, at least for now." By the time Heimo finishes telling me, his mood has improved, as if by uttering the words "We're leaving," he is one step closer to accepting the reality of his decision, however painful it may be.

"Are you okay with it?" I ask.

"Yeah," he says. "I guess. I don't like it, but it's the only way. The girls need to know how much I love them, that I'm willing to do anything for them, even if that means leaving the bush. This is my dream, not theirs."

* * *

A month later I meet Heimo in Fairbanks. He has come to town to sell his fur, buy supplies, and call Appleton East High School to find out if there's any way Rhonda can get credit for her fall term. Despite the problems she had, she got good grades. "It would be a shame for her to lose that," Heimo says. He has four days in which to do all this, and then he has to be back at the cabin for Edna's forty-ninth birthday.

It is 9:30 A.M. Dawn is on the way. The waning moon is silhouetted against a pale blue sky, which is now tinged with neon oranges and combustible reds.

"Remember last year out at the cabin?" Heimo asks. "How we waited for the sun? This year the sky was clear, no clouds. We saw it on January thirteenth for almost two hours. Now the sun's out for more than three hours. We're already gaining seven minutes a day. By March or so, it'll be ten minutes a day."

I haven't talked with Heimo since he called me to announce that he and the rest of the family were leaving the bush, but he is his old self again, smiling, animated, full of stories, flying around Fairbanks in his used Ford Escort, which he bought three years ago for running errands when he came to town. The car smells faintly of fur, and Heimo is apologetic. On the car's back bumper, he's plastered a sticker he's particularly proud of: "Wear Wolf—Eat Moose!" "This is how I am when I come to town," he says, cutting in front of a Chevy Suburban, seemingly daring it to hit us. "My mind races. I don't slow down till I get back out to the cabin. I've been in town now twice in the last month, once to get Rhonda and now. I don't mind coming to town once in a while, but that's way too much."

"How is Rhonda?" I ask, as he turns a corner and momentarily spins out and then fishtails on the icy street.

"She's good," he says, unalarmed. "She seems happy to be home, though she says she likes Wisconsin better than Alaska. She spends lots of time writing in her journal. She says she has to get her feelings out. Krin has finally managed to forgive her for 'blowing' it and ruining her chances of ever going down there, too." We both laugh at this, since Krin is known to carry a grudge longer than most. "Krinny still has her nose in books all the time. She just finished *The Hobbit* and now she's on the second *Lord of the Rings* book."

Heimo hands me a sealed envelope. "A letter," he says. "Rhonda never got to say good-bye. She made me promise I wouldn't read it, but I think I already know what's in it. She's glad to be home, but I think being at the cabin is harder than ever for her now that she's seen Wisconsin. She liked the lifestyle and she misses her friends. Coming back was kind of a rude awakening for her. Did I tell you about the snowmachine breaking down?"

By the time I answer, Heimo has already begun the story.

He and Rhonda were checking traps downriver, seven miles south of the lower cabin, when the snowmachine broke down. Heimo struggled to start it, but there was no spark, and it didn't take him long to realize that he and Rhonda would have to abandon the machine, walk to the lower cabin, overnight there, and then cover the remaining distance the following day. It was 20 below and 2:00 P.M. when they set out. An hour into the hike, Heimo knew they'd have to split up. The wind had drifted over the trail, slowing them down. "At this speed," Heimo told Rhonda, "we won't make the cabin until early evening. We'll be tired and sweaty and the cabin won't be much good because it will be as cold inside as it is outside. I'll go on ahead," he told her. "I'll break trail, and as soon as I reach the cabin, I'll build a fire."

Heimo hustled and made the cabin by 5:00 P.M and immediately started a fire in the woodstove. Then he went to the river and brought back a bucket of water. When Rhonda arrived in the dark two hours later, she was tired, cold, hungry, and dehydrated. The cabin hadn't even begun to heat up, so she sat as close to the woodstove as she could without singeing her clothes and drank cup after cup of river water. She threw up most of the water, but she knew her body needed fluids, so she kept drinking. Heimo searched the fifty-five-gallon drums that were outside the cabin and found two foam sleeping pads and five sheets. He was hoping to find some extra blankets, but the sheets would have to do. Rhonda was still chilled, so Heimo prepared two of the four packets of Mountain House freeze-dried food that he kept in his backpack for emergencies, and they ate, back-to-back, wrapped in the sheets. Rhonda was warmer now, but she had trouble holding the food down, and decided to save most of her share for the following morning.

At the upper cabin, Edna was worried. What's happened? Are they okay? Overflow, she thought, and then she couldn't get the idea out of her head—they'd gotten caught in overflow. She tried not to panic. It was 20 below, but at least Rhonda wasn't alone; she was with Heimo. Whatever the problem, Heimo would know what to do.

Heimo and Rhonda huddled together and slept as best they could. They woke early the next morning, but didn't linger. Heimo heated water for the freeze-dried food. They ate and were on the trail by 8:00 A.M. The plan was for Heimo to walk ahead. He'd reach the cabin and then he'd get the Polaris and drive back and pick up Rhonda. Fortunately, the wind hadn't drifted this section of the trail. It was still hard-packed, and the walking was easy.

Heimo was five miles north of the lower cabin when he heard the sound of a snowmachine. Edna had come to look for them. When Edna saw him walking alone, her heart sank. She stopped the snowmachine and watched, fighting off the dread she felt. "Heimo," she cried. Heimo ran to her. "No," he said, trying to calm her. "Rhonda's okay. Everything's okay." Then he hugged Edna and explained what had happened. He was sweating and he knew that he couldn't stop for long. "Go get Rhonda," he said. "Take her home and then send Krin to get me."

"Quite a homecoming for Rhonda, wasn't it?" he says, sliding through a yellow traffic light at the corner of University and Airport Way. "I felt bad for her, but that's life out here. You learn to accept stuff like that. It happens and you can't do jack shit to change it. Her first week back, her and I were checking a line. We had to go east across the tundra. The wind had wiped out my trail. I couldn't even find it. Rhonda had to walk in front of the snowmachine and make a trail so I wouldn't get stuck. We switched, but the machine was too heavy for her to handle. She was crying and carrying on, saying she hated it out here. I felt for her. In bed that night I was thinking about it, and I felt cruel for keeping the girls out here for so long. After that I was convinced that moving to town was the right thing. Rhonda will never want to live like this; I know that now. She says that when she leaves home she'll come back for a visit. But that's it! Once I guess I hoped that she or Krin might live out here after we are gone. But I don't kid myself about that anymore."

Heimo drops me off at the hotel where I've rented a room for us. Since Heimo stays with friends when he comes to town, he seems excited about staying in the hotel. "It says they have a pool, a spa, and an exercise room," he says, stopping in front of the lobby. "I'm going to do a hard workout later today and then soak in the whirlpool." I shut the car door and Heimo rushes off.

When I get to the room, I open Rhonda's letter.

"I think I liked it better in Appleton," she writes, "because I didn't have to crawl into a stupid sleeping bag every night, go outside to go to the bathroom, carry water, put wood on the stove, heat water for dishes, 4 a bath. It gets old after a while. Wisconsin was different. I would like to live in a small city instead of in the middle of nowhere because it's easier in many ways. It's nice to call a friend and hang out, watch TV, do something fun. Out here you just have moose and caribou, and wolf, wolverine and fox tracks." "And snowmachine breakdowns," I say out loud.

"I liked school," she continues. "No, that is an understatement. I loved school. I loved having friends. We've never had friends before. And I loved the freedom. At home it's always compromise and cooperation. That's part of living in the bush and living in a small cabin." Then the letter turns reflective. "I couldn't make it because I made some really bad choices," she writes. "I loved the freedom, but I couldn't handle it. It was exciting but it scared me, too, and I chose to do things, stupid things." What those "stupid things" were, she doesn't say, but it isn't hard to read between the lines. The temptations were there, and like a lot of other high school kids, she found them hard to resist.

The letter continues: "I joined the choir because I love singing. It was fun rehearsing and even more fun performing. I want to be a performer when I grow up. Ever since I was 7 years old I wanted to sing and act. After our Christmas program, I decided that I loved the stage. Though I screwed up, my time there was so worth it."

* * *

Heimo and I have just finished dinner. On the way back to the hotel, we stop in at Fred Meyer, Fairbanks's superstore, and Heimo buys a pint of Häagen-Dazs chocolate sorbet. "I eat one of these almost every night when I come to town," he says. "Three things I look forward to when I come in—soda, a hot shower, and sorbet. Only 480 calories and no fat, so it's easy on my arteries.

"Look at all these people," Heimo continues. "That's town. People everywhere. Don't get me wrong; I like people. After six years alone, you realize how important people are. It's nice for a while, seeing folks that you know and visiting. And it's easier. Living like we do is hard work, both mentally and physically. Sometimes I get tired and think it might be nice to give up trapping, maybe even live in town. But then I come to Fairbanks and see the reality of it, how most people live their lives, and I can't wait to get back to the cabin and start checking my lines again. I like town, but being in the woods, you might say that I find it . . ."

We're standing in the checkout line, and he pauses, considering his words. "You might say I find it healing."

When we get back to the hotel, Heimo sits at the edge of his bed. "Did I tell you I was at Richard and Shannon Hayden's today." The Haydens once lived year-round on the Sheenjek River, seventy miles southwest of the Korths by air. They raised all five of their kids in the bush, but now they live in Fairbanks for much of the year. "Shannon went to fish something out of the back room and then she comes and gives me this picture. It turned out to be a picture of Edna and Coleen." Heimo is silent for a moment. "Edna was holding Coleen in her arms, smiling from ear to ear. Coleen was a little girl, and Edna looked so young and happy. That was almost twenty years ago, but I remember it so clear. Just like that, I started crying. I had to turn my head. When I turned back I saw that Shannon had tears in her eyes, too. When Shannon saw that I was crying, she apologized for upsetting me. 'Apologize,' I said to her, wiping my eyes. 'I love it. Edna's going to love it, too.' "

It is Heimo's last night in Fairbanks. Tomorrow he will drive to Central, spend the night, and fly home with his friend Gene Hume. He's eager to get back out to the cabin. He has lots of fur to work on. Skinning, fleshing, stretching, drying, he rarely gets a break in winter. He starts as soon as supper ends, and he doesn't stop until Edna turns on *Trapline Chatter*. Heimo's plan for the rest of the year is to move the whole family to the lower cabin on April 1 and finish out the trapping season there, where the beaver and muskrats are plentiful. Then, in late May, he will go to Fort Yukon, to watch over the cabin, and Edna and the girls will go to Fairbanks or Central, find a place to rent. But before any of that happens, he has to bring Rhonda and Krin into Fairbanks so that they can take their state benchmark exams. The trip is scheduled for early March, and the girls are excited about coming to town. They'll sleep in and take hot showers every morning, and after their tests, they'll spend a day or two mall-walking. Heimo is less than excited—too many flights and too much of town. He worries about their money holding out, too. Edna isn't looking forward to it either. She'll be alone for almost a week. As much as she loves the cabin, she hates being alone. When the girls and Heimo are home, the cabin is full of activity. Heimo jokes, teases, instructs, irritates, and pontificates. The girls laugh, fight, dance, sing, and rap. Though Edna can't stand the rapping, it's better than silence. It's the silence that scares her, particularly at the upper cabin. It is said that a mother never recovers from the death of a child. Though Coleen has been gone now for almost twenty years, June 3 still haunts Edna. It is a memory she is able to hold at a safe distance when daily life is swirling around her. But when she's alone, she has too much time to think, and the images of that day replay themselves involuntarily. Especially at night.

"Bull-riding," Heimo says, sitting at the edge of his bed, remote control in hand. "I love bull-riding. Those guys are nuts." He watches three riders get tossed from their bulls, then he pulls off the lid from a pint of chocolate sorbet. We watch two more riders, and then he flips through the channels. Suddenly he turns off the television. "I miss Edna," he blurts. "Did I tell you we're trapping together again?"

In early January, Edna and Heimo were upriver setting traps for beaver. Edna set one side of the beaver house and Heimo set the other. When he finished, he waited for her at the snowmachine. Edna came back and she was smiling from ear to ear. "I love this," she said. "I love today, just you and me out on the trapline." She gave Heimo a hug. "Town's gonna be hard. I'm gonna be lonely without you, and I'm gonna miss it out here, too. You gotta promise me we'll come out here in July, though, for a month before the girls start school to shoot caribou and make drymeat. The girls and me will pick berries, and we'll make lots of jam. And we gotta remember to bring back a few gallons of Coleen River water when we go back to town. I hate town water."

Heimo finishes his pint of Häagen-Dazs and licks the back of the spoon. "You know, when Edna and me go back out in three years, we're going to live out of a tent and really cover country," Heimo says, sounding as if he is still an eighteen-year-old dreamer. "Whoever you talk to, just make sure you let 'em know that we're going back out. You gotta promise me that. It's what me and Edna love. We're going to die out there."

Though I believe Heimo when he says that he and Edna have every intention of going back, I can't shake the feeling that this is it, that it's over. The irony of the situation is that of all the things that might have forced him out of the bush, of all the things he's feared, it is love that has brought an end—if only temporarily—to his twenty-eight years in the Alaskan wilderness. But the truth is that in coming out of the bush, Heimo will be more representative of the modern Alaskan experience. People no longer come into the country—that era is gone—and the few who are there rarely stay. They leave with their memories, never to return. For most of them, the memories are enough. Heimo and Edna, however, may be the exception. Their good friends say not to doubt their resolve.

"Supper," Edna calls out.

Outside Heimo shuffles his feet, cleaning the snow from his boots, and ducks in through the door.

"Moose pockets!" he exclaims.

Edna wraps her arms around herself and shivers. "No dinner for you unless you put the blanket over the door. Hurry up; it's cold out there."

"Thirty-three below," Heimo answers. "I just did the weather." He sticks a log in the stove and shuts the door. The damper squeaks in the stovepipe when he adjusts it.

Krin puts down her pencil, folds and tucks a sketch into her diary. Then she grabs a mirror and fluffs up her hair. Rhonda has been listening and rhyming softly to a Nas CD. She clicks off the player. Heimo mixes a glass of powdered milk for himself, and Edna dishes out four plates of moose pockets and smothers them in gravy.

Twenty minutes later, dinner is finished. "Don't forget to do the dishes," Heimo says to the girls, putting on his parka. "Mom and me are gonna take a walk."

Before they are even out the door, Rhonda puts a cassette into the boom box and turns up the volume. Krin is already dancing.

"Ugh," Edna grumbles. "Rap."

Heimo and Edna wind their way through the woods. Above them the cold black sky is glossy with stars. The frozen snow pops under their boots. At the riverbank, they sit on their bench, holding hands, looking down on the Coleen.

"You and me belong out here, don't we, Mom?" Heimo says.

"Yup."

Selected Bibliography

Berger, Thomas R. *Village Journey: The Report of the Alaska Native Review Commission*. Hill and Wang, 1985.

Berry, Mary Clay. *The Alaska Pipeline: The Politics of Oil and Native Land Claims*. Bloomington: Indiana University Press, 1975.

Bluefarb, Sam. *The Escape Motif in the American Novel: Mark Twain to Richard Wright*. Columbus: Ohio State University Press, 1972.

Boeri, David. *People of the Ice Whale: Eskimos, White Men, and the Whale*. New York: E. P. Dutton, Inc., 1983.

Brunk, R. Glendon. *Yearning Wild: Exploring the Last Frontier and the Landscape of the Heart*. Montpelier, VT.: Invisible Cities Press, 2002.

Carius, Helen Slwooko. *Sevukakmet: Ways of Life on St. Lawrence Island*. Anchorage, Alaska: Alaska Pacific University Press, 1979.

Carrighar, Sally. *Home to the Wilderness*. Boston: Houghton Mifflin, 1973.

Carrighar, Sally. *Moonlight at Midday*. New York: Knopf, 1958.

Caulfield, Richard A. *Subsistence Use in and Around the Proposed Yukon-Charley National Rivers*. Anthropology and Historic Preservation, Co-operative Park Studies Unit, University of Alaska, 1979.

Coates, Peter A. *The Trans-Alaska Pipeline Controversy: Technology, Conservation, and the Frontie.*, Fairbanks: University of Alaska Press, 1993.

Crisler, Lois. *Arctic Wild*. New York: Harper, 1958.

Fussell, Edwin S. *Frontier: American Literature and the American West*. Princeton, N.J.: Princeton University Press, 1965.

Harris, Burton. *John Colter: His Years in the Rockies*. New York: Scribner, 1952.

Hazard, Lucy Lockwood. *The Frontier in American Literature*. New York: F. Ungar Pub. Co., 1961.

Hughes, Charles C. *An Eskimo Village in the Modern World*. Ithaca, N.Y.: Cornell University Press, 1960.

Jenkins, Peter. *Looking for Alaska*. New York: St. Martin's Press, 2001.

Kollin, Susan. *Nature's State: Imagining Alaska as the Last Frontier*. Chapel Hill: The University of North Carolina Press, 2001.

Krakauer, Jon. *Into the Wild*. New York: Villard Books, 1996.

Lewis, R.W.B. *The American Adam: Innocense, Tragedy, and Tradition in the Nineteenth Century*. Chicago: University of Chicago Press, 1955.

Lore of St. Lawrence Island: Echoes of Our Eskimo Elders. Unalakleet, Alaska: Bering Strait School District, 1987.

Madsen, Ken. *Under the Arctic Sun: Gwich'in, Caribou, and the Arctic National Wildlife Refuge*. Englewood, Colo.: EarthTales Press, 2002.

McGinniss, Joe. *Going to Extremes*. New York: Knopf, 1980.

McPhee, John. *Coming Into the Country*. New York: Farrar, Straus and Giroux, 1976.

Miller, Debbie. *Midnight Wilderness: Journeys in Alaska's Arctic National Wildlife Refuge*. San Francisco: Sierra Club Books, 1990.

Mitchell, Donald Craig. *Take My Land, Take My Life: The Story of Congress's Historic Settlement of Alaska Native Land Claims, 1960-1971*. Fairbanks: University of Alaska Press, 2001.

Murie, Margaret E. *Island Between*. Fairbanks: University of Alaska Press, 1977.

Nash, Roderick. *Wilderness and the American Mind*. New Haven, Conn.: Yale University Press, 1982.

Nelson, Richard K. *Hunters of the Northern Forest: Designs for Survival Among Alaskan Kutchin*. Chicago: The University of Chicago Press, 1973.

Our Voices: Native Stories of Alaska and the Yukon, edited by James Ruppert and John W. Bernet. Lincoln: University of Nebraska Press, 2001.

Pielou, E.C. *A Naturalist's Guide to the Arctic*. Chicago: The University of Chicago Press, 1994.

Pratt, Verna E. *Field Guide to Alaskan Wildflowers.* Anchorage, Alaska: Alaskakrafts Pub., 1989.

Ray, Dorothy Jean. *The Eskimos of the Bering Strait, 1650-1898.* Seattle: University of Washington Press, 1975.

Silook, Roger S. *Seevookuk: Stories the Old People Told on St. Lawrence Island.* 1976. (Available from Roger Silook, Gambell, AK, 99742.)

Slotkin, Richard. *The Fatal Environment: The Myth of the Frontier in the Age of Industrialization, 1800-1890.* New York: Atheneum, 1985.

Slotkin, Richard. *Regeneration Through Violence: The Mythology of the American Frontier, 1600-1860.* Middletown, Conn.: Wesleyan University Press, 1973.

Smith, Henry Nash. *Virgin Land: The American West as Symbol and Myth.* Cambridge, Mass.: Harvard University Press, 1950.

Smith, Kaj Birket. *The Eskimos.* London: Methuen & Co.,1959.

Stout, Janis P. *The Journey Narrative in American Literature: Patterns and Departures.* Westport, Conn.: Greenwood Press, 1983.

Turner, Jack. *The Abstract Wild.* Tuscon: University of Arizona Press, 1996.

Vestal, Stanley. *Jim Bridger, Mountain Man: A Biography.* Lincoln: University of Nebraska Press, 1946.

Wallis, Velma. *Two Old Women: An Alaska Legend of Betrayal, Courage, and Survival.* New York: HarperPerennial, 1994.

Webb, Melody. *Yukon: The Last Frontier.* Lincoln: University of Nebraska Press, 1993.